Children in Charge

Children in Charge Series

Children in Our Charge
The Child's Right to Resources
Edited by Mary John
ISBN 1-85302-369-8
Children in Charge 2

A Charge Against Society
The Child's Right to Protection
Edited by Mary John
ISBN 1-85302-411-2
Children in Charge 3

of related interest

A Voice for Children
Speaking Out as Their Ombudsman
Målfrid Grude Flekkøy
ISBN 1-85302-118-0

Children in Charge 1

Children in Charge
The Child's Right to a Fair Hearing

Edited by Mary John

Jessica Kingsley Publishers
London and Bristol, Pennsylvania

Elsa Dawson's chapter was originally published as 'Children and the right to play' in *International Journal of Children's Rights 1* (1993) pp.33–48. Copyright 1993 Kluwer Academic Publishers. Reprinted by kind permission of Kluwer Academic Publishers.

Zoran Pavlovic's chapter was originally published as 'Children's parliament in Slovenia' in E. Verhellen (ed) (1996) *Monitoring Children's Rights.* Copyright 1996 Kluwer Academic Publishers. Reprinted by kind permission of Kluwer Academic Publishers.

First published in the United Kingdom in 1996 by
Jessica Kingsley Publishers Ltd
116 Pentonville Road
London N1 9JB, England
and
1900 Frost Road, Suite 101
Bristol, PA 19007, U S A

Library of Congress Cataloging in Publication Data
A CIP catalogue record for this book is available from the Library of Congress

British Library Cataloguing in Publication Data
A CIP catalogue record for this book is available from the British Library

ISBN 1–85302–368–X

Printed and Bound in Great Britain by
Athenaeum Press, Gateshead, Tyne and Wear

Contents

List of Figures

List of Tables

Editor's Acknowledgements

Many of the papers included in this collection were first presented in their original form at the 'World Conference on Research and Practice in Children's Rights; a Question of Empowerment ?' held at the University of Exeter in September 1992. Other papers have been inspired by that gathering or report on work that has been developed within the spirit of concerns expressed there. It is only appropriate, therefore, to make acknowledgement here of the support that we received in holding that conference – held as it was at a time when children's rights were not very much on the public agenda in the United Kingdom despite the ratification of the UN Convention by the UK the previous December and the setting up of the Children's Rights Development Unit.

A number of individuals and organisations had the vision to support what at the time seemed a high-risk venture. Such individuals need to be thanked for inspirational support. The Assistant Director of Education for Devon County Council, Dr Paul Grey, supported us in concrete and facilitative ways and has continued to further the cause of the implementation of the UN Convention of the Rights of the Child in imaginative ways within the County Council. The Conference Manager, Ron Delve, Co-ordinator Hillary Olek and Graphic Designers Michael and Amanda Still held a risky undertaking together and ensured its success. The Conference Committee – made up of colleagues from various Departments in the University: Postgraduate Medical School, Department of Child Health, Psychology Department, Sociology Department, Law Department, School of Education and Department of Continuing and Adult Education – all demonstrated true interdepartmental co-operation and colleagues from the Dartington Social Research Unit of the University of Bristol, from the Faculty of Education at the University of Plymouth and the local Social Services Department reinforced that with real inter-institutional commitment of a high order and continued after the conference with input into the discussions of the publication possibilities for the conference papers. There remains only one regret. My original co-organiser, Christina Sachs, from Exeter University Law Department, was taken ill fairly early on in the preparations and although she did manage to attend some of the Conference, sadly she died before some of the fruits of that Conference could be harvested. We remember her life and work on behalf of children and families with affection and gratitude.

No acknowledgements of the birthing process of this collection would be complete without mention of the children and young people who acted as midwives to much of the work and many of the ideas that have emerged. First, the work of ten Cornish Schools and their 350 pupils who contributed in a dramatic form their views and feelings about certain Articles of the United Nations Convention of the Rights on the Child. To them, their adult allies, their teachers and the overall organiser, Rhys Griffith, my thanks for having raised our consciousness in such stimulating ways. The Young People's Evaluation Panel (Louise Pilcher, Joanne Kestevan, Louise Bridges, Kirstie Randall, Chris Hodder, Natalie Whitelock, Matthew Hendy, Molly Walker, Nicola Gregory, Felicity Thomas, Richard Partridge, Niki Dada, Vicky Maund, Alice Craven, Liz Beardsall, David Mance, Liz Palmer, Charlotte Murphy, Will Woodward and Rachel Bolt) made the aim of children's participation meaningful. I remain indebted to them for all they taught us about listening to children. To their schools: Kings

School, Ottery St Mary; Mount St Mary Convent, Exeter; Sands School, Ashburton and the teacher/chauffeurs who believed that what these young people were doing mattered – my appreciation.

The conference was financially supported by the Bernard Van Leer Foundation, the Elm Grant Trust, the Trustees of Westhill College Birmingham, University of Plymouth Faculty of Education, the School of Education of the University of Exeter, the University of Exeter Research Fund, Devon County Council Education Department and the Social Services Department, the Disabled Young Adults Centre, Cow and Gate Ltd, John Wyeth and Brother Ltd and Milupa.

Having expressed my appreciation for contributions of various kinds to the process of the development of this volume and the ones that follow, I wish to make specific acknowledgements for generous permission I have received from Kluwer Academic to reprint the article by Elsa Dawson which, whilst first presented at the Exeter Conference, later appeared in a more developed form in their International Journal of Children's Rights. The paper by Zoran Pavlovic was presented at a conference on Monitoring Children's Rights in Gent in December 1994. It will shortly be published by Kluwer Academic. Both the publishers, the Editor, Eugeen Verhellen, and the author, Zoran Pavlovic, have agreed to an edited version of that paper appearing here. I am grateful to the Center for Children's Rights at the University of Gent for their generosity in this. I would like to thank the technical and administrative staff within the School of Education for their support and, in particular, Michael Still as editorial assistant and my secretary, Angela Garry, for secretarial support, wizardry in all forms of new technologies and an unfailing good will when this preoccupation with children's rights began to encroach upon her own rights!

Finally and by no means least I would especially like to thank my children, Dan and Adam, my mentors who taught me everything I needed to know about Articles 12 and 13 but failed to ask!!

Foreword

We were members of the Young People's Evaluation Team (originally called the 'Children's Evaluation Team', but we changed that as we were aged between 11 and 16 years old) who were involved in the World Conference on Research and Practice in Children's Rights at the University of Exeter in September 1992, at which some of the papers in this book were presented and which inspired some of the other papers. We played a part in the early planning of the conference by giving our views on the proposed programme and, when the conference actually took place, we either chaired sessions or sat in on the presentations. Later, via closed circuit television so that we appeared on an enormous screen, we gave our views on these papers to all the people at the conference.

For such an event to run smoothly it needs to be given enough time and input of different ideas and options so that there is adequate time to respond, give support and work together towards a common goal. We had, therefore, a lot of preparation meetings after school but not as many as we would have liked. We can still remember the nerves, (at times) total dis-organisation, the difficulties and the fun we felt in having to assess, criticise and then talk about the speeches given. In this book two of our 'evaluations' are included after Chapters 9 and 15.

We are very glad that the three volumes of 'Children in Charge' covering the conference themes are being published as we hope that over time the books will achieve some of the publicity we did not achieve, despite our efforts. We feel that not only will they be a lasting memento for us of what we did but that it *will* mean that children's voices will be heard, understood and recognised with supporting evidence. It is also pleasing because we were concerned that the learning opportunities that the conference offered to us will not be wasted. Now others can learn from what we were part of.

Being at the conference and listening to the papers, virtually all of which are included in the three volumes of this series, really gave us a better understanding of just how difficult it can be being heard. It has made us aware that not only should we listen to children but to *everyone*. It made us realise how we were viewed by some adults. Now, although we not at all in positions of power, we hope we value the opinions of people who are younger than us. Both children and adults learnt to think with a more open mind. The conference altered our preconceived ideas of conferences. It touched on a subject that many of us had previously taken for granted and opened our eyes and educated us in areas where we were ignorant. It alerted us to some of the needs of all children, those less fortunate than ourselves in the developing and developed world. It gave us a chance to point out these rights in a way they may be recognised.

Children are often very perceptive and accurate yet are often dismissed without a proper explanation to a question. Now we always try to explain our answers as fully as possible for them to understand. Throughout feedback sessions we gained a lot of respect from many of the adults there. Some of the adults were quite surprised about the fact that we understood what was happening and held our own opinions on these issues. We had had the impression previously that some adults thought that children's views should not be valued because they could not understand all that goes on.

Not only did we work hard to change adults' views but hearing the papers also changed *ours* in various ways. One of us, for example, has become more assertive, personal development has been improved, as well as an increased understanding of what action is needed and the need for change. Another of us has become 'more confident in myself and in saying what I believe. It also taught me the value of team-work and the importance of listening'. More specifically, one of us felt that the conference had changed 'Perhaps the way I view other people's ways of life that I might not particularly agree with but must respect as their own individual choices'.

After the conference we would have liked more discussion about the results, findings and implications which we felt would have been good. The present volume and the ones that follow it give such an opportunity to an even wider audience. It was all a really valuable experience for the whole Young People's Evaluation Team not only for what we learnt but also for the growth in our confidence to let our opinions be known to 'the people in power'. We hope they, other adults and young people, will read these books and learn from them and change as we did.

Written on behalf of the Young People's Evaluation Team by
Rachel Bolt
Joanna Kestevan
Katherine Lewis
Kirstie Randall
Louise Pilcher

PART ONE

The Right to be Heard

Voicing

Research and Practice with the 'Silenced'

Mary John

Your children are not your children.
They are the sons and daughters of Life's longing for itself.
They come through you but not from you.
And though they are with you yet they belong not to you.
You may give them your love but not your thoughts,
For they have their own thoughts...

The Prophet by Kahil Gibran (p.13, lines 4–6)

Children's thoughts, how we access them, how we act on them and how we honour the thinking and the thinker in our research, interventions and relationships with children and how these thoughts shape us will be the focus of this first volume in the series on 'Children in Charge'. Interest in children was given particular momentum and focus at the beginning of this decade by the Convention on the Rights of the Child,[1] a legally-binding instrument which was passed unanimously by the United Nations General Assembly on the 20th of November 1989.

No other UN Convention has met with such a high level of support. Since it was passed some 175 nations have ratified it, which means that these nations have ostensibly committed themselves to protect and care for children. They have done more than this, however, and this forms an important focus in this collection of papers – they have committed themselves to *listening* to children as well. They have accepted that they can no longer make assumptions about

---

1 Information or a copy of the UN Convention on the Rights of the Child is available from UNICEF, 55 Lincoln's Inn Fields, LONDON, WC2A 3NB. TEL: 0171-405-5592. FAX: 0171-405-2332.

what children should or do think; children's *own* views and voices have to be heard and taken into account. This represents a highly innovative aspect of the Convention and a breakthrough in society's views about the status of the child. It has heralded, what Geraldine Van Bueren refers to in the first chapter of this collection as, a 'quiet revolution'. As a barrister very much involved in the drafting of that Convention and subsequent UN instruments, she makes it abundantly clear that the Convention serves as an important indicator of the climate of the times; a manifesto indicating what, in an ideal world, a child's life should be like. Moreover, the fact that Geraldine, a highly respected international lawyer and a distinguished scholar on the subject (Van Bueren 1993; Van Bueren 1995), was able to present the paper published here so that it could be understood by young people aged about 14 years, demonstrated her own commitment not just to listening to children but communicating with them in a reciprocal way.

The 'revolution' that Geraldine describes has been 'quiet' in quite another way. Children's silences come under scrutiny in this collection both from the point of view of the processes that have silenced them and the struggle they have had to be heard. We argue that children, now formally recognised as a minority rights group through the very provision of a UN Convention to protect their rights, share many features of such groups – one of which has been that their own subjectivities have been denied and a second that there has been, a paucity of research on those whose voices have been, as a result of this denial, silent. 'The views which permeate social science from the perspectives of the silenced are etic views: the views of those with power and access to control the naming process, even while being outsiders to marginal lives' (Lincoln 1993, p.29). It is the nature of this silence, an examination of the processes which create it and the structure, practices and research which liberates the voice of the child within the political process that holds this apparently disparate collection of papers together. In an approach further elaborated upon by Jeremy Roche, a lawyer, in volume two of this series, the relationship between voice and power is further explored developing Minnow's point:

> …power exercised in silence, is even less likely to know restraint; for silence, whilst sometimes eloquent, can seldom challenge power. Language, accompanying power, enables the powerless to challenge power. Without language, and especially without language recognised by the powerful, those who would challenge or resist power are quite disabled. (Minnow 1987, p.1904)

So, although the changes arising from the UN Convention have been subtle and the revolution it brought about has been muted, the fact that the Convention legitimised the recognition of the child's voice and listening to children has major implications which we both celebrate and explore here. Two major emphases in the Convention, however, were developments from earlier instruments such as the Declaration of the Rights of the Child adopted by the League of Nations in 1924. This represented a culmination of the work of Eglantine Jebb, founder of Save the Children, who had been an early campaigner following her involvement in trying to protect, in whatever way she could, the young victims and child refugees of the First World War. So concern about children's rights is not entirely new although it has only recently started to capture more generally the public imagination. The early Declaration of the Rights of the Child, which was later revised and adopted by the United Nations in 1979, stressed the need to protect and provide for children with the emphasis very much on their material needs. The image of the child contained in such declarations was not that of the citizen but that of the dependent weak member of society that had to be protected and provided for. The implications of equal opportunity policies, the re-thinking of the full inclusive implications of a democratic society and the slow ending of conceptions of children as 'property' rather than as persons in their own right have all led inescapably to an examination of where children, as autonomous individuals, fit in these oppor- tunities and the decision-making process. The inclusion in the recent UN Convention of children's right to be consulted and involved in matters con- cerning them is of interest to us here both from the point of view of how the terms of the Convention can be honoured, how the authentic voice of the child can be accessed and, more generally, from the point of view of what the inclusion of this new perspective tells us about how children are now viewed and what this says about society's changing values and stance on power relationships. Referring to the Convention, Richard Reid, Director of Public Affairs UNICEF,[2] said:

> The law on children's rights has three parts: provision (food, medical care, education, etc.), protection (from child labour, adult abuse, under the law, etc.) and participation by children. Few governments have any philosophic problem with the first two. It's the third part that worries them.

CHILDREN'S VOICES IN THE GLOBAL ARENA

It is, arguably, one of the most important features of the UN Convention on the Rights of the Child that, in addition to the traditional abiding concerns with the protection and provision for children, the Convention stresses this third element – children's participation. Particularly in Articles 12 and 13, the importance of participation is stressed. Article 12 makes clear that the child has the right to express his or her opinion and have that opinion taken into account in any matter or procedure affecting them, whilst Article 13 goes on to outline

---

2   Richard Reid, as quoted in Children of the World 1994, p.28.

the child's right to express his or her views, obtain information and access information regardless of frontiers. This endows the child with a new status in the international arena and poses the research and practitioner community with new challenges as to how to involve children, how to forge new partnerships with them, how to ensure that they become agents in their own lives and what processes of empowerment to engage in. The UN Convention has been a landmark in a legislative instrument that put children's participation firmly on the agenda; an agenda on which, following the UN International Year of the Child in 1979, children had begun to appear more prominently. The question remains, however, as to whether this aspect of children's rights is just a 'hurrah' idea or whether the policy-maker's rhetoric can match realities in children's lives.

The UN Convention can be seen as a benchmark for a change of priorities in our relationships, professional and otherwise, with children. It has provided, for some, the impetus to make many of our concerns about children take on a truly child-centred focus so that children are no longer seen as standing in the wings, waiting to become agents in their own lives and be taken seriously by the rest of the world. Waiting and watching, we argue, is not what they are actually doing; they are learning from the treatment meted out to them, learning whether or not their voice counts and, by implication, what their own worth is. By examining various paradigms of action with children, we can perhaps learn something about how to treat the generation of tomorrow as citizens of today. On one issue they have an undoubted vested interest. That is in the matter of the global environment – an environment that will be our legacy to them and in which they indisputably have an interest. One example of how children have become involved on the global scale in making their views known and have ensured that these views have had considerable impact has been in relation to environmental concerns.

At about the same time as many of the activities relating to the drafting of the UN Convention on the Rights of the Child, which was first formally suggested by Poland during the International Year of the Child in 1979, pressure was mounting in quite another quarter which was ultimately also to stress the importance of the involvement of children in world and in local affairs. In 1972, 70 governments met in Stockholm for a Conference which created the United Nation's Environment Programme (UNEP). The main task of this programme was to put pressure on governments to take more care of the environment. Environmental education was also encouraged through collaboration that was set up with UNESCO. In 1984 the World Conservation Strategy was published, aiming to explore constructively the issue of balancing protection of the environment with the world's need for food. The United Nations appointed a World Commission on the Environment and Development which produced the well-known report 'Our Common Future' which embodied, for the first time, the notion of sustainable development. In 1989 it was decided to hold a Conference on Environment and Development in Rio de Janeiro, Brazil. Chapter 3 by Kristin Eskeland in this volume describes children's involvement at that Earth Summit. In March of 1992, before the meeting of the Earth Summit in June, young people converged on San Jose, Costa Rica, to prepare for the Earth Summit. Three hundred young people were there from 97 countries; 75 per cent from developing countries, 50 per cent female and 10 per cent indigenous – an exact replica of the world's population. Out of this week emerged the Youth Statement to Rio which dealt powerfully with issues from poverty to pollution. Official youth were promised an hour. From the Report in Rescue Mission Planet Earth (Children of the World 1994) the experience of being 'heard' was as follows:

> Young people are half the world's population, so one hour in 14 days seemed fair. When they arrived, they were told they only had ten minutes. Two minutes in the TV cameras were turned off; reporters watching in the press room couldn't hear. When the youth tried to tell the eager press what they'd said, UN police arrested them for holding an 'illegal' press conference. So what everyone remembers is images of kids being hauled off by police, nothing of the statement. It said things like 'all Third World debt should be cancelled because rich countries had earned more than enough out of the period of colonialism'. A bit radical but that's the way youth should be. No diplomatic games.
>
> Children were also snubbed. A group called Voice of the Children had organised hearings all round the world. It was the Prime Minister of Norway's idea and she promised to bring six world leaders to hear their statement. None came. She did not even turn up herself... (Children of the World 1994, p.80)

Severn Suzuki did, however, speak and she tried to speak for children who had no voice at Rio 'and she was great; she got a standing ovation! But the voiceless children did not ask her to speak: the Director of UNICEF did. In truth, she represented herself' (Children of the World 1994, p.80). Following the Rio Summit, governments, non-governmental organisations and experts worked for a further two years on a document that 179 states could agree to. Agenda 21 was the result.[3] Whilst this is not a legally binding instrument, the fact that so many governments agreed to it is very important. From our point of view here, one significant feature of Agenda 21 is that, like the Convention on the Rights

---

3 The Complete Text of Agenda 21 is available in all six UN languages from the UN Information Centre, 21st floor, Milbank Tower, Milbank, London SW1P 4QH. Tel: 0171-630 1981, Fax: 0171-976 6478. Agenda 21 (and many other Rio documents including a plain language edition of Agenda 21: Agenda for Change which is 70 pages long with 2–3 page summaries of each chapter plus charts and diagrams) are available from Centre for Our Common Future, 52, rue de Paquis, 1201, GENEVA, Switzerland.

of the Child, it embodies the right to be heard: 'Each country should include children's concerns in all relevant policies for environment and development and support their involvement in the United Nations' (Agenda 21, chapter 25).

On the matter of children's involvement relative to Agenda 21, the Executive Director of the United Nations Executive Programme (Elizabeth Dowdeswell), despite the disasterous experiences in Rio, is very positive: 'I have absolutely no doubt that children are leaders where environmental matters are concerned. They have the power to educate their parents as decision-makers and change what's happening at an individual level' (Children of the World 1994, p.82).

As we have already seen from the children's experiences at Rio, they can only be 'leaders' if they are given the opportunity for voicing their concerns and if they are indeed listened to. Elizabeth Dowdeswell's optimism was born out, however, by the production by over 10,000 children in 200 groups in 75 countries around the word (members of the Children's Agenda 21 Task Force), as a result of thousands of hours work co-ordinated by an international team of 28 child editors, of a Children's Edition of Agenda 21 (Rescue Mission Planet Earth) by 'Children of the World' (Children of the World 1994) which is a powerful document and is commonly regarded as the best and clearest overview of the rather tortuous and complicated Agenda itself. It is lively, fresh and identifies the issues intelligently. Moreover, it makes clear that whatever statements are issued in relation to visionary manifestos they have to be realised in practice. Another message comes across in this impressive piece of work that counters the ill-thought-out criticism that children want rights without responsibilities. The many, many authors of this crucial guide to Agenda 21 have demonstrated that they do care about their planet, they care about what we are doing to it and what the legacy for them will be, and what *their* responsibilities are. In concluding their work they say:

> So you have reached the end of this book. But this is not the end of the story! Every one can take action for a better world.
>
> Often we think we are powerless. We think we cannot change anything until we grow up. Well, remember Samantha Smith: she helped to end the Cold War with her letter to Andropov when she was only 10. Joan of Arc drove the English out of France before she was 19. Mozart wrote half his music before he was 21!
>
> But this is not only about child prodigies. The daily efforts of each one of us are at least as important. What matters is the voice in your heart. Let it be heard! (Children of the World 1994, p.91)

Kristin Eskeland in Chapter 3 outlines the work of Voice of the Children International which has continued the work of ensuring that children have a voice on the global, national and local scene and demonstrates the way in which adults acting as allies can provide appropriate structures to facilitate and support children's self-advocacy.

The global dimension of concerns about children has been given further emphasis from another quarter by the World Platform of Action voted on at the close of the UN's Fourth World Conference on Women in Beijing. On the issue of children's rights it was agreed 'that children have the right to privacy when receiving health information and services but their rights must be balanced against the parent's rights and duties. Whose rights will dominate will vary according to the child's maturity'. What is not made clear is who will be the judge of the child's maturity. Such issues raised at the Women's Conference will be taken up in the second volume in this series – *Children in Our Charge* – where the critical tension between adults views of the child's best interests and the child's own choices will be creatively explored. Suffice it to state here that there is always lurking in the background the fear that giving rights to children could let things career out of control and that somehow, by giving them rights, other adult/parental rights might be infringed. In this volume, looking at the roots of personal powers, Rudi Dallos in Chapter 15 does look at the parent's role in the construction and destruction of autonomy and their pervasive influence on the child's sense of self. In the preceding chapter, Jaqui Cousins further emphasises the role of the primary caretaker – making it clear that talk of children's rights and respect for the child's choices can begin very early and have powerful consequences in the development of the child's sense of self. So parents need not necessarily be seen as controllers of the child's choices but also as very powerful and important facilitators right from the beginning in the process of the child's empowerment and emancipation.

This volume of *Children in Charge* attempts to capture the global spirit of the changing climate as regards the status of children yet, at the same time, demonstrates that whilst thinking globally we must be finding ways to act locally; that children's 'daily efforts' to voice their concerns and to be heard have to be seen within this global context. There is indeed an increasing body of literature on the pan-world's vision of what children's lives should be, but little of this is combined with the down-to-earth detail of what children do and can do at the local level. This collection, therefore, implicitly explores the counterpoint between thinking globally and acting locally. To this counterpoint is added an exploration of the resonances between local action in vastly different local contexts as, for example, in the last two chapters where work with street children in Mwanza and work with children who know the streets of Edinburgh is placed side by side. The similarities are striking, arising as they do from taking children seriously, from the value those children were given in the eyes of the adults who worked with them, believed in them and, importantly, learnt from the children's own realities. It was these realities which, in the case of the children in Tanzania, informed what interventions took place and it was these realities and the disregard of them by the statutory authorities that gives way to the researcher's note of despair in Richard Kinsey's chapter.

Judith Ennew (1995) claims that the UN Convention of the Rights of the Child was 'drafted during the same decade as an unprecedented increase in interest in groups of children called "street children"... In the juxtaposition of the Convention and the image of the street child, the entire discourse on children's rights stands revealed. The Convention, in the drafting process, the resulting text and its implementation, takes as its starting point Western modern childhood which has been globalised first through colonialism and then through the imperialism of international aid (Detrick 1992, Fyfe 1989, Boyden 1990)' (p.202). Her argument proceeds that 'One of the most crucial aspects of this nation [i.e. the UK] is domesticity. The place for childhood to take place is inside – inside society, inside a family, inside a private dwelling. This means street children are society's ultimate outlaws' (Ennew 1995, p.202). If we are considering provision for children then this might be the case, but we would argue here that when we are considering the voice of the child and the necessity to hear that voice then such listening is transcultural and, if truly practised, must rise above notions of what the child should be. Traditional epistemologies have excluded the possibility that children could be either 'knowers' or agents of knowledge. The listener that really listens to them becomes not only abused of this preconception but also begins to see the world with the acute observation of the child who also inhabits it. The last two chapters show how sensitive an audience for the child's voice can be in the 'developing' world whilst in the 'developed' world how deaf agents officially in place for the protection of the child can be to that child's own realities. The final chapter also tells us something about the researchers responsibilities in relation to children and, taken together, lodge a powerful case for listening to children.

CHILDREN AS A MARGINALISED GROUP

The UN Convention is an international instrument and the signatory countries are now, with varying amounts of vigour, monitoring the implementation of its terms and provisions. It has, therefore, served to put childhood on many agendas world-wide. The international comparative context has been an important one in setting activities within each country in the wider context and thus enabling each of us to establish how well or poorly we are doing. Start Hart's research reported in Chapter Two of this Volume, spanning as it does so many countries, also tells us how important specific children's rights are viewed to be by children themselves and their teachers in the countries studied and the extent to which such rights currently exist. Although this research is still at a fairly early stage it is clear that further detailed analyses will reveal the meaning of some of the data and inform us more thoroughly about cross-cultural variation and experience. It will also give us a sense of the extent to which children form part of mainstream concerns in particular countries and the extent to which their rights are now honoured. Within such a comparative context we have been able to learn from other countries new ways of involving children in the decision making processes of a society. Why is it, however, that children, global declarations apart, deserve our special attention at this time and why is it that they have come to be viewed as a minority rights group and what is the significance of this?

There have been a number of developments and trends common to most developed industrialised countries which have pushed children further to the margins of society. It is important to look at these trends in child-centred ways and this has been focused by a common concern with the implementation of the UN Convention of the Rights of the Child. The first trend has been the demographic transformation arising from the combination of low birth rates and rising life expectancy which has led to a decreasing share of children and an increasing share of adult and elderly persons in the total population. Thus the ageing of society and the financial responsibilities that this has entailed for the working population has raised issues of priorities in resource allocation in which often children come off rather badly and seem to be of relatively little account in the decisions. Moreover, looking further and more widely at the redistributive mechanisms, the relative deprivation of children, often connected with poverty in one parent-families and families living in difficult circum-stances, has raised questions which are common to many developed countries about taxation, social and family policies (John 1993; 1995) and, in the developing world, the priorities laid down by foreign aid have raised questions about the extent to which such policies are child-sensitive enough. These issues are taken up in detail in Volume Two of this series.

From another perspective, growing attention is being paid to disturbing symptoms and, at times, pathological phenomena in attitudes and practices toward children at risk, physical, sexual and emotional child abuse, child labour, children in areas of war and violence, child vagrants, street children and international trafficking in children. The plight of children such as these – who are placed at the margins of society and whose rights are violated – has served to heighten the focus on children as a minority rights group. Children's rights have also become something of a growth industry. With the intensification of monitoring the UN Convention, the process of realising the Convention has been as important as its content and is now influenced by activities such as research projects, conferences, international gatherings and expert meetings. Whilst these meetings have heightened awareness about children and their rights there is no denying that it now also has the danger of becoming yet another 'machine' for which children are the fodder and in which they have no voice. The tendency in these meetings, however, has been to concentrate on structural aspects of provision and the dominant discipline has been the law.

The research community working with minority rights groups has had under investigation some issues which are highly relevant to, but which have not yet been systematically applied to, children. Whilst children have often been *the focus* of research, thinking and interventions, it is only relatively recently that children have been perceived as a minority rights group. As a result they have not yet seriously come within the purview, except perhaps rather obliquely, of the research in the area of minority rights. So, even by the research community, they have been marginalised! In work with such groups there has been a notable blind spot in relation to children's rights. This is not entirely because of an omission on the part of the researchers, but, like other minority rights groups, until they become consciously focused they are somewhat 'invisible':

> The incipient ideas about childhood as excluded or marginalised or dependent in real life were immediately confirmed, since children were also excluded, marginalised, and dependent in the available material. Even in child studies, children are sometimes invisible as they are perceived as 'becoming adults'. Information is scattered because it is collected from the viewpoints of the family, the school, women's activities and opportunities, professional and/or bureaucratic interests, etc. and is therefore adult-centred.

> The nature of children's representation in research and documentation thus becomes a significant token of the nature of children's participation in real life. Children's near absence in public statistics and social accounting signifies their lack of importance in the minds of authorities and adult society in general. A description of children which takes seriously their own life expressions, might question the validity of conventional wisdom. (Findings of Programme on Childhood, European Centre for Social Welfare, Policy and Research, Vienna 1995, p.4)

Not only have children been missing from official statistics and public accounting but their views, their experiences of life, their worries and their concerns have also been absent. In black consciousness movements, in the world of disability and in the lives of women, a first stage of consciousness-raising was the celebration of the personal; the sharing of subjectivities and direct experiences. In the world of children, such a stage has still to be marked and celebrated by the stories born of their own experience of the world and, just as in the other minority rights movements, the recognition, not of the uniqueness of that experience, but of it as part of the common experience as part of life on the margins. The translation of the child's articulated experience into its political significance will also mark a stage in the emergence of this the last of the minority rights groups to receive our attention. Yet even this transformation from the personal to the political will meet with all the resistances which are now the common experiences of other minority rights groups – the denial, the personalisation, the paternalism and de-skilling of the speaker – and, in the case of children, there is an additional factor. Just as disabled people were 'denied a body' in the way in which they have been regarded as of neutral gender and their sexuality denied, so children's 'innocence' is protected by the denial of them as political beings. The politics of childhood from the child's point of view has still to be written. In this collection we have just the beginning of a literature which sketches the early stages in re-conceptualising and re-negotiating power relationships.

PARTICIPATION AND EMPOWERMENT

> Documents should not be dismissed because their authority is symbolic rather than statutory. Acknowledging the legitimacy of a group's claim to rights is itself part of a process of empowerment; rights are levers which the empowered group must pick up and put to work. In the mid 70s equal opportunities legislation gave women and black people a set of such levers with which to prise open opportunities in education, at work and in a range of social settings. Moreover, conceding moral claims is undoubtedly a prerequisite for, and might prompt, a firmer statutory guarantee for children's rights. The symbolic significance and desirability of the Convention is difficult to deny. (Franklin 1992, p.105)

How have we been able to use the UN Convention of the Rights of the Child as a tool or lever in the process of children's empowerment and, indeed, have children been able to avail themselves of such 'tools'? Stuart Hart (the author of Chapter 2) opened the 1992 proceedings of the 15th International School Psychology Colloquium in Istanbul by reiterating the words of one of its founders, that we have four choices in relating to children: to do things *to,* to do things *for,* to do things *around,* or to do things *with* them. He suggested that the knowledge we have gained of children's capabilities encourages us to give them more opportunities for participation and self-determination giving more emphasis to doing things around and with them than previous generations. Similarly encouraging messages come from his namesake Roger Hart's essay for the UNICEF International Child Development Centre on 'Children's Participation' (Hart 1992). Commenting on projects in Kenya, India, the Philippines and Brazil involving street children and preventative programmes for children at risk of becoming street children, Hart discovered that, for a number of countries, children's participation is becoming fundamental to their approach to improving children's rights. This is certainly evident in the work described in this volume in Peru and Tanzania. Whilst this appears to be encouraging news, and indeed Roger Hart's model 'The Ladder of Participation' which demonstrates graphically the models of participation and non-participation he outlines, his concluding comments are disturbing. He suggests that in looking at where to begin in fostering young people's understanding and experience of democratic participation, the schools would seem to be an obvious place. The schools are thought of as an integral part of the community and, of course, many of our great educational philosophers have argued that it is here that the seeds of true democracy are sown – although in practice this is found to be rare.

Hart claims that, although in many countries one can find exciting experimental schools 'there is no nation where the practice of democratic participation in schools has been broadly adopted. The most fundamental reason seems to be that, as the primary socialising instrument of the state, schools are concerned with guaranteeing stability; and this is generally understood to mean preserving the very conservative systems of authority' (Hart 1992, p.43). This point is examined in this volume exploring to what extent democracy is learnt through practice and what these practices have been which have involved the participation of children. Zoran Pavlovic's chapter makes it clear that no democracy can call itself a democracy if it is not inclusive, that is that it includes children in the decision-making processes of that society. To this end, he describes the work of the Children's Parliament in Slovenia. In Chapter 9, pupils describe their school – in which democratic principles are incorporated to a very large extent in the way the school is run by the pupils themselves.

In fact, as Hart points out, in the educational sphere acknowledgement of children's participant status has been patchy. In the United Kingdom, for example, the Children Act 1989 made much of their importance, and was referred to by Ronald Davie in 'Listen to the Child: A Time for Change' his Vernon-Wall Lecture, to the 1991 Annual Meeting of the British Psychological Society (Davie 1993), as embodying, more than any other single document, the spirit of taking the child's perspective seriously and giving it due weight. Professor Davie outlined how, in a variety of spheres (including the educational one), the child's voice was beginning to be heard. Nevertheless, the Children Act was followed not long after by an Education Act (1993) that does not once mention children and a Parent's Charter which must be one of the few charters not to mention the 'customers' of their practices or the 'point of delivery consumers'! This unevenness reflects different rates of change and some difficulty, not just in society, but also within the research and practitioner community in re-framing children as a minority rights group and re-focusing some of the concerns in research with other minority rights groups onto work with children.

This first volume collects together some of the work of people operating in different domains who are working in a particular way with children and some writing by children themselves which are transformative of traditional power relations between children and adults and researcher and researched. The twin themes of participation and empowerment form an integrating focus throughout. This collection has developed out of presentations at the first 'World Conference on Research and Practice in Children's Rights; a question of Empowerment?' – a Conference which was a flagship event in that for the first time anywhere in the world, as far as we were aware, children themselves were actively involved in the planning, the proceedings and the evaluation of a meeting about the UN Convention. The Young People's Evaluation Panel critiqued various papers given at that Conference and their very presence made many of the presenters aware of how very far from children's lived realities their work and research had departed. As postscript to Chapter 9 and Chapter 15, which were presented in their original form at the Conference as workshops, the comments of the young evaluators have been included. The Conference acted as a catalyst for gathering together some of the other work that appears in this collection. As a result of their participation in the Conference, the Young People's Evaluation Panel drew up a list of activities they wished to undertake following the Conference. They were vigorous in pursuit of these but sadly the experiences of empowerment they felt they had had at the Conference were not reflected in the responses to their initiatives. They wrote to all the major national newspapers regretting that there had been no coverage of the Conference, which they regarded as a very significant event on the international scene, and offering to write an article about it to make up this omission. Not a single newspaper replied. They also wrote to a local television station offering to make a programme about Children's Rights as part of one of the programme development opportunities on offer by the station. Again their offer met with silence. They tried to hold a Children's Hearing – having been inspired by the work of Kristin Eskeland reported on here – but they were similarly disappointed in their search for support. Whilst this created some disillusionment amongst the Panel members, it also raises questions for those of us who raised their expectations and the extent to which we should have built into this follow-up support, for, as we shall argue, empowerment and participation need ongoing constructive alliances.

MODELS OF PARTICIPATION

When children's participation is considered, Roger Hart's model the 'Ladder of Participation' is often quoted. It is a 'ladder' which shows children's involvement in the decision-making process with, at the bottom, tokenism moving up various stages ('rungs') to a situation where decisions are initiated by children themselves. There are problems with this ladder metaphor, which is based on Arnstein's 'Eight rungs on the ladder of citizen participation' (Arnstein 1979), in that it can be seen as reinforcing traditional notions of patriarchy. The ladder is offered and the child, with various assistance from the adult, is 'empowered' to move up it into mainstream society and mainstream citizenship. This is an old model of rights which one might call the model in which rights are 'bestowed' by the powerful on the less powerful. Surely the rights discourse is about transforming power rather than giving a less fortunate member of the community a helping hand up into the world of the dominant majority. For helpful models of participation and empowerment we have to look beyond models emerging from consumer involvement to models emerging from the struggles of minority rights groups.

Steve Biko (Aelred Stubbs 1983), in writing about black consciousness, made it clear that in his experience there are three fundamental pre-requisites to empowerment – black responsibility, unity and a people's movement. If we look at how this might be used in analysing the growth of a political movement amongst children, there also has to be some sort of *responsibility* for educating other members of the marginalised community about their status and position and alerting them to the collective nature of their oppression. During this stage the rhetoric of in-group/out-group polarisation is strong. In other minority right groups it is expressed through the immediacy of samizdat pamphlets and publications. Chapter 8 – outlining the work of Underground Power – is included in this collection as an example of this genre in the field of young people's rights. It is typical of the early stages of the political process of educating the group and ensuring unity. This chapter gives the full-flavour of the angry stage of in-group solidarity and out-group vilification – the 'arse kicking' (sic) of the vested power interests and the marginalising forces and the taking of responsibilities for educating the group about their position in society. This can be viewed as an essential stage in the growth of a political movement where experiences have been coloured by exclusion and powerlessness for so long. Difference is accentuated and in-group similarities celebrated. In the case of children, Biko's stage of 'responsibility' has a particular significance as 'children', having become politically aware, then pass out of the constituency and move from the role of oppressed to the status associated with the perpetrator of oppression, namely adult status. Thus it becomes important that young people within their own constituency 'educate' the younger members who will have to take on the mantle of responsibility.

Unity involves making sure that the members of the minority rights group at least speak with one voice to the outside world. It involves each member identifying with the marginalised group and seeing their own personal strug-gles as part of a general oppression. Christina Safilios Rothschild (1976) describes this well in the case of disability in the early days of the development of the political movement of disabled people. She sees a first step as the disabled person being able to identify with the group – a difficult step in that it involves identifying with the most stigmatised group (echoes of this difficulty are seen in the Underground Power paper in the assertion that they are not 'children' but 'young people'). There has to be identification with other children and presentation of a united front to the world. The next stage, in Biko's words the *people's movement,* is when the group starts to make itself visible in the community and turns its attention outwards from an inward-looking, power-building movement for solidarity towards pressing for recognition. It involves 'getting alongside people in their daily lives'. The movement then, in turning outwards, begins to be felt as a political force in the community. Jo Bird and Kunle Ibidun describe the Carnival they held and the campaign they mounted for voting rights for young people. The turning outwards towards the community, however, can have two forms. The first is where the group complains about the treatment meted out to them but sees responsibility for effecting change as that of the society rather than themselves. This is only one remove from the dependency that is the traditional view of members of minority groups and, in particular, children – all that has been added is the voice of the complainant and a complainant who feels they have rights. It is the dissatisfied consumer not the participant in the decision making process who speaks thus. Flexing newly recognised muscles as an individual who has just acknowledged and realised that they have rights can, in its early days of political consciousness, take this form. Indeed Zoran Pavlovic in Chapter 6 in his description of the Children's Parliament in Slovenia describes just such a situation. He recounts how, in the 1990 Parliament on the theme of 'A Healthy and Safe Environment for Children', whilst children displayed a considerable level of awareness and understanding of the serious ecological problems threatening the planet as well as problems nearer home in their own localities, the children were accusatory, accusing adults for such a state of affairs. 'They demanded serious changes but they were not able to see themselves as competent agents of change.' By the third Parliament this had changed in that the children, having found that they had been accepted even when they were not pleasing the adults, became more co-operative and realistic in their discussions and demands. They demonstrated a better insight into which issues could and should be dealt with at school level, which they needed to discuss with the local authorities and what really needed to be addressed to State level politicians. Although Zoran does not specifically say so, he implies that the children were also becoming aware of their own responsibilities in the processes of change they were advocating. This acceptance of responsibility for change forms the second approach to looking outwards from the internal solidarity of the minority group towards societal responsibilities.

A second form that turning outwards to the community can take, which roundly grasps responsibility for change, is evidenced by Penny Townsend. In Chapter 7 in this volume she tackles head-on the accusation that children wish to have rights but are not prepared to take on the contingent responsibilities. She gives ample evidence of how, within a local community, young people have shouldered responsibilities and given a particular insight and impetus to the activities they have undertaken. Penny, in talking on behalf of the Devon Youth Council about the issue of young people's participation, frequently makes a useful distinction between different approaches to how the peer group is used and the balance of adult/child power and responsibility in such approaches. It is this model which has guided the inclusion of some of the papers in this volume. They are as follows:

- **Peer Pressure:** Instances of this approach to participation are seen when members of the peer group are used to put pressure on other members relying on the internal politics of the peer group for some of its effects. Chapter 12 by Alex Mellanby about the 'A Pause' project is an example of this sort of approach in that members of the peer group are trained to work persuasively with younger members of the group in relation to the young person's attitudes and behaviour in relation to early sexual experiences. In this case one might feel that the end justifies the means but it does raise questions about the infiltration of the peer group and the use of the internal politics of such a group in the service of adults.

- **Peer Education:** Here young people are used to educate their peers but the script for such education has been determined by adults. Here pressure is not a predominant feature nor an essential part of the dynamics. Examples of such an approach to the participation of the child are the account Elsa Dawson gives in Chapter 13 on the work of ANYI (the Association for Integrated Child Development) with older pupils being trained to teach younger children to play. Similarly, many of the activities of the Child to Child Trust are based on this model of involving children.

- **Peer-Led Work:** This sort of work is concerned with delivering messages arising from the insight and concerns of the peer group, but using adult-supplied resources, skills and training to address the issues and facilitate the work. It quite clearly demonstrates children guiding and focusing adult thinking, in some instances in quite sophisticated ways, with young people taking on some of the responsibilities of the education and empowering of their own group. The later stages of the Children's Parliament in Slovenia described in Chapter 6 is an example of this approach – as is, at the more local level, Sands School (Chapter 9). Similarly, Sarah McCrum's approach (Chapter 5) in making radio programmes with children reflects this sort of balance of power with the children guiding and shaping the agenda rather than simply mouthing predictable ideas that the producer had started out with in making a programme. Sarnia Harrison's work (Chapter 10) on the leaflet she prepared for other young people whose parents were going through the process of divorce is a further example of a young person accepting a responsibility in relation to support by education of the peer group. The Devon Youth Council have demonstrated the difference that a peer-led approach typifies and how, by starting with young people's realities, adult interventions may have a more realistic chance of success. The Youth Council have been working on a SCODA (Standing Committee on Drug Abuse) project locally. Adults were pressing for a 'total abstinence' approach whereas the peers leading the operation made it clear that a 'harm minimisation' campaign, at least as a first stage, was likely to be more effective. In this peer-led work described in Volume Three the Youth Council have found that a 2–3 year gap in age is most effective.

Activities within such a model of peer participation have demonstrated much about peer competence and also about the extent to which adults are themselves prepared to work in new roles with children.

BRIDGE BUILDING AS A MODEL FOR PARTICIPATION

Roger Hart has proposed a 'ladder' as a metaphor for the various stages in children's participation and entry into a democratic society. It has been a model that has been widely used. Earlier it was suggested that such a metaphor is unfortunate in all the implications it has of bestowing rights on a passive receiver. From much of what has already been said about children's participation it is clear that we need a model which is much more dynamic, which takes account of the politics of child participation and which also encompasses the construction of creative alliances with adults which forms the true basis of an emotional democracy on which, it could be argued, children's participation must be based.

Giddens' (1992) views on the establishment of emotional democracies are relevant here. He asserts that what characterises self/society relations in the late modern age is a move from prescribed bounded roles (and here one might think of those of adult/child) in relationships towards an emotional democracy where the self-in-relationship is not clearly prescribed but negotiated and sensitive to the needs of others. Whilst he himself does not deal with children, it is arguable that such a view is generalisable to them with the rendering of the child/adult boundary less clear. Giddens points out that many have found this fluidity too threatening and have tried to reach for control by putting back the clock, trying to get back to basics and old established family structures and values. He also talks of the pathological consequences in terms of exit-behaviours or aggression and violence that failure to cope with such a democracy involves. This has bred heated controversies about the proper rearing of children, and indeed about the nature of children themselves. Bob Franklin (1995), in a memorable phrase, suggests that 'Society constructs the children it needs' and goes on to point out that 'instead of policies to protect children, the government and the media have preferred to protect the community from children' (p.5). This could be interpreted as the backlash from a movement towards emotional democracies that include children.

Looking further at what sort of model could encompass the politics of children as a minority rights group, their entrainment with adults in processes of empowerment and their full membership as citizens in a democratic society,

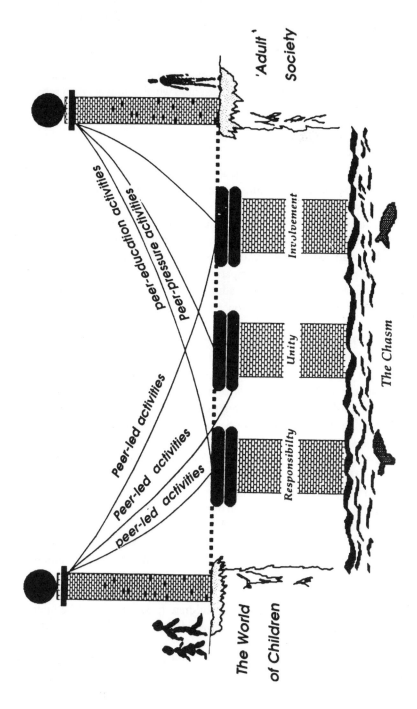

Figure 1.1 Building the bridge of participation

it is possible to see that the model must be a dynamic one and, I would argue, must encompass a radical change in one point of its development. If the Responsibility, Unity and Community Action which we used as a model for the early stages of the political life of children as a minority rights group were seen to be pillars to support a bridge that have to be put in place before the chasm between the world of the child and the world of the adult from which they are initially excluded in any powerful sense can be spanned, then we can see that, having built a strong movement (in which they may need facilitation and support), the children are then in a position to act collaboratively with adults in a variety of ways. They move from the solidly established base of their own in-group politics to negotiative and collaborative activities with adults. At this point there is a radical change in the character of the operation – the pillars are in place and the collaborative work of spanning the chasm can begin.

Thus a bridge can be built which involves firm foundations within the group and, for its ultimate success, the collaboration of both parties. In considering the form this collaboration might take, Penny Towsend's characterisation of different types of peer partnership activities is helpful. Finally, bridge building as a model for the participation of children is a useful one as it underlines the individual, collaborative and negotiative elements of the process – a process in which children are not passive but active constructors. In the case of children as a minority rights group, transforming power relations involves constructive and insightful relationships with children and with adults; it requires that they communicate and both are 'heard' and understood.

RESEARCH WITH THE SILENCED

In looking at research activity in relation to minority rights groups concerns, an analysis of the research methods themselves are important. Exciting work is emerging in qualitative research on 'voice', or 'voicing', the concerns of the silenced (prefigured in an early paper by Lincoln 1993). This takes a position that minority rights groups do not speak for themselves as the effects of the oppression they have experienced has been internalised such that they become 'silenced'. Not only are they invisible but also they are not heard. Moreover, the emphasis in this research paradigm is that 'voicing' is not about hearing what the underprivileged have to say and acting as their advocate, speaking for them or speaking on their behalf, but rather developing research methodologies on the basis of partnership, which in turn involves a new role in the power structure for the researcher – a move from the plunderer of information to facilitator which enables the child to be an active part of voicing their concerns. This involves a number of dilemmas for the researcher. One of these own concerns the construction of texts about the silenced. The problem used to be whether such material from the 'native's point of view' should be included at all. Now the concern has shifted to how best to represent that point of view

(Van Maanen 1988). Sarah McCrum, in Chapter 5 of this volume, describes how, in her research using the media as her form of representation of children's voices, she encountered problems of how best to get near to what the children really felt; what were their concerns. She makes it clear that the power of the mediator must not go unquestioned in such research.

There are further research issues associated with representing minority groups. Although many representations of such groups have been a-historic, we must acknowledge the history of silence and accept that '...emergent social science might shed its seeming a-historicity and presumed objectivity in favour of commitment to change and empowerment and social transformation' (Lincoln 1993, p.31). For the researcher to enter the field in the role of agent of social change is fraught with problems; ethical, moral, procedural and disciplinary. This is not the place to discuss these in the detail they require and, moreover, as Lincoln points out, the present state of affairs in research in this area makes it clear that the roles of researcher, researched and text will change radically but the shape those changes will take 'remain the least systematically explored arena in the contemporary literature on (research) method' (Lincoln 1993, p.32). Not only are there methodological issues but also ethical issues that arise and the political positions adopted will have to be delicately approached to ensure that the 'research itself does not further erode the rights of, alienate and indeed silence the silenced.' (Lincoln 1993, p.39).

Much of the research reported here is not in the sophisticated language of the professional/career researcher. This is partly to do with the fact that the history of research in children's rights is such a recent one and only slowly is a body of knowledge being built up about how to involve children. What is important in new paradigm research is that it captures the spirit of work going on on the ground; that it has a sort of authenticity – whether this be with traveller children in the far South West of England, with imaginative child-centred work with children on the streets of Tanzania, or on the streets of Edinburgh. This is work which is at an early exploratory stage of hunch-chasing rather than hypothesis-testing. It is not its translation into the language of the researcher but the resonances this work with children displays which helps to score our understanding of how, in reality, we can make good Articles 12 and 13 of the United Nations Convention of the Rights of the Child.

The implications have been that to work in this way with children we have to learn to look at the world with their eyes and hear their own articulations of their experiences and, importantly, communicate with them. Ultimately one would hope that the 'from above' and 'from below' perspectives will have been eliminated and also the suffering that sharpens the focus of powerlessness.

> We have for once learnt to see the great events of world history from below, from the perspective of the outcast, the suspects, the maltreated, the powerless, the oppressed, the reviled – in short from the perspective of those who suffer... We have to learn that personal suffering is a more

effective key, a more rewarding principle for exploring the world in thought and action than personal good fortune. This perspective from below must not become the partisan possession of those who are eternally dissatisfied; rather we must do justice to life in all its dimensions from higher satisfaction, whose foundation is beyond any talk of 'from below' or 'from above'. Dietrich Bonhoeffer *Letters and Papers from Prison* (1971, p.17)

REFERENCES

Arnstein, S.R. (1969) 'The Ladder of Citizen Participation.' *The American Institute of Planners Journal 35,* 216–224.

Aelred Stubbs, C.R. (ed) (1988) *Steve Biko. I Write What I Like. A Selection of his Writings.* Harmondsworth: Penguin.

Bonhoeffer, D. (1971) *Letters and Papers from Prison.* Ed. E. Bethge. London: SCM Press.

Boyden, J. (1990) 'Childhood and the policy makers; comparative perspective on the globalisation of childhood.' In A James and A. Prout (eds) *Constructing and Deconstructing Childhood: Contemporary Issues in the Sociological Study of Childhood.* London, New York, Philadelphia: The Falmer Press.

Children of the World (1994) *Rescue Mission Planet Earth. A Children's Edition of Agenda 21.* Peace Child International in association with UNICEF. London: Kingfisher Books.

Davie, R. (1993) 'Listen to the child: a time for change.' *The Vernon-Wall Lecture reprinted in The Psychologist, June 1993* or available as a booklet from the British Psychological Society, St Andrews House, 48 Princess Road, Leicester, LE1 7DR.

Detrick, S. (1992) *The United Nations Convention on the Rights of the Child: A Guide to the Travaux Préparatoires.* Dordrecht, Boston, London: Martinus Nijhoff Publishers.

Ennew, J. (1995) 'Outside childhood: street children's rights.' In B. Franklin (ed) *The Handbook of Children's Right. Comparative Policy and Practice.* London: Routledge.

European Centre for Social Welfare, Policy and Research (1995) Publicity Leaflet. Vienna.

Franklin, B. (1992) 'Children and decision making: developing empowering institutions.' In M.D. Fortuyn and M. de Langen (eds) *Towards the Realisation of Human Rights of Children; Lectures given at the Second International Conference on Children's Ombudswork.* Amsterdam: Children's Ombudswork Foundation and Defence for Children International.

Franklin, B. (1995) 'Children's rights a progress report.' In B. Franklin (ed) *The Handbook of Children's Right. Comparative Policy and Practice.* London: Routledge.

Fyfe, A. (1989) *Child Labour.* Cambridge: Polity Press.

Gibran, K. (1926) *The Prophet.* London: Heinemann.

Giddens, A. (1992) *The Transformation of Intimacy. Sexuality, Love and Eroticism in Modern Societies.* Cambridge: Polity Press.

Hart, R.A. (1992) *Children's Participation: From Tokenism to Citizenship. Innocenti Essays, No 4.* Florence: UNICEF International Child Development Centre.

John, M. (1993) 'Children with special needs as the casualties of a free market culture.' *The International Journal of Children's Rights 1*, 22.

John, M. (1995) 'Children's rights in a free-market culture.' In S. Stephens (ed) *Children and the Politics of Culture.* Princeton, NJ: Princeton University Press.

Lincoln, Y.S. (1993) 'I and thou: Method, voice, and roles in research with the silenced.' In D. McLaughlin and W. Tierney *Naming Silenced Lives. Personal Narratives and the Process of Educational Change* (pp.29–47). New York and London: Routledge.

Minnow, M. (1987) 'Interpreting rights; an essay for Robert Covern.' *96 Yale Law Journal 8*, 1860, 1904.

Programme on Childhood (1995) Leaflet *Childhood and Society* European Centre for Social Welfare, Policy and Research,. Berggasse 17, A-1090 Vienna, Austria.

Safilios Rothschild, C. (1976) 'Disabled persons' self-definitions and their implications for rehabilitation.' In G.L. Albrecht (ed) *The Sociology of Physical Disability.* Pittsburg, PA: University of Pittsburg Press.

Van Bueren, G. (1993) *International Documents on Children.* Dordrecht,Boston, London: Matinus Nijhoff Publishers.

Van Bueren, G. (1995) *The International Law on the Rights of the Child.* Dordrecht: Kluwer.

Van Maanen, J. (1988) *Tales of the field: On Writing Ethnography.* Chicago, IL: University of Chicago Press.

PART TWO

A Listening Culture?

CHAPTER ONE

The Quiet Revolution
Children's Rights in International Law

Geraldine Van Bueren

Over the past ten years or so what I shall call a 'quiet revolution' has taken place in first formulating and then establishing children's rights firmly on both the diplomatic and international legal agenda.

It may seem odd to focus on international law as it is commonly assumed that international law has similar qualities to those perceived in Mahatma Ghandi's view of 'Western civilisation'. When asked by a journalist, 'Mr Ghandi, what do you think of Western civilisation?', Ghandi replied, 'I think it would be a good idea'. Many people, likewise, think international law is a good idea but retain a scepticism about its achievements.

International law is often regarded as remote and ineffective and in many areas this is undoubtedly true. However, as far as specific children's rights are concerned international law is providing a trail which many States are beginning to follow. The United Nations Convention on the Rights of the Child is the first globally-binding treaty protecting children's civil, political, economic, social and cultural rights in both peacetime and armed conflict. In essence, the Convention on the Rights of the Child provides a Bill of Rights for Children which, by August 1995, 174 governments had accepted. The Convention's 41 substantive articles enshrine a broad range of rights from rights to privacy and freedom of religion and expression, to preventing child abduction, economic and sexual exploitation and prohibiting all unjustifiable forms of discrimination against children. The Convention seeks to protect children from torture, cruel, inhuman and degrading treatment and all forms of neglect and abuse. The Convention is concerned with developing preventive health care and recognises the rights of children with disabilities to active participation in community life. The Convention incorporates specific provisions on child justice and provides for equal access of all children to cultural, artistic and recreational activities.

The rights are many and varied and although they are not exhaustive, the Convention is significant because it is the first time in many years that the international community has spent any significant period considering the status of children and their entitlements. The Convention has also been significant, not only because of the rights which it enshrines, but as a symbol and a catalyst in introducing practical measures to improve the lives of specific groups of children. The symbolic nature of the Convention should not be underestimated; it legitimises the concept of children's rights, making the question 'do children have rights?' outdated. However, even whilst the Convention was being drafted states were asking what precisely are the rights of children. The many rights of the child can be divided into 'the four Ps': prevention, provision, protection and participation and it is the participatory rights of children which have contributed most to this quiet revolution.

One area of doubt was whether children can possess political rights or whether political rights only appertain to adulthood. What do we mean by children's political rights? Let's define our terms. Political rights are the rights which ensure that children are able, if they so wish, to participate at various levels in the promotion, formulation and enactment of policies. At first sight it appears that children do not, under international law, possess political rights. If one considers the highest form of political expression, the right to elect a government through the ballot box, international law is admittedly not very helpful as far as children are concerned.

Article 25 of another major human rights treaty, the International Covenant on Civil and Political Rights 1966, which entered into force in March 1976, guarantees every citizen the right to vote. There is nothing to prevent a State Party defining children above a certain age as citizens. Indeed, article 27 of the 1987 Constitution of Nicaragua gives children above the age of 16 the right to vote, and Nicaragua's pioneering example has been followed by Brazil. International law, however, does not guarantee children the right to vote. A petition to any of the international or regional human rights tribunals, from a child of a State Party, which does not enfranchise children, alleging a breach of their right to freedom of political expression, would fail.

International law also does not recognise the right of children to stand for elections. In the case of W, X, Y, and Z, v. Belgium (a very catchy case name) the European Commission of Human Rights observed that, when Belgium established a minimum age of 25 for those wishing to stand for election to the House of Representatives, Belgium could not be regarded either as imposing an unreasonable or an arbitrary condition by, in effect, preventing everyone under 25 from standing for election. It is because international law does not enshrine the child's positive right to vote or to stand in elections that some wrongly assume children do not possess political rights. However, let us remember that the definition of political rights does not limit itself to the ballot box and standing for election. It concerns an input to policy promotion, adoption and implementation at all levels.

One initiative has been taken by the President of Venezuela. Once a week a car leaves the Presidential residence to go to a poorer section of the capital. The car picks up a 12-year-old boy and takes him back to the President. He is one of the President's advisers on the environment and reports on the changes in the quality of the environment in his neighbourhood. Now, this may be dismissed as tokenism, but Venezuela is challenging the assumption that young children do not have anything to say of political significance. In fact, on local issues that also concern children, the former Norwegian Child Ombud found that children sometimes have a superior knowledge of local conditions and service provision.

The United States Supreme Court has also recognised that children have, and are entitled to exercise, their political rights. In the case of Tinker v. Des Moines School District, the Supreme Court upheld the right of school students to wear black armbands in school to protest against the Vietnam war. The Court held that school students cannot be punished for expressing their views, even if they are political views, unless the school authorities have reason to believe that such expression will 'substantially interfere with the work of the school or impinge upon the rights of other students'. Although this was a case decided under American national law, the relevant provisions of the Constitution of the United States are similar to international legal provisions and hence this landmark decision has implications for children outside of America.

In Lothian, an area in Scotland, children were consulted by the local authority as to whether they wanted a Charter of Children's Rights and if so, which rights did they wish to be incorporated. Lothian became the first local authority in the United Kingdom to adopt such a Charter of Children's Rights. The Lothian Charter could not have come about unless attitudes towards children and their entitlements had changed. International law has provided an impartial framework for arguing for these changes.

Venezuela and Lothian are examples of children exercising their right to freedom of expression, both in speaking out, and in being heard, on political issues. Yet there are dangers in quiet revolutions. Quiet revolutions can sometimes go unnoticed.

At the much heralded World Summit on Children held at United Nations headquarters in September 1990, 70 political leaders met to discuss the lives of children. The leaders at the World Summit adopted a Declaration on the Survival, Protection and Development of Children. Although this Declaration acknowledges that 'the well-being of children requires political action at the highest level', the Declaration assumes that this must be by adults and does not involve children themselves. Fortunately this is a non-binding Declaration and the assumption that political action for children is the exclusive terrain of adults is being continually challenged and shown to be wrong by the children themselves. In particular, as we shall see later, by children in Brazil.

In addition to children expressing themselves through political channels, another important international legal right for children when it comes to their political rights is the right to freedom of association and assembly.

Article 15 of the Convention on the Rights of the Child provides that 'States Parties recognise the right of the child to freedom of association and freedom of peaceful assembly'. When Article 15 was originally proposed for inclusion in the Convention, Poland objected. Poland objected both for cynical reasons and because they and a number of other states genuinely could not see the relevance of the right to freedom of association and assembly to children. They are, after all, rights more often associated with trade unions. But the right to freedom of association is equally applicable to children to associate in a wide variety of voluntary organisations from scouting, guiding or a Youth Council, as described elsewhere in this volume (Townsend, Chapter 7), to campaigning for nuclear disarmament and peace or for the establishment by children of a school union. Some of the street children of Brazil have shown how important this political right is for children.

The Brazilian street children have effectively exercised their right to freedom of association; that is the right to meet together to plan policies and discuss political issues. In May 1986 the first National Street Children's Congress was held in Brasilia, the capital of Brazil. Four hundred and fifty children came from groups throughout Brazil and the location of Brasilia was designed to raise the awareness of public authorities of the problems which street children face. This was followed in 1989 by the Second National Congress of Street Children with 700 children, not only from Brazil, but also from other Latin American states. The children met with national politicians and among other issues discussed was the draft of what is now the Brazilian Child and Adolescent Statute.

The right to freedom of association is particularly important for children because it is a right which increases the power of individuals by conferring on them the right to participate in a group activity. This right to freedom of association, therefore, has a particular relevance for the more vulnerable members of society and hence children. In Brazil, from 1989 onwards, the street children succeeded in attracting both national and global media attention. There they marched through the streets of the capital protesting at the lack of government action, and even government complicity, in the murders of street children. The placards they carried, including the ones which said 'we don't want to be a social problem', were far more eloquent than any adult statement. Hence the right to freedom of assembly is particularly relevant for children because children do not generally have access to the mass media. Nowadays it is through access to the media that issues become forced on to the political agenda.

These are the kinds of issues from the raising of specific problems to be placed on the political agenda, to the meeting with politicians, that children do and are capable of doing successfully. To ignore the political rights of the child is not in the best interests of children. Not to acknowledge the exercise by children of their political rights is to deny the bravery, and the pain, of child political prisoners – be they Turkish, Palestinian or Kurdish schoolchildren.

One of the reasons for this quiet revolution in children's rights is that, as well as being a symbol, the UN Convention on the Rights of the Child has also acted as a catalyst for reforms in the area of children's rights.

In the aftermath of the Romanian revolution there was a belief that children were being exploited and taken out of Romania for adoption. Reports circulating in the western media alleged that up to 150,000 children were abandoned in institutions. The facts were very different. Some children were indeed institutionalised under horrifying conditions and a humanitarian response was needed, but the vast majority of children were not abandoned. Many were traumatised and needed special family environments and a large percentage were HIV positive.

In fact, the most sought after children for adoption were under the age of three and they were only in their hundreds in institutions. Yet thousands of babies were adopted abroad. Because of the lack of suitable babies for adoption, i.e. babies without living family members, many prospective parents from western states made deals directly with biological parents who were prepared to give up their children for cash. The pressure on these economically deprived parents became intense. The exodus was so great that by the beginning of 1991 over a quarter of all children adopted internationally came from only one country, Romania. Over half of the Romanian children adopted abroad were under six months and many had not been in the care of an institution but obtained directly from their families.

Romania invited Defence for Children International and International Social Services to report. Their report confirmed that the level of adoptions had reached the level of a 'national tragedy'. Romania acted quickly to comply with international law which is contained in a United Nations Declaration on Fostering and Adoption as well as in the Convention on the Rights of the Child. The law states that the first priority is for children to be cared for by their own parents. Inter-country adoption should only be considered if no suitable solution is found in the child's own country, and all adoptions have to be governed by the best interests of the child and not the best interests of the prospective adopters. In addition, in no case should the placement result in improper financial gain for those involved in the adoption. Romania's immediate response was to suspend inter-country adoptions, create an agency and a national legal structure to ensure protection and then to allow inter-country adoptions within this tight structure (Van Bueren 1995).

Albania has also undergone social turbulence. Albania knew of the successful application of international law in Romania and similarly, in 1992, invited Defence for Children and International Social Services to help draft legislation on inter-country adoption. Between February 1991 and March 1992, 279 children were taken out of Albania. 90% of these children went to only three countries; 160 children were taken to Italy, 54 children to Greece and 49 to the United States. Which, apart from anything else, seemed to point to a certain degree of organisation in these three receiving states. As in the case of Romania, once there were no more children available from institutions, families were approached directly. Albania acted very swiftly. It was concerned over the trafficking of Albanian children and suspended several judges and lawyers, as well as initiating legal actions against some of the directors of children's institutions (Van Bueren 1995).

A number of other countries are contributing to this quiet revolution by taking the international law on children very seriously. Some of them are doing so with scarce resources and have imaginatively adapted their policies to fit their available resources. Examining examples from the sphere of education is instructive. The right to education on the basis of equal opportunity is so fundamental that Article 28 of the Convention makes all other aspects of the right to education dependent upon it. Yet at present over 100 million children are without basic schooling – of whom two to three are girls, many of them living in rural communities.

Bangladesh, as a step towards universal free primary education (which it is under a duty to introduce progressively), in the early 1990s adopted a policy of free education for all girls up to 14 years of age who live in the non-metropolitan areas. It is too soon to judge the success of this policy but in Bangladesh, as in many other developing states, girls do not have access to education for a number of cultural, economic and political reasons. Bangladesh's policy has removed one of these hurdles; the obstacle of unaffordability.

A number of other countries, not all of them wealthy, are also taking time to examine the provisions of the Convention. A number of states have established law reform committees reviewing national legislation to bring their national laws up to the required international standards. These include Uganda, Tanzania and Zimbabwe. Mozambique has adopted its own Declaration of the Rights of the Mozambican Child and Sri Lanka has developed a national five-year plan for Sri Lankan children with specific targets for child development. In addition, the Organisation of African Unity has become the first regional organisation to adopt its own treaty on the rights of children in Africa.

These are only the beginnings and it is not time for complacency. There is still a need to increase government and public awareness of the negative consequences of beliefs and attitudes which deny children their rights. This is why Article 42 of the Convention is so useful. Article 42 provides that states parties are under a duty to make the provisions and principles of the Convention widely known by active means to both adults and children.

At its most extreme, this undervaluing and consequential invisibility of children endangers their lives. The lack of concern, and even irritation, over street children in Brazil and Guatemala contributed to the atmosphere in which it was possible to clear the streets of children, not through love, but extermination. Street children were routinely murdered with, initially, no public outcry. The children are seen as an embarrassment rather than as lacking opportunities to share in the exercise of their rights to shelter, adequate food and education. Now, in part because of the international outcry, Guatemala, a signatory to the Convention the Rights of the Child, has brought proceedings against at least six police officers for the murder of street children. However, a number of child witnesses to the murders have had to be taken out of the country for their own protection. To avoid such a situation arising in Costa Rica, the Costa Rican El Defensor de law Infancia is helping design programmes for Costa Rican police to sensitise them to children's rights. Training for police on the rights of children is important, not only for working with street children, but for child justice generally.

There has also been an unheralded revolution in the international law on child justice.

The Convention on the Rights of the Child places a duty on states parties to promote the establishment of a minimum age below which children should be presumed not to have the capacity to infringe the penal law. Inevitably, when establishing minimum ages there is arbitrariness, but the minimum age for criminal responsibility ought to be linked to the child's development and maturity. If the age of criminal responsibility is too low or non-existent then the concept of responsibility becomes meaningless. At present there is a wide disparity in age, even within the continent of Europe. In Ireland criminal responsibility begins at seven, in the Ukraine at 14 and in Sweden at 15. As bright as Irish children are, are we really saying that they mature eight years earlier than the Swedes and seven years earlier than the Ukrainians?

International law also seeks to persuade states that children should be diverted away from formal justice processes partly because of the vulnerability of children within the juvenile justice system. A comparative study of children in adult prisons throughout the world revealed that a common feature in all the national surveys was the lack of protection of children in the pre-trial stages of criminal proceedings. The study reported that:

> Extensive powers of the police, vague provisions for the protection of rights of arrested or detained persons and practically non-existent accountability of officials directly or indirectly responsible for ill-treatment of children caused the taking of children into custody and their pre-trial detention to be emphasised as a primary concern for the protection of children. (Tomasevski 1986)

The Convention establishes as the aim of child justice systems the entitlement of children to be treated in a manner consistent with their age, the desirability of promoting their re-integration and assumption of a constructive role in society. Society's needs are viewed as being satisfied if the child is shown how to re-integrate and assume a constructive role in society. The emphasis in the Convention is on the 'promotion of the child's sense of dignity and worth' and this cannot be undertaken where a state party is adopting policies solely with punitive and deterrent characteristics. International law also de-prioritises institutionalisation because of its many adverse effects. Children are particularly vulnerable to negative influences because of the combined effect of a loss of liberty and separation from their accustomed daily social life. With its new focus on the re-integration of children, international law seeks to assist children in beginning to believe that they are valued members of the community. This has the opposite effect of institutionalisation, which risks alienating them.

In addition to the restrictions which international law places on states depriving children of their liberty, international law also prohibits specific forms of punishment from being imposed on children. These include the imposition of the death penalty and life imprisonment without review for those under 18. The age which is significant is the age at which the offence was committed. A state is not entitled to wait until a person passes his or her eighteenth birthday and then perform the execution. If a person commits a crime below the age of eighteen that person can never be executed for that crime. In the past decade only seven states have executed its juvenile offenders; Iran, Iraq, Nigeria, Pakistan, and the United States. One execution was also reported in Bangladesh. Barbados, which was included in the list, has since raised the minimum age to 18.

With the exception of Iran and Iraq, the United States has executed more juveniles in recent years than any other country. An Amnesty International Report on 23 juveniles sentenced to death in the United States found that the majority of the offenders came from 'acutely deprived backgrounds; at least 12 had been seriously physically or sexually abused; ten were known to be regular users of drugs or alcohol from an early age. At least 14 of the 23 juvenile offenders suffered from mental illness or brain damage. Most were of below-average intelligence but despite this the trial juries had no opportunity to consider the defendant's mental capacity or background as factors mitigating against a possible death sentence.' Despite the fact that the Supreme Court has ruled that age should be considered a 'relevant mitigating factor of great weight', Amnesty International found '...that in some cases the defendant's age was not fully mentioned or fully considered'. Although the United States is not a party to the Convention on the Rights of the Child it has signed the Convention and pressure is mounting within America to abolish the death penalty for children.

The Convention will continue to act as a catalyst for action because it raises the profile of children and reduces their invisibility. Furthermore, the Committee on the Rights of the Child, which is the independent body entrusted with monitoring the Convention, ought to help maintain this more visible profile. The Committee is made up of ten experts in the field of children's rights serving in their personal capacities. States report on how they have implemented each of the articles in the Convention and are questioned in public on their reports – as was evidenced in the widely published comments on the United Kingdom's first submitted report (HMSO 1994). The Committee will also be able to facilitate the provision of technical advice and assistance to states who have difficulties in implementing specific provisions in the Convention.

The weakest part of the Convention is that it does not, despite the urgings of Amnesty International, enshrine a right of individual petition. The intention is that each of the government reports will be made 'widely available' and so be used to stimulate national debates on the rights of children. It does, however, mean that the committee does not have the jurisdiction to respond to individual children's complaints.

Children should not be afraid of bringing cases to international fora. A number of children have already taken their cases to Strasbourg, to the European Commission and Court of Human Rights. Children also pleaded their case at the United Nations in Geneva whilst the Convention on the Rights of the Child was being drafted. A group of Canadian children argued successfully for the right of indigenous children to have the right to practice their own culture, language and religion and this was incorporated into the Convention.

Less successful, but very well organised, was the petition from children presented to delegates urging states to prohibit child soldiers. The children's petition organised by the Swedish youth branch of the Red Cross argued that, they, as the youth of the world, wanted 18 to be established as the minimum age for child soldiers. In this, unfortunately, they did not succeed. The Convention only reiterated the standard of 15 as the minimum age with a duty to recruit the oldest first amongst 15- to 18-year-olds. However, this is an issue which is not likely to go away – particularly as there are plans to raise the age limit by drafting an additional Protocol to the UN Convention.

The Quiet Revolution has also led to the creation of national and local officers to implement the rights of the child. A number of countries including Norway, Costa Rica, New Zealand and Sweden have Ombuds or Commissioners for Children. The Ombud is one way of protecting the rights of children. A Children's Ombud can scrutinise legislation to ensure that it protects children's rights. The Ombud can lobby on behalf of children and can, unannounced, visit children's homes and children's detention institutions. Coalitions of non-governmental organisations have also been formed to monitor the Convention in their own countries and to submit alternative reports to the Committee on the Rights of the Child.

More is still needed if the Convention on the Rights of the Child is to be a useful practical tool. The Convention can only be pleaded in the national courts of 'those states which have incorporated the Convention or its provisions directly into national law'. If children wish to bring, for example, a case in British courts relying solely on a provision of the UN Convention they would be unlikely to succeed.

I would like to call for countries to incorporate the Convention on the Rights of the Child into their national laws. Incorporation would mean that the UN Convention could be used where it would be most effective; in the courts. As we in comfort contemplate and discuss children's rights, children are still dying in Somalia and their lives are at risk in Bosnia and Rwanda. It is tempting just to be despondent and to cast aside international law as useless.

However, international law has its limits and it is just as damaging to argue that international law ought to remedy all ills as it is erroneous to assert that international law achieves nothing. The truth lies midway between the two. As we have seen, international law, can and, has helped specific groups of children.

Children's rights in international law have passed through a quiet revolution. We have come a long way since the 1870s when in New York Mary Ellen was chained to her bed by her parents. There was no law at that time protecting children and the only way Mary Ellen could be helped was by claiming she was a member of the animal kingdom and entitled to the protection of the statute protecting animals. The Quiet Revolution has come a long way since then. But we still have a long way to go. Children and adults working together on these issues can help contribute to the progress.

REFERENCES

W,X,Y and Z v. Belgium 6745 6/7 DR 2, 110.

John F. Tinker v. Mary Beth Tinker, Minors v. Des Moines Independent Community School District (393 U.S. 503).

Declaration on the Survival, Protection and Development of Children. World Summit for Early Childhood Education, World Congress, 1992. 'Working for all children, their survival, protection and development.' Mesa and Flagstaff, Anjona.

United Nations Declaration on Fostering and Adoption. Adapted by the General Assembly 2 December, 1986. Published by United Nations Department of Public Information, DPI/14, August 1987.

Death penalty and juvenile offenders (1991) New York, Amnesty International Publications.

HMSO (1994) The United Nations Convention on the Rights of the Child. The UK's First Report to the United Nations Committee on the Rights of the Child. London: HMSO.

African Charter on the Rights and Welfare of the Child. OAU Assembly of Heads of State and Government, 1990. Adis Ababa: OAU.

Tomasevski, K. (ed) (1986) *Children in Adult Prison. An International Perspective.* London: F. Pinter.

For a detailed analysis of the international law see:

Van Bueren, G. (1995) *The International Law on the Rights of the Child.* Dordrecht: Kluwer.

All the details of the international instruments can be found in:

Van Bueren, G. (1993) *International Documents on Children.* Dordrecht, Boston and London: Martinus Nijhoff Publishers.

CHAPTER TWO

Children's Rights

Cross-national Research on Perspectives of Children and their Teachers

Stuart Hart, Moshe Zeidner and Zoran Pavlovic

The United Nations Convention on the Rights of the Child sets standards for the protection, nurturance, development, and participation of children. This treaty is clearly a major step forward in the collective progress of civilised people toward caring for and respecting children as persons. It requires much more careful planning, action and evaluation for child rearing than any nation has previously achieved.

Over 175 nations had ratified this international treaty by the time of this writing.[1] They have assumed the responsibility to upgrade child life-conditions in the direction of the Convention's standards and to regularly report on their progress in doing so. While all dimensions of the treaty must be given attention, arguably the child's progress toward participation and self-determination in a democratic society is a major, and possibly overriding theme, because it is both a formative and summative goal of the treaty (see particularly articles 12–15, 29, and 42). Like Piaget, the drafters of the Convention appear to have recognised socially responsible autonomy as the superordinate goal of human development (Hart and Pavlovic 1991; Kamii 1991).

There are four basic alternatives for adults to influence the lives of children: to do things to them, for them, around them, and with them (Catterall 1970). The UN Convention explicitly and implicitly encourages all four of these strategies. The fourth, doing things with children, is essential to enable children to responsibly participate in decisions about issues which will or may influence their lives. In setting goals for meeting the standards of the Convention, and

---

1   This chapter was originally presented in September 1992 at the UN convention; and was written in this form in September 1995.

for monitoring progress toward those standards, most nations will follow traditional patterns of gathering information from adult-constituted governmental and non-governmental agencies, and from adult authorities. This will not be sufficient if the spirit of the Convention is to be realised. It is essential that information is also gathered directly from young people as persons whose opinions are important. Strong cases have been made for soliciting and incorporating the views of children in efforts to achieve children's rights (Hart 1991; Melton 1987; Verhellen 1989). This chapter describes a cross-national research project which has been gathering information on the perspectives of children and educators about the importance children's rights deserve and the degree to which they have been established.

DEVELOPMENT OF THE PROJECT

In 1986 the International School Psychology Association (ISPA) began exploring possibilities for conducting children's rights research which would give particular emphasis to the views of children. The chairs of ISPA's child development/services and research committees (Stuart Hart and Moshe Zeidner), over a two-year period and with the advice and encouragement of psychologists from a wide variety of nations, determined the major objectives and scope of the project.

Originally the project was intended to periodically gather data from young people aged 7–8, 12–14, and 17–18 years; and from teachers and parents of these age groups to determine:

- their perspectives on the importance that should be given to a selection of children's rights and the degree to which those rights are presently supported,
- the techniques being used by child rearers (parents and educators) to socialise their children,
- the documented perspectives, commitments and practices of the institutions of society regarding children's rights.

The main objectives of the project have always been to investigate the conditions of treatment of children, conditions of desired treatment for children, and the discrepancies between these conditions within and across nations. Practical considerations led to planning for this research to be conducted through a series of stages, building from relatively narrow to broad research goals, with each stage giving direction for modifications and refinements in later stages and, if successful, stimulating resource, dissemination, and application support for subsequent stages.

The first stage of the research was designed to explore the perspectives of 12- to 14-year-old persons, because of their pivotal developmental position, and of teachers of that age group. Hart and Zeidner, two of the authors of this chapter, worked closely together in planning the project in 1987 and 1988. In 1990, as Zeidner experienced constraints on his schedule, Zoran Pavlovic, the third author, began to assist in the project and has recently become a co-prin-cipal investigator.

INSTRUMENT DEVELOPMENT

The questionnaire instrument for the first stage of the project, presented in Appendix 1, gives attention to all the major themes of the United Nations Declaration of the Rights of the Child and to what, in 1988, was the proposed form on the United Nations Convention on the Rights of the Child. The questionnaire includes 40 items which cover protection, nurturance, participa-tion and self-determination. These items were developed through a process of proposals being made by Hart and Zeidner, several rounds of advice and consent by an international reference group of child development specialists and researchers, and review and recommendations made by Irwin Hyman (Temple University) and Mike Jupp (Director, Defense for Children International-USA at that time).

The questionnaire asks the responding youth or teacher to indicate, for 12 to 14-year-old persons, (a) the degree to which the rights exists, and (b) the importance the rights should be given on five point scales. A sixth option is provided for use if the subject does not have a response or does not think the item applies. Appendix 2 presents the response scales for existence and impor-tance. The items were written to match the reading and conceptual levels of 12- to 14-year-old persons, and, through pilot work, were found to be processed effectively by 11- and 12-year-old learning-disabled students. Re-sponses provide the opportunity to make comparisons of the level of importance and existence between items, and for items across home and school settings; and for discrepancies between the level of importance and existence within the school and within the home, and between the home and school.

Two forms of the questionnaire, with items in random order and alternating responses for existence and importance and home and school were found to be sufficient for the project's purposes. This decision was made after reviewing findings for pilot work in the United States, with the items in hierarchical sequence, and two years of data gathering in other nations using four alternate forms with items in random order and responses for existence and importance, and home and school in all possible sequences. In addition to responding to the rights questions, each subject was asked to provide identifying demographic information including age, sex and grade. Country, community type and school type were either entered by subjects as directed by those administering the questionnaire or coded by the teachers or field research leaders. Respondents were given the opportunity to voluntarily indicate their father's and mother's highest level of education, their own religion; and to indicate on the back of their answer sheet whether there are rights which have not been covered in the questionnaire and whether there are some groups or people not treated fairly in regard to rights.

The questionnaires were used in their original form in nations where English was the primary language. In other nations it was required that researchers translate the questionnaire into the primary language(s) of their country and back-translate from their language version to English to verify for the co-principal investigators that the essence of each question was respected.

SUBJECTS

Through the communication channels of the ISPA, interest in participating in the research was solicited. Populations from a nation were included in the research when a national field research leader or leaders volunteered who had access to sufficient resources, and the ability to enlist participation from schools in a variety of community types and geographical locations capable of producing desired data.

For each participating nation the following subject characteristic criteria were set as goals: 400 or more subjects, students aged 12 to 14 years, equal numbers of males and females, equal numbers from the lowest socio-economic status level (within the lowest quartile of socio-economic standing) and the modal socio-economic status (the largest middle income group in the country) and rural-small town and suburban-urban community types. Socio-economic status was to be indicated by school type as judged by the lead researcher and/or the educators of the school involved, and by the father's educational level. The teacher population for each country was to equal fifty or more, preferably to be from the same schools as selected students, and to be teachers of the 12- to 14-year-old age group.

METHODS

Prior to participation in the research, each national field research supervisor, prominent social scientists within their own countries, had the opportunity to review the purposes, procedures and instrumentation for the project. They were able to request that certain items be modified, omitted, or added to the questionnaire. None of the countries for which data is reported eliminated any of the elements of the basic instrument, although some did add questions. One modified the administration procedure to have individual subjects respond to subsections of the questionnaire rather than the questionnaire in its entirety, and two countries expanded their data gathering to other-aged students and to other adults, the results of which are not dealt with in this report. The Office for the Study of the Psychological Rights of the Child (OSPRC, Indiana University-Purdue University at Indianapolis, USA) was the co-ordinating center for this research project and as such it provided materials for instructing those who would administer the questionnaire, for gaining school system approval, for gaining parental approval for the involvement of each child, and for informing the child of his/her rights regarding participation in the project. Additionally, the OSPRC provided machine-scoreable answer sheets to all researchers wishing to use them and data processing services, which were partially underwritten by the ISPA.

The questionnaires were administered by teachers, school counsellors or colleagues of the national field research supervisors in school classrooms and required 35 to 45 minutes to complete. Results were generally sent to the OSPRC for processing.

FINDINGS AND INTERPRETATIONS

Data gathering for the first stage has been completed and its processing begun in 13 countries: Belgium, China, Czech Republic, France, India, Iran, Lithuania, Poland, Slovakia, Slovenia, Thailand, USA, and Russia (previously USSR). Data gathering is also complete in Brazil, Denmark, and Iceland, with processing yet to occur, and data should soon be available from Australia, Greece, Portugal, and Venezuela. As will be seen in Appendix 3, the national data populations vary greatly in their size.

With few exceptions, the findings presented in the following sections will not identify the particular country from which they originate for the following reasons. The opportunity to complete analyses sufficiently characterising the data populations and comparing the data between countries has not yet been accomplished. In addition it was agreed that each field research team would have the opportunity to analyse thoroughly its own data and to formally agree to have it included in identifiable form in reports before this would occur.

General findings for a few of the major issues will be presented here. Students will be referred to, interchangeably, as students or children. The first major phase of analysis for student and teacher data has been done for the first five countries to report data, while only a beginning has been made in analysing student data for the additional eight countries for which data has been more recently reported (see Hart and Zeidner 1993 for a more extensive presentation and discussion of findings from the first five countries reporting). The goal here is to provide a sense of the possibilities for this research as exhibited in this early stage of analysis. Results are presented in both parametric and non-parametric statistical terms. The question of the appropriateness of particular statistical techniques for this data continues to be debated.

IMPORTANCE OF RIGHTS

Findings

Student data results for the first five countries to report found average ratings of importance for specific rights for home approaching *very important* to *of greatest importance*, and for school *important* to *very important*. For the 13 countries which have reported data, composite average home importance ratings range from a low of 3.29 to a high of 4.54, *important* to approaching *of greatest importance*, and school importance ratings range from a low of 3.22 to a high of 4.32, *important* to *very important*. Data from the 13 countries shows a broad range of responses, and in fact, when the data for each country is considered, some countries are found to have importance ratings for particular items averaging as low as 2.44 for home and 2.68 for school and as high as 4.81 for home and 4.67 for school.

The items identified as most important by children, in the top 20 per cent, are quite similar across these findings for the five-country composite and for the 13 countries, and for home and school. They emphasise safety, protection and help in times of danger, physical necessities, love and affiliation, support for development and self-respect. The following items were indicated to be given priority by children across all data: 6, 7, 9, 11, 18, 25, 26, and 40 (see Appendix 1 for item statement). Item 35, the right to have a place to study, was also given importance, being in the top 20 per cent for 6 and 5 of the 13 countries for home and school respectively.

An analysis of the range of rank positions (i.e. difference between the lowest and highest rank across the 13 countries) for these eight items found the majority to be under 30, with some under 20 (HI items 25, 40; SI items 11, 26), and one above 30 (HI item 7: the right to grow up strong and healthy in mind and body). This suggests that while these items are generally considered to be quite important, significant differences exist in the relative importance given them within different countries. Discrepancies between rankings across countries for the 160 item-comparisons possible found 121 to be at 20 or greater rank positions of difference. The greatest discrepancies between rankings across countries, all of 30 rank positions or higher, were given to items 4, 7, 13, 15, 16, 20, 21, 27, 28, 33, 35, 36, and 38. Seven, more than half of these items, focus on participation, choice and/or privacy rights.

Teacher judgments of the importance of rights have been analysed only for the first five countries to report. Teacher responses indicate they generally agree with students on the relative importance of rights in the home to support or respect basic human needs. Teachers differ more in the rights that rank in the top 20 per cent for the school, with students ranking the rights to a healthy mind and body (7), learn what is right and wrong (26), and a place to study (35) much higher than the rankings of teachers; and teachers ranking the right to be with people who love you (25) much higher than students. In the early five-country composites, teachers were found to vie somewhat lower values than students to rights in the home, and lower but closer values to rights in the school.

Interpretations and comments

All rights appear to be judged to have at least some importance by children. Both the early and more recent data indicate that children and teachers generally give greater importance to rights in the home than in the school. This may be due to the fact that the first critical years producing the base for further development occur in the home where affiliation and commitment are personal and strong and that this is sensed both intuitively and recognised generally. Rights given the greatest importance by both children and teachers emphasise basic human need fulfillment of the type conceptualised by Maslow (1970), somewhat validating the foundational nature of these rights. The more extensive life experiences of teachers may lead them to be more moderate in their judgements, supporting their generally lower ratings of importance in comparison to children. This finding suggests that developmental and age trends will be worth analysis for both children and teachers as data from a broader range of those populations becomes available. The differences in average scale values and rank positions given to rights by children of different countries (of statistical significance in both cases) indicate that there is much to be learned about the conditions which produce these varying perspectives. In some countries the realities of life and the persuasions of cultures and subcultures may encourage quite different hopes and expectations. Differences in the children's ranking of the importance of rights (derived from average scale values) across countries appears to be substantial for a majority of the items, and particularly large for higher order privacy, participation and choice rights. Among the explanations for this finding which deserve further study are the possibilities that great variation is being expressed by children in this 12–14 transition stage toward more adultlike identity and expectations for rights, and that these variations are strongly associated with cultural differences in conceptions of children as persons versus property and/or the age at which, if ever, autonomy rights are to be conferred.

EXISTENCE OF RIGHTS AND COMPARISONS WITH IMPORTANCE

Findings

In the five-country composite, on the average across items, students were found to rate specific rights in the home to exist from between a medium and a large degree to between a large degree and fully supported, and in the school to exist from a medium to large degree. Average scale values for existence in the home for the composite were all found to be significantly higher than those for existence in the school. The 13 country data reveals a similar pattern, with existence ratings for the composite of items for the home ranging from 3.29 to 4.36 and for the school from 3.20 to 4.45. Differences in findings for comparisons between the 13 countries were found to be quite pronounced, e.g. for some countries findings for home and school are reversed with existence ratings generally higher for school, others produced quite similar ratings for home and school, and some countries had school ratings dramatically lower than home ratings.

As with the importance findings, the rights judged to exist at the highest levels concentrate on basic human needs. The items which find clearest support for existing at higher levels across data for home settings are 6, 9, 11, 20, 25, and 26 and for school settings are 5, 13, 19, 10, 26, and 35. Only item 26, the right to have a chance to learn what is right and wrong in order to become a good person, is indicated to generally be of high importance and to exist at a high level by students across all data, and with differences in ranks across countries relatively small.

Items for which existence is judged to be lowest across most of the five and 13 country results deal with rights to: be given help by experts when you are confused or feel bad (1), have people look after you and speak up for you when you need it (3), be treated fairly when people think you are wrong (4), be able to play and make believe (14), have time and a place to be alone without being bothered by others (21), have money to spend as you choose (23), make choices that fit your age about how you will behave (24), be respected as a person free to act in you own special ways (27), be able to live on your own when you are ready and choose to do so (36). Average scale values for the importance of rights were higher than those for the existence of rights for the home and for the school, and significantly so, for all but three items for the five country composite. The 20 per cent of items for which the discrepancies were greatest dealt predominantly with participation and self-determination issues, and with respect and support from adults. Also, those items which were found in the bottom 20 per cent for existence, but were not in the bottom 20 per cent for importance, were all participation and self-determination rights. While the thirteen-country composite data indicates a clear majority of the items are rated higher on the importance scale than on the existence scale, for some countries many items were rated higher for existence than for importance. Data for 11 of the 13 countries shows more items with importance judged higher than existence; in 80 of 80 comparisons for two countries, and in 70 or more of 80 comparisons for seven countries. For the two countries showing the opposite pattern, one had only 12 and the other 33 comparisons for which importance was scaled higher than existence.

Teacher findings for the five-country data indicate they judge rights to exist in the home, on the average, from slightly below a medium degree to slightly above a large degree; and in the school from below a medium degree to a large degree. Teachers, on the average, judged for the majority of items (33 of 40) that home existence was higher than school existence, but for only 16 items were the differences significant, 14 for which home existence was higher (items 2, 3, 6, 7, 9, 14, 21, 22, 24, 25, 30, 31, 34, 38) and two for which school existence was higher (1, to be given help by experts…and 39, to be given as much help as you need in order to learn). Discrepancies between importance and existence as judged by teachers are significant and in favour of importance for nearly all same-item comparisons for both home and school settings. The top 20 per cent of items for which these discrepancies are greatest emphasize healthy and full development and respect for the views and decision-making ability of children.

Interpretations and comments

Rights have been judged to exist at lower levels in school than in home environments, and generally to exist at levels below the importance given to them. These findings, with few exceptions, appear to hold across national, student and teacher data. Particular emphasis needs to be given to exploring the conditions and reasons for children to view rights providing adult help, trust and respect, and opportunities to make choices about their own behaviour to be relatively poorly supported.

To the degree it is accepted that existence and importance scale meanings allow for comparison between what is and what should be, these findings identify discrepancies which can give direction to efforts toward improvements. The relatively low levels of existence, and the stronger discrepancies between importance and existence levels for privacy, participation and self-determination rights supports targeting them for special attention in plans to intervene and upgrade. It raises questions about the degree to which children, during this transition period of development, are conceived and treated as persons progressing toward autonomy.

Clearly it is not sufficient to focus on composite or across-country findings. It appears that quite significant differences exist in the perceived levels of existence of rights and in comparisons of desired and existing conditions between countries. The conditions which lead students in one country to find existence quite discrepant from and below importance levels, while those in other countries find them quite similar, or even that existence exceeds expectations, deserves careful analysis and very probably further research. Advancement of children's rights may be well served by inquiry into the correlational and causative factors, and the concrete associates of the divergent views. Many hypotheses for these inter-country differences deserve to be explored – including misunderstanding of the response options, tendencies to set very low expectations and/or to feel you deserve less than you get, genuinely good conditions which exceed expectations and fear of responding in a manner which might incur criticism for one's country. Consideration must also be given to the degree to which it is justified to make comparisons between findings for the two scales.

GENDER DIFFERENCES IN PERSPECTIVES ON RIGHTS

Findings

Only student results for the five countries have been analysed. Females have been found to generally give rights higher score values than males. While four of the five nations' results exhibited this general pattern, one nation showed the opposite pattern, with males giving higher scale values than females. Considering differences in direction for the 40 item sets, females gave higher values for 35 home importance items, 35 home existence items, 28 school importance items, and 32 school existence items. The only items for which differences were significant were: for home importance, items 1, 20, 36 and 40, emphasising being given help by experts, your own special name, a choice to live on your own, and bodily protection; for home existence, item 20, having your own special name; for school importance, items 18 and 20, emphasising being given help under dangerous conditions and having your own special name; and for school existence items 20, 25, 26, 31, 32, 38 and 40, emphasising having own special name and being with people you love. For all four categories, having your own special name or identity is given significantly higher scale values by females.

When discrepancies between the levels of importance and existence of rights are considered, males tend to identify larger differences in 51 of 80 comparisons; with one home item, 13, and five school items, 16, 25, 26, 31 and 32, approaching significance. Caring and respectful relationships between people and fairness seem to be emphasised. However, these findings appeared to result primarily from the very strong gender differences found for one nation, the very same nation for which male ratings were higher than female ratings.

Interpretations and comments

Interpretations of male and female differences must be highly speculative at this time. With a large cross-national subject population it appears that females judge rights to be at higher levels of existence and importance, and with smaller discrepancies between what is and what should be, than do males. However, since the pattern for one nation's findings was discrepant from that of other nations in ways which would influence overall findings, more data and more analysis is needed.

SOCIO-ECONOMIC STATUS RELATIONSHIPS

Findings

The socio-economic status of students was investigated under two conditions of its determination:

1. By student report of the highest education level reached by the student's father, with a high father-education (HFE) group defined as those whose fathers completed approximately 9 or more years of formal schooling (the equivalent of the USA high school education or greater), and a low father-education group (LFE) defined as those whose fathers completed 8 or less years of education (the equivalent of a USA middle school education or lower).

2. By school community socio-economic status for the students, as judged by the school's teachers or field research leader to be modal school-community status (MSCS), representing predominantly the largest middle income group of the society, or low school-community status (LSCS), representing the lowest quartile income group of the society.

For the five-country composite, under both definitions, those in higher socio-economic groups tended to give higher scale values to both the importance and existence of rights for home and school settings. The findings were particularly strongly supported under the school community status definitions (for which approximately 40% of the student population had been defined), achieving 100 per cent discrimination for the importance of rights both in the home and school. Statistical significance of differences was found for the majority of items, predominantly favouring the high socio-economic groups but with a somewhat mixed pattern.

As to the discrepancies between existence and importance as related to socio-economic status, findings were strongly different under the two definitions. Eighty comparisons were possible under each definition (i.e. 40 comparisons of home importance versus home existence and 40 comparisons of school importance versus school existence). The lower father-education group (LFE) differences exceeded the higher father-education group (HFE) differences for 50 out of 80 cases, six of which were significant for the home setting, and with larger discrepancies for the LFE group; while the higher socio-economic status school-community group (MSCS) differences exceeded the lower socio-economic status school group (LSCS) differences in 72 out of 80 cases, 36 of which were significant; 21 for the home setting and 15 for the school setting, and with larger discrepancies for the MSCS. While these patterns held for the majority of the five countries analysed, quite different results and opposite patterns were found for some of the countries.

Interpretations and comments

It appears that students of higher socio-economic status give higher ratings to the importance and existence of rights in both home and school settings. They may set higher expectations based on having received better treatment than those of lower socio-economic status. Status and esteem perceptions may influence these expectations and evaluations. The strong tendency for students in higher status school communities to indicate greater differences between existence and importance than students in lower status communities, when they are in school communities sufficiently homogeous to be so characterised, suggest that school community climate may have important effects on perspectives. The fact that quite different pattern exist in some countries and that this is a very early stage of data analysis for partial results, supports the conclusion that these important variables deserve further study.

COUNTRY TO COUNTRY COMPARISONS

Findings and comments

The analysis of the first sweep has indicated that a comparison between countries is not a simple issue. When a general level of the scores for two countries is different, what should these general tendencies be attributed to? Does higher level present a better position of children in one of the countries, or less critical attitudes and smaller expectations? Or is it a typical response to the survey material? When general level differs, how should differences at individual items be understood?

For example, Pavlovic (1994),[2] comparing student data from Belgium and Slovenia found a generally higher level of scores in Belgian data, except for the existence of rights in the school. Further analysis showed that many of these differences can be explained by controlling independent variables, which argues for giving more attention to the development of precise definitions of independent variables for application in the future. Some 'country specific' differences remained unexplained. Taking this uncertainty regarding the real meaning of differences in absolute scores between the countries into consideration led to the conclusion that it is probably more promising to observe the differences in relative ranking, particularly of the importance of rights than the differences in cultural value hierarchy of rights.

This process has, in fact, only just begun. The whole international data pool is just reaching completion. In the near future, the national directors will be presented with full results displaying absolute scores and relative rankings of individual items for each participating country. The national teams will be asked

---

2   This work was done in cooperation with Eugeen Verhellen, Frans Spieschaert and Geert Cappelaere of the Centre for Children's Rights in Gent, Belgium.

to communicate their own understanding of the findings – after they observe carefully which similarities and differences with other countries they find expected or, on the contrary, surprising. The first glance through such tables, based on an uncompleted data pool, revealed a wealth of intriguing details demanding qualitative interpretation.

Apart from studying how the participants from a particular country ranked the rights, as compared to the collection of other countries, it may be particularly interesting for national teams to carry out more detailed comparison to another single national set of data. This procedure can 'sharpen up' the features of the 'country profile' that may remain concealed in the former one. For example, in the previously mentioned comparison of Belgium and Slovenia (two European countries similar in some respects but fairly different in others) it was found that at the same age, Belgian children seem to be somewhat more peer oriented and Slovenian more family oriented, although the two sets of ranks generally didn't differ dramatically.

Finally, for some of the listed questions the average scores and the relative ranks don't reveal all the story. By looking at the relative frequencies (percentages), some of these questions can present indirect measures of different forms of child maltreatment in a given population. How many children are there who will choose very low marks when asked about their rights to be protected from people and situations who could hurt their emotions or body, or from unfair work?

Every score in this study gets its full meaning and significance when observed from the proper angle in a meaningful comparison. On a national level, comparisons are made between students and teachers, students of different ages, importance and existence of rights, home and the school. But, ultimately, there is an interest in finding out about the particularities of one's own country in an international context. Although there is a lot of qualitative interpretation needed in reading the data, the value of the collected information for that purpose just keeps revealing itself as we proceed to deeper levels of analysis. This study should prove itself to be a useful tool for measurement of the progress of the rights of the child on an international level.

GENERAL CONCLUSIONS AND PROSPECTS

The early progress in this research makes it clear that there is a strong international interest in clarifying the children's rights perspectives of children and the adults who influence their development, and that data relevant to these purposes can be gathered. The research design, instruments and procedures appear to be working well enough in this first phase of research to provide useful data and to provide the information necessary to refine and expand the project in the directions originally intended. School students of ages 12 to 14 consider rights following the basic themes of the UN Convention on the Rights of the Child to be important, to be more important generally for the home than school setting, and to exist at levels generally below the importance given to them. Rights respecting basic human needs fulfillment have been found to be rated higher in importance than other rights, while participation and choice rights have been judged to exist at levels lower, and more discrepant from, the importance given them relative to other rights. To varying degrees, the sex, socio-economic status, and country of the students are related to their rights perspectives.

Available data suggests that teachers judge both the importance and existence of rights to be below those levels indicated by students. Teachers and students were found to strongly disagree about some rights (e.g. students gave much more importance to learning right from wrong than did teachers) while agreeing strongly on others (e.g. the relatively low level of existence in comparison to importance for participation rights).

As interesting as some of these results are, however, it must be noted that only a partial analysis has been made of the data from the first five countries which reported, analysis of the new larger 13 country data pool has barely started, and that at least seven more countries are expected to provide data for this first phase of research. The relationships of some variables, such as community type and religion, to rights perspective have not yet been analysed. The findings presented here will probably grow both weaker and stronger, clearer and more complicated as more data is available and further analyses are completed. Certainly, the interpretations so far discussed must be considered interesting, even enticing, but highly speculative.

While a thorough analysis of the data from the first stage of this research is being pursued and its results disseminated and debated, refinements of the design, instruments and procedures must be undertaken in preparation for the next stage. Discussions among involved researchers have for some time focused on questions about whether items should be dropped, added, or modified; whether the response options should be altered to increase the validity of comparisons between desired and existing conditions more directly; and whether changes should be made in the response scales to strengthen the interval qualities of the scale. Already it has generally been agreed that the questionnaire should be divided into subsets, possibly four, and that students would be asked to complete only one subsection, such as indicating importance for home items, with other students completing the other subsections. This would reduce administration time and contamination by response set, while requiring larger numbers of respondents.

The long range hopes of the authors and the national research team leaders is that the project will be expanded to cover all major school-age developmental periods, and that teachers, counsellors, and parents of these age groups will make up the adult respondent population. It is further hoped, and plans are being made in this direction, that the research will become institutionalised in all the nations which are States Parties to the UN Convention so that it might become a regular part of their programmes to evaluate and report the status of achieving the Conventions standards and progress toward that goal.

REFERENCES

Catteral, C.D. (1970) 'Taxonomy of prescriptive interventions.' *Journal of School Psychology 8,* 1, 5–12.

Flekkoy, M.G. (ed) (1991) *Models for Monitoring the Protection of Children's Rights: Meeting report.* Florence, Italy: International Child Development Centre, UNICEF.

Hart, S.N. (1991) 'From property to person status: historical perspective on children's rights.' *American Psychologist 46,* 53–59.

Hart, S.N. (1993) 'Children's rights in a civilised society.' In M.A. Jensen and S.G. Goffin (eds) *Visions of Entitlement: The Care and Education of America's Children.* New York: Geneseo.

Hart, S.N., and Pavlovic, Z. (1991) 'Children's rights in education: An historical perspective.' *School Psychology Review 20,* 3, 345–358.

Hart, S.N. and Zeidner, M. (1993) 'Children's rights perspectives of youth and educators: Early findings of a cross national project.' *International Journal of Children's Rights 1,* 165–188.

Kamii, C. (1991) 'Toward autonomy: the importance of critical thinking and choice making.' *School Psychology Review 20,* 3, 382–388.

Maslow, A. (1970) *A Theory of Human Motivation.* New York: Harper and Row.

Melton, G. (1987) 'Children, politics, and morality: The ethics of child advocacy.' *Journal of Clinical Child Psychology 16,* 357–367.

Pavlovic, Z. (1994) *Country Profiles of Belgium and Slovenia: Cross-cultural Study of Children's Rights.* Llubljana, Slovenia: Institute of Criminology.

Verhellen, E. (1989) 'A strategy for a fully fledged position of children in our society.' In E. Verhellen and F. Spieeshchaet (eds) *Ombudswork for children.* Leuven, Belgium: ACCO.

APPENDIX 1
Children's Rights Survey Items

1. To be given help by experts when you are confused or feel bad.
2. To live with and spend time with each of your parents, unless it may cause serious harm to you.
3. To have people look after you and speak up for you when you need it.
4. To be treated fairly when people think you are wrong.
5. To be a good friend to others.
6. To be given medical help when you are sick.
7. To grow up strong and healthy in mind and body.
8. To influence decisions about what will happen to you.
9. To have food, clothing, and a place to live.
10. To have the information you need to understand difficult choices.
11. To be respected for your religion, language, color, race and social group no matter what they are.
12. To have your needs and wishes considered in plans and actions that might affect you.
13. To have the opportunity to have good friends who care about you.
14. To be able to play and make believe.
15. To be able to be with friends you have chosen.
16. To be encouraged to respect people of other religions, language, colours, races or social groups.
17. To develop all your abilities and talents.
18. To be given help quickly when very bad things happen (such as war, fires, earthquakes, floods, starvation).
19. To be able to go as far in school as your talents and efforts allow.
20. To have your own special name from birth.
21. To have time and a place to be alone without being bothered by others.
22. To be protected from having to fight in a war before you become an adult.
23. To have money to spend as you choose.
24. To make choices that fit your age about how you will behave.
25. To be with people who love and care about you.
26. To have a chance to learn what is right and wrong in order to become a good person.
27. To be respected as a person free to act in your own special way.
28. To be able to choose your own religion or beliefs about life.
29. To have your own ideas and opinions which others listen to and respect.

30. To have your rights supported by people in charge.
31. To be given attention and guidance by adults who want the best for you.
32. To be protected from having to do work which is unfair (dangerous or wrong for your age).
33. To learn to take more and greater responsibilities as you grow older.
34. To be protected from people and situations which might hurt your feelings.
35. To have a place to study.
36. To be able to live on your own when you are ready and choose to do so.
37. To do work that makes life better for yourself and others.
38. To have opportunities to show love to others.
39. To be given as much help as you need in order to learn.
40. To be protected from people and situations which might hurt your body.

APPENDIX 2
Importance and Existence Scales

IMPORTANCE (for persons my age, the right should be given the following level of importance)
(1) Of no importance
(2) Of some importance
(3) Important
(4) Very important
(5) Of greatest importance
(?) Does not apply/don't know

EXISTENCE (For persons my age, the right exists to the following degree)
(1) Not at all
(2) To a small degree
(3) To a medium degree
(4) To a large degree
(5) Fully supported
(?) Does not apply/don't know

APPENDIX 3
Country Sample Sizes

Belgium	570
China	1090
Czech Republic	580
France	190
India	380
Iran	390
Lithuania	450
Poland	2800
Slovakia	530
Slovenia	130
Thailand	340
USA	500
USSR	360

PART THREE

Finding a 'Voice'

CHAPTER THREE

Voice of the Children
Speaking Truth to Power

Kristin Eskeland

The Voice of the Children Campaign has been an exciting learning process, from one single Children's Hearing in Bergen, Norway in 1990 to an international campaign with non-governmental organisations (NGOs) in more than 40 countries participating.

The objectives of the first children's hearing was to give children a voice at an international conference. In 1995 the Voice of the Children is first and foremost an awareness-raising campaign, to empower young people to participate in democratic processes in their local communities and to fight for their own rights and concerns.

BACKGROUND

- Voice of the Children was started in 1990, with the Children's Hearing in Norway.

- This was followed up with the Global Children's Hearing in Rio during the Earth Summit in 1992 with participants from 20 countries.

- In 1993 Voice of the Children helped organise a similar process and a children's conference in Austria, in connection with the UN Conference on Human Rights in Vienna.

- In October 1993 Voice of the Children organised an International Peace Festival for Children in connection with the Olympic Games at Lillehammer, Norway.

- Voice of the Children has, in co-operation with United Games of Nations and Peace Child, organised several meetings for young people from different parts of the former Yugoslavia. The idea behind these meetings has been to help young people communicate across 'enemy lines' and to start local projects at home.

NGOs in 40 countries are registered as participants in the campaign. The idea is to collect children's concerns, experiences and ideas and to help the children present them to local and national leaders. According to the UN Convention on the Rights of the Child, all children have the right to be informed and to participate in making decisions concerning their lives. Voice of the Children is a way of involving children in democratic processes and giving them the opportunity to speak up about their problems and their concerns. In addition, it is important to encourage children to participate actively in local projects to change their situation for the better.

VOICE OF THE CHILDREN AS A TOOL

There are thousands of NGOs around the world working for children. In most of the 175 countries that have ratified the Convention, committees have been established to make sure the Convention is implemented. But in very few instances have the adults asked the children about their experiences and their problems. The work of Stuart Hart and his colleagues described in Chapter 2 is one exception. The idea of having children's own concerns as the starting point, however, is not yet common. We do not want to establish Voice of the Children branches all over the world. Our aim is to promote, within existing NGOs and institutions, the idea of children's participation and children's right to be heard. We see Voice of the Children as a tool for anyone who wants to promote children's rights, their right to be heard and their right to participate on their own terms.

OBJECTIVES OF THE CAMPAIGN

- To strengthen the movement for children's rights.
- To empower children to participate in democratic processes.
- To encourage children to develop and implement local projects.

GUIDELINES FOR VOICE OF THE CHILDREN

NGOs all over the world are encouraged to participate in the movement for children's rights. All children have the right to express their concerns and tell their stories to people in power. Children are worried about the future. They know a lot about the problems; there is no way of escaping all the negative information about the state of the world. Many children are worried about the environment in general, others are concerned about their individual rights, the problems of poverty in the world, or their own lack of education or clean drinking water. Lots of children have serious anxieties about war between countries, others suffer from violence and abuse in their local communities. No matter what their concerns, they have the right to be heard and to be taken seriously.

The great challenge for the adult facilitators is to make sure the children's real concerns are focused, not on what the adults think is good for children. Children's own experiences and their activities at the local level must be the starting point. Adults may be facilitators and helpers, but no manipulation, coaxing or bossing is acceptable. No matter how well organised a campaign may seem, it is a failure if it could be described as a show staged to please the adults, or if the children end up voicing the views of the adults.

In Norway where all children go to school, we asked all the pupils a question and invited them to make their own replies on postcards, with statements, questions, poems, drawings. Our question to them was simple: 'What would you like to tell people in power about your concerns?' We received 6000 postcards within a few months. In some other countries and cultures this method would only reach the élite and middle class children. Each country needs to choose their own methods to ensure that all the different groups of children are included.

The most important aspect of this campaign is what takes place locally, that the children speak about their own experiences from their daily lives. We would like as many children as possible to be involved, not only school children from urban areas, but street children, working children, rural children, minorities and handicapped children. The children should run the campaign themselves in a democratic way. Adults may be partners and facilitators.

The Guidelines which have been produced present a lot of ideas on how to organise a Voice of the Children campaign. But each country and culture should feel free to use the advice in their own way. What is suitable in a country like England may be completely useless in India or Uganda, what would be a good idea in Bangladesh may not work at all in the USA.

VOICE OF THE CHILDREN IS A PROCESS

Both children and adults need to understand how difficult it is to succeed. Even if people in power give encouraging, positive answers, the children might still be disappointed by a lack of practical results. The children should ask for concrete commitments and then return to the politicians in a year's time to challenge them again. The process will therefore have these stages:

1. Collect children's concerns, choose the most representative ones.

2. Decide on local actions, What can we do ourselves?

3. Present the concerns, ask for commitments.

4. Check up on practical results, repeat the process after a year's time.

FROM 1990 TO 1995

So what has actually taken place since the first Children's Hearing in Norway in 1990 and the International follow up in Rio in 1992? What are the children's concerns, what are they saying to us?

CHILDREN'S HEARING IN RIO

When we organised the Global Children's Hearing in Rio in 1992, the 20 young people who participated had a lot of different ideas and concerns. From the Appeal to World Leaders, which was the result of all the national campaigns, I have selected these statements:

- We want to inherit a clean earth. We would like our grandchildren to know: What is a tree, a fish, a dog. Leave us trees to climb in.

- Ecology is not just trees, animals and rivers, it is also hunger and the homeless.

- We want every girl and boy in the world to get an education. We want to be educated in such a way that we get the courage to speak our minds.

- We don't want our cities to be ruined by cars. Make it easier for us all to use our bicycles.

- We don't want our world to drown in rubbish. Make it easier for people to recycle their rubbish.

- Please give us clean drinking water. Without water there is no life.

- Everybody has a right to live in peace. Instead of making bombs, improve the standard of living in the world.

- The Earth is a single country, and all people are its citizens. We have to share this planet, so don't be selfish. The Earth is more valuable than all the money in the world.

At the Global Children's Hearing the children who perhaps made the deepest impression on the audience were Ana, 11-years-old from Colombia, Marthe Olive, 12-years-old from Rwanda and Sayda, 12-years-old from Guatemala. Ana said in her quiet, unassuming way:

> What concerns me most on my reservation is the violence against the indigenous people. More and more of them are being killed. For me it is horrible when they kill five, four, three or twenty-five at a time.

Marthe Olive talked about the war in Rwanda, which at that time was unknown to most of us:

> I come from Rwanda. I want to talk about the problems that I have in Rwanda. For years the children in Rwanda have been unhappy because

of the war. They have seen children like themselves die. Lots of families are scattered. They have left their possessions to get away from the guns and the bombs. Now they have no shelter, no food, no clothes. They have nothing. Some children have become orphans and no one takes care of them. Others, their schools have been destroyed and they do not know where to go. We do not want to live in this war, this misery. Wars kill innocent people, they spread disorder and hatred. They slow down development. Children do not like war. Children in Rwanda want the war to end very soon so that people can live in peace. Thank you.

And Sayda from Guatemala closed the Hearing:

Children are tired of seeing so much violence. We don't want any more war. We want peace, fraternity and harmony among all human beings. Look at what you are doing to the world we live in. You are making the world such a bad place, and children so sad. It is terrible. God left us such a beautiful world, and was it only for us to destroy it from end to end? No! That is not right. For God's sake, let's realise what we are doing. Please!

CHILDREN'S TREE OF HUMAN RIGHTS

In June 1993, 37 young people, mostly from Central Europe, but also a few from the so-called Third World came together in Austria, for a meeting in front of the Human Rights Conference in Vienna. Voice of the Children had, in advance, asked all our partners around the world what children considered the most important human rights. We received input from 25 countries. The young people who came together in Austria produced The Children's Tree of Human Rights, a document which they introduced this way:

In all of the 25 countries children have sat together to find out what they feel are the most important human rights for them and what promises they would like their leaders to keep for them, if they had the chance to ask. This document is based on the input from the children who could not be here.

Their concerns were:

- Adults make war, children pay.
- Too many dangers to children, not enough protection.
- Too much discrimination.
- No food, no future!
- Adults are unemployed, children are forced to work.
- Millions cannot read and write.
- The gap between rich and poor gets bigger.

- If we destroy our world, we destroy ourselves.
- Do we have to shout to be heard?

The whole group made a wonderful, colourful tree, three metres high, weighing one and a half tons, where all the concerns were painted on the branches and all the promises they wanted adults to make were painted on the fruits of the tree. The tree was transported to Vienna and erected in the Conference Hall.

CHILDREN'S PEACE FESTIVAL

In October 1993, Voice of the Children organised an International Peace Festival for Children. The project was part of the cultural build-up before the Olympic Games in Lillehammer, Norway. Eighty-eight children from 35 countries spent nine days together. They had fun, met Norwegian kids, participated in workshops and produced plays and songs. The results were presented in a big concert hall. The children told us, through their dances, songs, plays and exhibitions, about their backgrounds, their ideas their hopes and their pains. From the Appeal to World Leaders which they produced through a very impressive democratic process I have chosen these points:

- We want more co-operation and communication between and within countries.
- More tolerance for other cultures, religions and races.
- We want an end to illiteracy, more and better schools and teachers
- Every child has the right to basic needs: food, water, shelter and clothing.
- Children should be protected by law against physical, sexual and mental abuse.
- Stop the killing of street children.
- Corporal punishment should be abolished.
- Children should not be forced to work
- Stop excessive consumption, don't buy disposable products.

They end their document this way: 'We want an international day of access. This day will give us an opportunity to interact with politicians to raise our concerns, and to help make the world a better place'.

THE POST PESSIMISTS

Out of these two meetings came the Post Pessimists. Young people from different parts of the former Yugoslavia asked us to organise a meeting for them. They wanted to get to know other young people across the new borders, they wanted to try to understand what was going on and they wanted to see if it would be possible to be friends in spite of the conflicts. Voice of the Children, in co-operation with United Games of Nations and Peace Child, started organising a series of meetings with young people from Kosova, Serbia, Bosnia and Croatia. It has been a great experience. These young people are by no means 'Yugo-nostalgic', they do not want Tito's Yugoslavia back. But they do want to be able to communicate, they want to be good neighbours, they want their human rights, they want to become friends, they want 'to live, not just to be alive'.

As a result of the three meetings, the different groups have started several local projects in their home towns; rock concerts, newspapers, exhibitions and meetings. Many of them have become real friends and their groups have managed to stay in contact with each other. To date we have organised three meetings, and more are planned. Each time most of the participants are new, but we keep the continuity from one meeting to the next by inviting a small group of 'veterans' to take part as leaders. Each time we learn something new; each time the participants reach a higher level of understanding; each time they come up with new ideas for local projects. And each time more young people come to love each other, completely disregarding 'enemy lines'.

YOUNG VOICES

Most of the children who are involved in the International campaign are between 12 and 15 years of age. Many do not particularly like to be called children at that age. We have, therefore, named the new campaign Young Voices.

There are groups and NGOs all over the world participating in the campaign. Adults are beginning to see that the Rights of the Child means more than giving children food and shelter; it also means making sure that children are allowed to participate in democratic processes. UNICEF is getting directly involved in many of the activities to implement the Convention. Different presentations, plays and hearings are taking place in so many countries. In India a big national campaign is being planned involving street children as well as rural children and urban school children. In Uganda, Malawi and Tanzania similar processes are under way. In Bangladesh and Nepal national movements are starting in the Autumn of 1995. In Latin America the NGOs have been active for a long time making sure that children are being heard in their own right. If all goes well, and if it is possible to raise the money, Young Voices hopes to organise an International Event in New York to celebrate the 50th Anniversary of UNICEF in 1996. Children who have participated in the process in their own countries will be invited to raise their concerns at the UN. For although the local processes are the most important part of this campaign, it is also of great value that children from different parts of the world can come together and are given the chance to speak directly to the leaders of the world.

FURTHER INFORMATION FROM

Voice of the Children, PO Box 8844 Youngstorget, 0028 Oslo, Norway. Telephone: 47 22 03 77 75 or 76, Fax: 47 22 11 17 70, e-mail: Kristin.Eskeland@npaid.no

CHAPTER FOUR

Representing of Ourselves
The 'Voice' of Traveller Children

Cathy Kiddle

People arriving at the Plymouth Arts Centre, Devon in the United Kingdom for the private view of an exhibition of Josef Koudelka's photographs were surprised to find two exhibitions on show. In the main gallery was Koudelka's work, photographs of Gypsies from all parts of Europe taken over many years. In the café alongside the gallery were more photographs of Gypsies, but these had all been taken and processed over the previous few months by a group of Gypsy teenagers then living in the city. The novelty of the second exhibition attracted much of the attention of the gallery clientele and many comments.

The morning following the private viewing a dozen members of the city's Gypsy community, mothers, fathers and young children, came into the Arts Centre to see their children's exhibition. It was the first time any of them had been in there. As the Gypsy population in England is treated with hostility by the house-dwelling majority, they tend to keep to themselves and do not readily approach our institutions. For them to venture into the gallery was remarkable. Within moments their unaccustomed and unusual presence dominated the space. For an hour they made the place their own, animating the normally quiet atmosphere of the gallery with their direct comments on the photographs, making comparisons between the two exhibitions and displaying enormous pride in their children's achievements.

This exhibition, which was first shown at the Arts Centre in 1985, had not been planned. The idea grew from a photographic project carried out by a group of teenage Gypsy Travellers. Their families were among some Gypsies stopping in the city on a piece of waste ground, under threat of eviction. They had no legal place to camp, though by UK law at that time the County Council should have provided an official site for them. While they waited and campaigned for a site they camped without security or facilities in appalling conditions anywhere they could.

The major obstacle to site provision has always been the negative stereotype of Gypsies held by house-dwellers, who are liable to get a distorted view of the Gypsy way of life, if they get one at all. The official camp sites which do exist tend to be tucked away in isolated or industrial areas and, beyond work arrangements, there are few opportunities for ordinary social contact between house-dwellers and Travellers.

The general public sees mostly the unofficial campsites perched on waste land or roadside verges; on any available space. These tend to be untidy as there are no sanitary or rubbish disposal facilities. Also, the space outside the trailer is used as a work area, for sorting scrap, cleaning metal and so on. The startling contrast of the inside of the trailers (the only space the families can control), the shining chrome, mirrors and glass, the scrupulous cleanliness, is not seen by passers by. They form their opinions, re-affirming the stereotypes, from seeing only the outside conditions, which they themselves have forced onto the families by opposing official sites.

I had been working as a teacher with the Gypsy families in the city for several years trying to ensure that the children had access to education despite the lack of an official campsite. While the primary age group were mostly attending local schools, the secondary children were more difficult to settle in schools as, due to their travelling, none of this group had had more than a few weeks primary school experience. I was working on various bridging projects with these children, concentrating on helping them to acquire basic literacy skills and to improve their low level of self esteem, hoping to integrate them into secondary schools eventually.

In the autumn of 1984 I was approached by an art student, Sara Hannant, who, as part of her course work, was expected to initiate an art project in a local community. She was keen to learn more about the Gypsies in order to base her work within this group and asked if there were any opportunities to work with me. We discussed the idea of a photographic project, which seemed favourable from various points of view. The teenagers were very interested in photographs but they had not previously had the chance to learn the processes of developing and printing. Sara could come into the group primarily as a technician, an enabler for the project, not an intruder. I felt that photography would be an ideal vehicle for other work and we might also make some images that would be useful for the families' campaign for their site.

We put the suggestion to the group; they were keen to take some photo-graphs and interested to learn how to develop and print them, but my idea for the subject matter was rejected straightaway. No one wanted to focus on the mud, the squalor, the broken water tap, the proximity of rubbish dumps, the reminders of what they had to live with day by day. What the children wanted were pictures of themselves. All Gypsy Travellers love family photographs. They treasure and add to them whenever possible as living, growing family histories. Theirs is primarily an oral culture, each generation passing on the family traditions and lore through conversation and storytelling accompanied by the photographs they keep. The children already figured in their family archives of photographs, but now welcomed the chance to take control of the process, to choose where and how to photograph themselves, to make their own images and to represent themselves.

Much thought was given to the composition and setting of each photo-graph. Each teenager decided which aspects of their home, environment and life they wanted to show to others; how they would present themselves. They were acutely conscious of their negative public image. Regularly in the media and in personal contacts they heard themselves scorned and reviled as dirty people, as parasites, as undesirables. They wanted to deny this image, to show themselves as they really were. More important, however, they wanted pictures of themselves for themselves, realisations of a self-image.

Working one day a week, with the encouragement and technical assistance of Sara and myself, the young Travellers gradually produced their portraits. After a disastrous first session in the darkroom, when everything came out black because light was getting into the room and the safe light was faulty, the results were more impressive than any of us had imagined. The teenagers had captured a sense of themselves and they were delighted. Their achievement went beyond individual prints. Seen as a collection of photographs, the pictures gave a positive identity to this small group of Gypsies.

It was at that stage of the project we discovered that Koudelka's photographs were to be shown in the city later in the year. The coincidence was too good to be ignored, so we approached the Arts Centre with the idea of holding a simultaneous exhibition of the local Gypsy photographs. Our suggestion was taken up and approved and, after a few weeks of preparing and mounting the prints, the exhibition came into being.

By now I had realised that the statement the young people had insisted on making for and about themselves was far more powerful an assertion of their right to maintain their own culture and its richness than any I would have contrived. After initial embarrassment that they were on show to whomever might walk into the Arts Centre, publicly presenting their pictures gave the Travellers a greater confidence and pride in themselves. They took a profes-sional interest in Koudelka's images, recognising their quality and despairing of ever being able to achieve as much themselves. Yet they also understood that they had been regarded as worthy of displaying their work alongside his. Their community had asserted its right to be given space among other communities, to be seen on its own terms. It was that dignity, a pride in the community, that the parents carried with them when they found the confidence to walk into the Arts Centre to see the exhibitions that day.

It was that dignity that I recognised as the real success, and sought other ways to develop some of the ideas and processes of working in subsequent projects. The exhibition has continued to be requested and shown throughout the last ten years in many different contexts – schools, teachers' centres, arts centres and galleries. Its inclusion in the World Children's Rights Conference at Exeter University in September 1992 was a testament to its continued relevance, but I was most pleased that some of the Gypsy children who had taken the photographs of themselves were willing to attend the conference. By that time they were young adults, yet they were willing to stand by the images of themselves that they had created as children, discuss their exhibition and its implications with other children, young people and adults, and take pride in their work.

The young Gypsy Travellers who came to the Exeter Conference have remained in, or frequently returned to, the Devon area throughout the years since the exhibition was made, so it has been possible for me to keep in touch with them. About two years ago, however, I met a young Gypsy woman again whom I had not seen since the summer after the original exhibition, to which she had contributed as a teenager. Her family had moved away and had been travelling in the London area. She was now married, had a young son and tended to travel to areas frequented by her husband's family. We met at the wedding of one of her cousins which took place in Exeter. After the initial surprise at seeing each other again, I admired the baby and she enquired, 'Do you remember our exhibition? That was good wasn't it?' That she should remember it and speak of it so readily was the good thing to me. In her life it had been a unique opportunity, a chance to represent and speak for herself, and she would not forget it.

It is all too easy to be exploitative of another's culture and an ever present danger in working in the way I have described. There has to be a constant awareness of motive and a sensitivity to need. The safest way it seems to me is to allow the children's voices to be heard, to let them lead as far along the way as they want to go, to be there with encouragement to explore and as a practical enabler for them.

Recently I was supporting a ten-year-old New Traveller child in school. His life to this point had been one of continual disruption. In his early years Joe had lived in a house and attended school where both his mother and his teacher found his behaviour difficult to understand or to deal with. A traumatic birth was thought to have some bearing on his troubles, but no one could offer any easy solutions. After trying a succession of schools, psychologists and child guidance clinics, Joe's mother turned her back on institutions and professionals and went on the road travelling with a group of friends to try to sort things out for herself. They moved around the country in a horse drawn waggon, spent more than a year in a bender-tent[1] and Joe rarely had more than a few weeks at a time in school.

---

1   A bender-tent is a construction made from pliable tree branches bent over in an 'n' shape
     with the two ends pushed into the ground. A weatherproof covering is put over this frame
     and weighted down.

Figure 4.1 Gypsy women will take pride in the inside decoration of their trailers whatever outside living conditions might be (Photograph taken by Adeline Reilly)

Figure 4.2 Lucy chose to be photographed by a gleaming mirror in her trailer. One of her domestic responsibilities which she enjoys is to keep the chrome polished and the mirrors shining. Jason, the photographer, designed the image so that he would appear in it too (Photograph taken by Jason Smith)

Figure 4.3 From a young age Gypsy Traveller boys will know how to strip down an engine
(Photograph taken by Jason Smith)

Figure 4.4 Gypsies often travel in an extended family group. Teenagers have photograped a
group of their young cousins and nephews playing fishing (into the road)
(Photograph taken by Andrew Loveridge)

Figure 4.5 Caring for the little ones (Photograph taken by Adeline Reilly)

When I met the family, as part of my work with Devon Traveller Education Service, Joe had been completely out of school for nine months. His mother had decided that the family needed a period of stability again, had rented a house for the winter at least and wanted to put Joe back into school. Joe himself was willing to give it a try, but beyond his innate learning difficulties and the lack of any recent regular opportunity to attend school, he was also acutely sensitive to the possibility of being teased, bullied or called names because of his recent travelling lifestyle.

After considerable discussion with the class teacher it was decided that I would give a few hours extra support each week to Joe in class to help him to settle in and that I would focus my work on helping him to develop basic literacy skills as he was a virtual non-reader. It seemed to me that as Joe was almost ten years old a language experience approach would probably work best for him, but I was well aware that he might not want to share his recent experience with me. We started with his love of animals and how to care for them and before too long had a story about a hedgehog he had found injured. I asked Joe when it was that he had rescued the hedgehog and he replied that it was when he was living in the bender. This was the first time he had made any mention of his travelling life.

When I went into school the following week the class teacher drew my attention to a carefully coloured drawing on the wall, which was labelled 'Joe's Bender'. It seemed that a child sitting near to Joe and I the previous week had overheard our conversation and had asked Joe what a 'bender' was. Joe had been embarrassed and defensive not knowing what to say or how to explain and the class teacher noticing what was going on had joined in the discussion. He said how interesting the construction of a bender was and perhaps the other child would understand it better if Joe made a drawing. The drawing provoked more interest in the class and the teacher was able to do some science on the properties of materials following a discussion when Joe explained that hazel branches were the best to use as they would bend rather than break.

Other children recounted their camping experiences and described different kinds of tents and the focus of attention was shifted from Joe to the design of tents and he was comfortable in the group, able to take a full and demonstrably knowledgeable part. Before long some practical building experiments were taking place on the patch of grass between the classroom and the playground.

A few weeks later I came into contact with another family of Travellers who were still living in bender-tents and who were in fact just about to construct a new enlarged one with windows. I bought them some film and they agreed to photograph the bender at various stages of its construction. When the set of photographs was complete I took them into school to show Joe and ask his opinion of this design. He showed the photographs around the class and to the teacher. The class teacher saw the opportunity for a permanent resource and asked to have a set of the prints, pointing out that they would enable him to discuss the design ideas with other classes after Joe had moved on. 'Maybe we could make a book about it', suggested Joe, to whom this idea was now very familiar through our other literacy work, 'then you could keep it in the class library'. For the next few sessions our work focused on Joe preparing a text to go with the pictures which would describe the building of a bender-tent. In the end we made multiple copies of the book using a colour photocopier as many teachers asked for copies as an extra resource for 'homes' topics and Joe was well pleased.

It took a long, long time for Joe to settle in school; his difficulties were many and complex. However, following the work on the bender-tent his sensitivity and defensiveness about the travelling period of his life was significantly lessened and he no longer worried about being victimised because of his family's lifestyle. He and others had seen the relevance of what he had to offer and he had been able to share it with pride. Beyond this, other children had benefited from Joe's experience and knowledge through the class teacher's imaginative inclusion of the work into curriculum studies.

It is clear that most children – and many adults – start from an extremely low information base in Gypsy and Traveller issues. Until relatively recently there were few accurate and straightforward resources which could be used, but this is no longer the case. Now many materials are available in various media for use in curriculum development and there are opportunities throughout the National Curriculum for Traveller perspectives to be included as part of general study. The question now arises about where these materials come from and how far Gypsies and Travellers themselves are able to be involved in their production. Otherwise we are back to the issues of exploitation.

It was possible to take the exploration further with a small group of Showmen's children when they were travelling with the fair for a period of about a month around towns and villages in North Devon. The Showmen follow a regular seasonal work pattern, spending the winter months from about mid-November to mid-March in winter quarters and then travelling a relatively fixed route from just before Easter to the end of the Bonfire Fairs, which provide their back-end run. Sometimes the travelling season is extended to include a Christmas Fair. For the Showmen's children in the South West this means attendance at schools local to their winter quarters each winter when they return and the completion of packs of distance learning work taken with them to continue with their studies as they travel through the summer. These packs of work are generally prepared by class teachers with help from Traveller Education Service teachers. Each will contain about three weeks' work to be returned to school after completion when a new pack will be sent out. Sometimes it is possible for Traveller Education Service peripatetic teachers to visit the children on the fairgrounds during the summer months to encourage and support them in completing their distance learning work.

This support work is currently done in the North Devon area by Devon Traveller Education Service teacher David Williams. During a month when one particular fair was in North Devon moving between three different locations, Dave was able to give support to the same group of children for this extended period visiting them for teaching sessions about three times each week. In the group were two teenage boys of fourteen and fifteen, one of whom it was particularly difficult to motivate to work on his school pack. Already, during the travelling season, Peter felt adult and was given some adult responsibility on the fairground and he was not inclined to demonstrate the inadequacies of his literacy skills to the gaff lads,[2] hired in for a season's labour, if he could help it.

In looking through the work that Peter had been given to do, Dave decided to focus on a task which asked Peter to describe one of the rides on the fair. Dave pointed out to Peter that it was unlikely that his classmates and teacher back in school would have any idea of the intricate technology of the fairground rides and the careful structural design that was involved in making a machine that could be built up and taken down quickly every few days, yet still be strong

---

2   Gaff Lads are seasonally employed casual workers, not from a shoman's family.

and secure enough for its constant use by the general public. He suggested that Peter might like to introduce his family's 'Noah's Ark' ride to his class through a series of sketches, labelled diagrams and notes.

The idea caught Peter's imagination and also that of Mark, the other teenager in the group, who decided to work in the same way on introducing his family's 'Big Wheel'. The boys made careful and detailed drawings of the rides, in section and bird's eye view. They focused on levers and pulleys, levelling and gearing mechanisms. At the end of each of his sessions Dave took the boys' work away and put it onto a computer and returned it to the boys to extend during the following session. He found that they were working on the designs between sessions and Peter had been out to buy a throwaway camera to photograph the Noah's Ark as it was being erected. He wrote notes to accompany each stage.

The families of the two boys became interested and involved. They told of the history of the rides and how they had come into the family; they brought out old photographs for comparison and these too they allowed to be scanned and turned into computer images for the project work. At the end of the month there were three booklets on the Noah's Ark, the Big Wheel and the Waltzer. Each one described the machine in terms of family history, its place on the fair, its design, its construction and the way it is transported. The booklets were produced finally on the computer with both drawings and photographs included.

The top copies of the booklets were sent back to Peter and Mark's schools in their work packs, but as the results were excellent, photocopies were made of the work which was kept in original form on disc. The boys each kept copies for themselves and their families and agreed that Dave could make copies for further use by the Traveller Education Service with other children and in other schools.

It seems that the positive results of this project work extend across three areas. First it was good for the children. Through this work, which was motivating and relevant to them, they were able to find a voice for themselves. Always, back in his school in the winter, Peter felt inadequate knowing that the constant interruption of his schooling meant that he fell farther and farther behind his peer group in terms of academic work. Now he had been able to present a strong and positive view of his world to his classmates which demonstrated his skills, responsibilities and knowledge. When Peter reported that on his return to school for a visit mid-season to collect more work, he had seen his project booklet opened out and displayed all around the classroom walls, the increase in his self-esteem was almost palpable. Through this work he and Mark had each also learned more for themselves of their own family history and had a greater appreciation of their own heritage, in which their families had been able to share by their involvement with the project. Peter and Mark's parents were glad to bring their families' business and traditions to a wider audience as they are well aware that there is a general ignorance of their world which often leads to a negative reaction from some people when the fair moves into town.

The second positive result, then, of this work was that it did contribute to a greater understanding of the Showmen's world among the other children and teachers in Peter and Mark's schools. A considerable amount of information was offered within the booklets that the teachers in school were able to incorporate into work in several different subject areas. The fairground is a particularly rich resource for all kinds of artistic, practical scientific and technological study. What this project offered to others beyond this was a sense of the cultural heritage which was coming to Peter and Mark through their families.

The wide-ranging and integrated work of the Traveller Education Service makes it possible that a third positive dimension can extend from this project. If we can produce copies of the boys' booklets finished to a high standard then we can, with the families' permissions, make them available as a material resource to other schools. It may then be the case that not only will many house-dwelling children have the opportunity to learn more from and of the fairground world, but also that other Showmen's children in different areas may find the booklets in use in their schools when they return for the winter months. They will receive the positive message that their lives and culture are accepted and respected alongside all others, but more important than this, their culture will have been brought to them by their own people.

It is this point which is the most significant. There is a humiliation in being introduced to your own culture by an outsider to it. It is for this reason that whenever possible the Traveller Education Service in Devon will work with Gypsy and Traveller people, both children and adults, to produce any resources that are developed.

I, and I am sure all other teachers who work with Gypsy Traveller families, am continually being asked if a certain family or group of families are 'real' or 'true' Gypsies, as if there could somehow be somewhere a pure undiluted strain of people from India – not one of whom had ever married outside their group in the last 1000 years. The late nineteenth and early twentieth century image of the carved and decorated horse drawn waggon is a strong and enduring one which remains dominant in the public imagination. It seems hard for people to believe that the families seen on the roads today in shiny white and chrome trailers or cream and gold Weippart caravans from Germany share the same heritage and have simply adapted to changing circumstances, work opportunities and economic demands as all communities have had to move with the times. I wanted to produce a simple resource for use in Primary Schools which would show visually the changing accommodation which Gypsy Travellers have used over the last 100 years, starting from bender-tents, through open-lot and barrel-top waggons to the chrome and the more recently popular Weippart trailers. My aim was to demonstrate through these various homes how a community has changed in some ways, yet has maintained distinctive traditions and values.

To test out and develop this idea I turned to a young Traveller, Danny, who ten years before had been one of the youngest participants in the photographic 'Pictures of Ourselves' project. Now an independent 19-year-old, he still had the interest and skill in sketching that he had shown from an early age. I asked him if he would be prepared to make a series of line drawings of tents, waggons and trailers as I have described to show how the accommodation of Gypsy Travellers had changed since Victorian times. Maybe he could draw on the experience of his own family as a starting point. Danny himself had been born in, and has always lived in, a series of trailers pulled by motors, but his father had been born in a horse drawn waggon and his grandfather had made his living as a waggon maker. The furthest back that he knew his family history was to his great grandparents, who, about 100 years ago, had been living and travelling in Wales in bender-tents.

Danny agreed to experiment with some sketches and suggested a parallel series of drawings from candles, through gas lamps to generators showing how the energy sources for producing heat and light had similarly changed over the years. I talked to his father to make sure that he was happy with the idea of Danny doing the drawings for me. I found him more keen on the idea than I had anticipated.

Danny, his father and I collaborated on the text. I prepared a kind of chronological frame and structure within which the individual drawings and aspects of life could be described, then handed this over to the family. They put in the flesh of the text with as much individual detail as they chose. In this way I hoped we could achieve the general sense of an adapting community which was my original purpose, together with the human interest of one family's story and the way they coped with change. The final section was left to Danny. The narrative had reached the present day and the realisation that new restrictive legislation was going to force yet more changes on the next generation. He completed the text with his own aspirations and hopes for the future.

In terms of legislation in the UK, attitudes towards Travellers are hardening. The 1968 Caravan Sites Act has been repealed, so local authorities no longer have a duty to provide sites for Gypsies. They may build them if they choose, but no longer will central grants be available for this purpose. The Criminal Justice Act also makes trespass a criminal offence and makes it possible for those occupying land unlawfully to be moved on more swiftly than before; under threat of immediate arrest on refusal to go. It is more difficult than ever for the minority communities to be heard amid the continued hubbub of hostility from the house-dweller.

In these circumstances there is a desperate need for the children of these minority groups to have a way of finding an identity and a voice. Denigrated by the public at large, there has to be some way for them to develop a positive self-image. Through educational opportunities such as the photographic project, the oral history project and others I have detailed, some small steps can be taken to a greater sense of dignity, to respect the child's voice and right to an identity. We need to continue searching for others.

CHAPTER FIVE

A Voice in the Media

Radio – Children Speaking for Themselves

Sarah Mc Crum

C:[1] I think kids should have a right to speak out to other people and to adults 'cause they always seem to be interviewing adults about kids and they never seem to interview kids and they never get to express the way they feel towards different issues and stuff.

M: I think that the parents mostly think that the children don't know what they're talking about. I don't think that they feel that they're ready for the world or anything really.

P: And they don't know what they're talking about. They think that we don't know anything – like certain subjects…like politics that we learn in school and then it's on the news and then you say something about it and they say, 'Oh be quiet, you don't know what you're talking about!' And yet we do know what they're talking about…

C: 'Cause whenever they have different issues about teens problems, you always see them interviewing the teachers or something in the schools, and they do talk to the kids sometimes but that's not as important, it seems, 'cause they're just like five seconds and they're off talking to the Principal…

SARAH: So what effect does that have if it always means the young people are less important?

---

1 All quotes from children have been edited to make them easier to read, leaving out repetitions, stumbles and digressions.

M: Well, they don't get their side of the story.

C: They always look at one side of the story, not both. They'll take the teachers or the parents but they never take aside the students to talk to them about these issues and it kind of makes us feel down.

M: The only teenager they interview is their friend or their next door neighbour. They don't really talk to the actual child.

C: But it also might have an effect on the kids 'cause then they start thinking less about themselves, and their self esteem won't be as high, because they'll think, 'Well, I'm not worth talking to anyway so why should I bother to talk?'

SARAH: What difference would it make?

G: Well, one day all the kids, they're going to grow up and be the people in the news, and if they don't start out young, and if they don't do anything when they're young, and they have no clue of what's going on, then further in their life where they get into businesses and jobs and more important stuff that are newsworthy, then they'll be...

C: Yeah, they'll be...they won't be open about it, will they? They'll just be really quiet 'cause they learned at a young age that what I have to say is not important, so why bother talking?

P: The kids now should stop it and tell everyone, 'Hey, you need to talk to us too so that when we grow up we'll – (otherwise) if we grow up we won't think about interviewing children – (so that) we'll know how they feel so we'll interview them more.

(13- and 14-year-olds in Rankin Inlet, Canada)

It is by listening to conversations like this one that I have learned how to make radio programmes with children and young people. They have been far better teachers than any professional radio training organisation, but it is easy, and almost fashionable amongst children's organisations, to talk about listening to children. It is quite a different thing to do it effectively. Throughout all my work with children in radio I have been exploring one major theme – how can I, as an adult and professional, work with children in a way that gives them the opportunity to speak for themselves whilst making programmes that will be broadcast by adult-controlled organisations. It is not just a question of technical standards, which are fairly straightforward with modern equipment. The big difficulty is that what seems most natural for children (and probably most adults too) is often almost the opposite of the way most broadcasters work.

L: They came at home and they had a camera too and it was twice
            or three times they came and they wanted us to talk about how
            the people here are educated, the children, and how do the
            parents help and the teachers and homework and these stuff for
            the students. Maybe I was afraid because the way he asked was
            not very good.

SARAH: What do you mean?

L: Well, you couldn't say what you wanted to say about Israeli
            people and what you don't like actually and who you don't like
            and why you don't like. You just had a question and you had to
            answer.

SARAH: So how exactly did you know that you couldn't say the things
            you wanted?

L: Because the things that I said were not ideas that I had and
            anybody could answer, not only me… So I think he had to ask
            a question, a free question or leave like a question to me to
            answer so…

SARAH: So was it like you knew what he wanted you to say or…

L: Yeah.

SARAH: Aha it's difficult that isn't it? What did it actually feel like for
            you?

L: On radio repeating what he wants to say but in my voice.

            (A 13-year-old Palestinian girl talking about a television interview)

Probably the most common situation for a radio reporter working with children
is to be given an assignment by a producer who will have a very clear idea what
he or she is looking for. For example, I was once asked to make a recording
with some children for a radio programme about the sense of smell. The children
were to shut their eyes, smell various objects – a strawberry, some soap, an
onion, etc – and describe the smell. At first the children found it quite
interesting. I was a new person and a break from the normal classroom routine
and what we were doing was fun for a while, but very quickly they began to
fidget and lose concentration. In response I tried giving them the strawberries
to eat; I asked them to sit still and concentrate; I appealed to their desire to be
'on the radio' and begged them to help me get it done as well as possible; I
gave them a break and then tried to start again; but none of these tricks really
worked. I managed to get the material the producer needed – after all he was
probably only going to use about one minute in all – and the children and I
parted on friendly terms, but we were somehow dissatisfied. We all knew that

we had not done as well as we could; the children had been close to being 'naughty' (in school terms) and I was 'failing to keep discipline'.

My first response to this situation was to blame myself for not giving them enough fun, not preparing carefully enough, failing to suit the task precisely to the children's age or to vary the activities enough – as an ex-teacher I felt I should have known exactly how to achieve my goals with a group of 6 nine-year-olds. Alternatively I might have blamed the children for being silly or not intelligent enough; I might have accused them of lacking respect for an adult, and a visitor; or I could have blamed their school for a lack of discipline.

Looking back on it now, I can see much more clearly what the problem was – it is easy to detect it even in the description above. I was far more interested in my role than in the children. *I* set up the task; *I* knew what *I* wanted to hear from them; *I* decided what kind of behaviour was appropriate, and *I* was the only person who knew when we had finished when *I* was satisfied that *I* had what *I* needed. In fact I was using the children because they had virtually nothing to gain from the encounter: after all we smell things all day every day so that was nothing new. Many adults might argue that it was a wonderful opportunity for the children to be on the radio and to learn a bit about the media. I suspect that what they learned about the media is that reporters are people who come and tell you to do rather silly things, and expect you to perform like circus animals. And they made it quite clear that being on the radio was not all that appealing if that was what people would hear from them. The children knew, without putting it into words, that I was far more interested in my agenda than theirs and they showed me, in their own way. It was probably lucky that I missed the signs at the time, because I would have had to go back to my producer and tell him that the children did not think much of his idea and did not want to participate on his/my terms. Once you begin to listen to the subtle messages of children you have to start working in a different way.

A: They (journalists) should think about what we want instead of what is convenient for them and what they think – what they think might not be convenient for us and most of the time it isn't.

SARAH: Anything else?

E: Same thing – give us as children a choice to do what we want and say what we want.

(12-year-olds in Barbados)

Having vowed never again to use children in the way I described above, I finally got what I had been wanting for a long time – a chance for children to make their own programme. I had learned much more about what they are capable of and what they enjoy and I began to get the feeling that they could do just about anything if I only gave them the opportunity. I offered a class of

10-year-olds in London the chance to make their own 15 minute radio programme on any subject they might choose. I went in a few times and showed them how to use the tape recorder; they practised interviewing each other and got used to talking on tape and listening to their own voices. Then I left the tape recorder with them so they could use it whenever they wanted. I gave them permission to take it home in the evenings and left plenty of tapes and batteries so nothing would inhibit them. They seemed very excited about the idea and I expected great things. In fact nothing happened at all and I realised after a few weeks that they were barely using the tape recorder. I was very disappointed, because I felt that I had understood something very important about children – their need for freedom to express their own views; their competence to do things which adults generally suspect they cannot do; their desire to be trusted.

When I thought about this afterwards I realised that even with the freedom and trust that they wanted they still needed a framework and a point to what they were doing. And whilst they were quite capable of making a programme themselves, they had never done it before. If someone said to me 'You can make a programme about anything you like,' even as a professional radio producer I would find it hard to know where to start. I did not want to tell the children what theme they should choose for their programme and what they should record: I did not know what was important to them, and I really did want them to choose for themselves. I was genuinely happy to learn from them and respect their views and ideas, but in some way I was saying that I did not want them to learn from me, and that I did not want to contribute my own ideas or experience. I knew far more about radio than the children so I was much more confident than they about what might work and what might not. I failed to share that knowledge with the children. In a way I was not listening again. I had listened to children enough to know that they wanted to speak for themselves and that they were capable of making radio, and then I stopped listening and became caught up with my own ideas, rather than responding to what was in front of me – I needed to 'listen' to their inactivity and confusion.

In the end I realised what was happening – I started listening again – and those children went on to win an award for the programme they made for BBC Radio 5 about racism. Looking back now, however, I am aware again of just how much power I had in this situation – the power to initiate the contact, to set the ground rules, even the power to grant them permission to use my tape recorder. Their power lay much more in their reaction to me, or their lack of reaction.

SARAH: So what are people doing wrong, what are all those journalists and people doing wrong?

M: They talk for us, you know. They're telling us as a child you're supposed to be like this, like this, like that but that's not how children are, you know… Every child is different, you know, even though somehow he might be the same. I think what you're doing now is correct: I think children should be able to talk freely on their own and say what they think and not what the grown-ups think.

S: And the journalists before they start talking about children and everything, I think they should do like what you're doing and come and ask the children what they think about it and say things which probably don't make much sense and just saying things that they don't know but they just think about it and that isn't nice, you just talk about things which you don't know.

E: And sometimes they also say how it used to be when they were small but things always change.

S: Yeah, exactly, it's a different generation.

SARAH: Another question that I'd like to ask you is if you were gonna give some advice to journalists about how to make it easier for children to express themselves, perhaps if you get a journalist who hasn't worked with children much and they don't really know very much about it, can you think of a way that you could help them to help you?

S: By telling them we're human.

    (four sisters aged between 7 and 14 in Windhoek, Namibia)

SARAH: What were you expecting when you thought you were going to make a radio programme?

M: I was expecting to have to read something off or something like that. I thought it was all done for us and you'd have to read it off.

SARAH: Is it better if it's not all done for you? Does it make a difference, do you think?

C: If you read it then you can't really get the emotions that you want to when you're talking because first of all if you're reading you sort of talk a… bit… like… that and it don't sound human, but when you're talking you can get it out properly. You can say what you want to say, really, and you can't just – 'cos if you writ it down you'd have to get it exactly right and you'd have to see whether it's in proportion and things like this, but

when you're talking it's much easier because you can just relax
and just speak as you think about it.

(10-year-olds in London)

Again and again the word 'human' comes up – children want to be treated as
humans; they want to be allowed to behave in a human way and to show other
people that they are human. It is very shocking that they should even need to
talk in these terms, and it is tempting simply to deny what they are saying by
suggesting it is exaggeration. If, on the other hand, we try to listen to what lies
behind their words, I think it gives a clue about one of the most important
aspects of working with children. It is easy, once you have discovered the power
of listening to children, to become ever more skilled as a listener, until you
become a kind of professional listener. I think that the minute this happens you
stop being human, in the way children mean it. Being a good listener puts you
in a tremendously powerful position. You can work sympathetically with
children; they trust you, to the extent that they often tell you very personal
details about their lives, which they clearly need to express to someone; the
quality of work is usually much higher as a result; it becomes easier to predict
and even forestall problems; as you get better at it you make less and less
mistakes. Yet it is these very problems and mistakes that can give children the
chance to see you as human, as weaker than them in some ways, as vulnerable
or simply wrong. There are many things that children know far more about
than me – or any adult – not least themselves, their own lives and their culture.
By negotiating a way through problems, admitting weakness and dealing with
mistakes, children and adults can be truly equal (human), because each person
in the discussion has a unique perspective. It is a very subtle balance. If you do
not listen well to children it is unlikely that you will feel comfortable negotiating
with them. If, on the other hand, you listen too skilfully and professionally, the
skill can become a protection and a way of controlling children even more.
They are never professionals. They bring their whole selves into their work
with any adult, which adults often do not. I think children assume that adults
are like them, but to be like them we have to be prepared for every meeting
with a child to be a new experience. Of course we learn all the time and become
more skilled at listening and working with children but I have found that when
that gets in the way of direct contact (which can mean letting down my own
defences and even changing my life in the light of what I have learned from
children) I feel that I am not engaging with children in the way that they are
engaging with me.

> SARAH: How would you like to see journalists working with young
>   people?
>
> A: To actually be there for the young people, 'cause most of them
>   they're just – they should set an example, because most of them

aren't setting examples to the youth, so most of the youth ain't gotten a choice. They're set bad examples and the youth follow them and they get involved in all sorts of bad stuff.

(A 16-year-old in Barbados)

G: Well we could help them, (adults) like when we grow up we're probably gonna want to try out the things we thought of as children, but they may not work. But if we give them ideas and help them understand what we mean, then they may be able to try it, and then if it doesn't work, we can progress, like keep thinking up new ideas.

N: What I wonder is that we're complaining now but when we get to be adults are we gonna listen to the children, when we get older?

SARAH: Are you?

G: I think we need to be taught that we *can* listen to children because maybe subconsciously we're gonna learn from what they're doing; and that if they act like they are listening to us maybe we'll learn to listen to our child, maybe it will help.

(13-year-olds in Barbados)

Another project gives some clues as to how this can work more successfully. I was talking with a group of ten-year-olds one day, consulting them about a programme I was planning. We gradually moved away from this discussion and they started chatting about television. The subject of single parent families came up and they commented on how rarely they saw such families on television. Thomas suddenly said 'Sometimes you just want to tell other people about it, like people you meet in the street, but you can't really.' I realised immediately that this was a sensitive subject for him and an important one too. It occurred to me that it might make a good radio programme. We continued to talk for a while and, as I had suspected, he brought the subject up again. This time I suggested that if he really wanted to tell people what it is like living in a single parent family he could make a radio programme about it.

This beginning to the project reveals a number of crucial factors. Thomas came up with the idea completely spontaneously – we were not even trying to have programme ideas – so I was absolutely sure that I was not putting anything into his mind. At the same time it was my experience of radio that suggested here was a potential programme. I knew little about single parent families, and nothing about Thomas' feelings, but I did know about radio, and it was this particular combination of his and my skills, experience and interest that came together. If I had just 'left it to the children' there would never have been a radio programme. On the other hand if I had been pumping them for ideas, I am sure that such a sensitive topic would not have been raised.

During the first recording session, a few days later, it was quite clear who was in charge. The three children who were taking part had prepared themselves so they would be able to manage 'without getting too emotional'. I never needed to ask any questions because they felt so clearly what they wanted to say. All I needed to do was listen with complete attention to everything they said and give support when they felt shaky – it was not easy for them to speak openly about such a personal subject. I feel that if I had tried to direct the discussion I would have lost the children's trust very quickly, and yet if I had not been listening and fully concentrating, the children also would not have been able to speak freely, if at all.

C: When we first started off we didn't feel as used to it and we didn't feel relaxed – we were all uptight, sitting up, and we weren't really getting our emotions out but in the last few stages we really got our emotions out and if we couldn't have edited it it would have been a whole different story – we wouldn't have got the message across properly.

SARAH: Can you explain a little bit about how you edited it...

C: Well, what we did is first of all we recorded and then we listened to it, and we found bits that we didn't like. So we recorded again and we added it to the things that we did before, and we listened to it all the way through, and then there were certain things that we didn't like or weren't really relevant...

M: We also had to discuss what we wanted and what we needed most of all and things like that and if there was a sentence that we didn't want to use we cut part of it off and put another bit in.

B: Sometimes when you breathe for a long time or when you say 'ok like' and things like that then you cut it 'cos they don't sound very good.

SARAH: Do you feel as though you had control over what you were doing?

M: I think we did have control because we chose the subject and we chose to work on it and do things about it and to talk about it on the radio – that's why I think we had most control over it.

(10-year-olds in London)

A couple of weeks later, after we had finished editing the tape together and the children were happy with the programme, they found they had not said everything they wanted so they asked if they could write a magazine. They were really excited at the idea of interviewing children all round the school about their experience of living in single parent families. I was extremely worried about this – it might be very traumatic for some children, particularly if they had no chance to volunteer to take part, but were simply approached out of the blue. We discussed the problem together – again a combination of their ideas and enthusiasm with my experience of working with children. When I came back a few days later they told me they had found a solution. They had formed a small group of children in their own class who wanted to take part. They had not needed to ask anybody – these children had been curious about our work anyway and when they heard about it they asked if they could join in – a perfect result. I could never have achieved it because I do not spend enough time with the children, and yet it might also not have happened if I had not told them of my worries.

The real pleasure was to watch them interviewing their friends (classmates who they may have known for five years but who had never, ever talked about this subject with their friends before). They were so sensitive, so supportive. The interviews were very moving and revealed much of the strength and the pain of these children. As I watched the three who had been working with me I realised how much they had learned in a few weeks. They were listening in a way that children can, but very rarely do. They worked exceptionally hard at helping their friends to trust them and feel it was safe to be open, and I watched them learning as they were listening. Again they did it so much better than I could have, and differently too, building on the experience they had had with me.

Having finished the magazine, Thomas told me he wanted to make some recordings with children, again about living in a single parent family, but without me there. He knew that children would speak differently with him alone than with an adult there. Not only did he now have the confidence to tell me I was not needed, but he also recognised his own strength and capability. He still needed some help and support, but he had reached a point where he could ask for what he wanted.

B: I think it's good for children to make radio programmes because children have different points of views to what the adults have and sometimes the adults – like with wars, because it's usually the adults that cause the wars, not the children, and the children – if they come from the country that's fighting they have to suffer the oppression and say their family may be getting killed and something like that – they have to go through a lot.

SARAH: So what you're saying is that we should hear from the children's side as well.

B: And they should see what the children think about the situation.

C: Children should be allowed to make radio programmes
         because…they (adults) need to listen to children because we
         always listen to adults, and sometimes I think 'Why is it that we
         always have to listen to adults and if we do something wrong
         then adults shout at us but if the adults do something wrong we
         can't shout at them?' And it really gets on my nerves because
         they've got to listen to us as much as we listen to them.

SARAH: What do you think they would get out of listening to you?

C: Well, sometimes we feel differently from them and like a lot of
         times adults have more things on their minds than us so they
         don't really think about some things like this as much but when
         children have got the time to think about it we can really get
         our emotions out whereas adults, they don't listen to us because
         they think that only their view is right because they're the
         adult and they're the grown-up and they're the oldest person in
         the family and that's going to matter more

B: Because grown-ups are just really older children, aren't they? Just
         because they've passed a certain age limit they think they can
         control everything else but I don't think that's really fair.
         Sometimes children have got a lot more solutions to some
         problems, and problems (of their own). Then it's the adults that
         go completely the wrong way and it's the children who suffer –
         they don't get a proper education or something like that
         because some adult at the top has said 'All right we're going to
         stop your money or we're going to do this to you or we're
         going to shoot your Dad or your Mum or something like that'
         – why should they have to be oppressed?

C: Well as Roald Dahl said, adults are just giants that tease children.
         In one of his books, I remember reading it, he said that children
         should be allowed to tell adults things that they don't know
         and things that they do know but they haven't really thought
         about it, 'cos all they are are children that have sort of grown
         up, like they've got to an older thing – they've got older, so
         they're bigger, and they earn money and they've got more
         things to think about. But the thing is, sometimes children
         know more about different things than adults do, but adults just
         won't listen to them because they feel they know more just
         because they've got to pay bills and everything – it ain't always
         right because not every one knows everything about everything.

                                                      (10-year-olds in London)

PART FOUR

Adults as Allies

CHAPTER SIX

Children's Parliament in Slovenia[1]

Zoran Pavlovic

INTRODUCTION: CHILDREN IN A SOCIETY

Society should foster persuasive, inclusive rather than exclusive myths[2] so as to be able to use the intelligence of the whole system. So, what about the myth of 'children's rights', is it such a myth? It certainly includes *children*, but it can be understood in so many different fashions, depending on the 'mental health' level of the particular group or society. It can be understood as a call for the protection, or just the opposite, for liberation of children, and many other things. If we fall out of balance, we will lose from the picture a specific nature of the child as a human being, person in permanent development and change, in need of belonging, protection, assistance, support and tolerance for his/her mistakes, as well as in need of respect of his/her individuality and his/her point of view, freedom of feeling, of exploration, of going away and coming back, of acquiring his/her own independent empirical experience. A balanced and integrated view of the child's nature opens a possibility for a better integration for a care-giver as well, and for the society. Fragmented views lead to a one-way communication and one-way process of giving and taking, to the feeling of a zero-sum game, where one must lose for the other to gain, to a myth of children's rights as an exclusive one.

---

1 A longer version of this paper was presented at the European Conference 'Monitoring Children's Rights', Gent, December 1994. The full text appears in E. Verhellen (ed) (1996) *Monitoring Children's Rights*. Dordrecht: Martinus Nijhoff.

2 'Myth' is understood as an abstract bit of common condensed wisdom, which fills in a blank in our mental map of the world, which we, being limited empirical creatures, cannot draw out relying only on our experience. Myths are ideas and stories that enable human beings to co-operate and work together as a society. Value of a particular myth must be assessed by asking, how effective it is in helping to integrate human behaviour (individuals to become more integrated, groups to become more co-operative). Skynner and Cleese (1993) point at the two aspects to that effectiveness.

Living with a child may make an adult's life more difficult or at least more complicated, but definitely richer. An adult may have to give up some of his/her comfort, but in return, gets full wealth of new life unfolding right in front of him/her, whatever one makes of it, after all. And for society, a life without children would be equal to imminent death. If the myth of 'children's rights' did not mean a better quality of life also for parents, kindergarten, school and all other levels as well, because of everything children give and teach us, it would not really be inclusive. We want to see it as an inclusive myth, indeed, as a new positive utopia, a hope for a better future for everybody. Yet, we so often make it to be a zero-sum game, whenever we make it sound that being pro-children's rights means being against somebody else's rights or interests.

Therefore, the 'children's rights' myth has the powerful potential of becoming an inclusive myth, but there are still lessons to be learned before it actually does. On the other hand, is it a persuasive myth?

The UN Convention on the Rights of the Child comes readily into the picture at this point. It has now been signed and ratified by so many countries that it looks like the best possible confirmation of the persuasiveness of the myth. Yet, do all these countries take children's rights really seriously? Didn't they, during the World Summit on Children in 1989, discuss the Gulf crisis behind the curtains? Didn't they sign the Convention because it sounded nice at the time, while making significant reservation to preserve national legislation intact? Well, even so, the Convention itself and the international process related to it will probably *persuade* countries to take it seriously. Some of them may not have meant it seriously at the time, but they have officially involved themselves in certain commitments. Gradually, as monitoring mechanisms evolve and mature, the international persuasiveness of the myth will grow and also the international pressure to initiate real changes. It may be a slow process, but is, nevertheless, bound to have a profound impact on the particular societies involved, and on the meaning of the universality of human rights as well.

How about 'democracy', is that a persuasive and inclusive myth? It is certainly persuasive, as recent history of Eastern and Central Europe clearly displays. But is it inclusive?

There have always been people and forces who find their vocation to drive somebody out of the participation in public affairs, or out of the country, or out of the Earth, because they were of the wrong skin colour, wrong place of birth, wrong age, wrong gender, or wrong whatever. 'Democracy' has, historically, hardly been an inclusive myth. Yet, gradually, the inclusive understanding seems to be prevailing – at least as long as a society is doing relatively well. In times of adversity the majority usually puts some tighter control on women, foreigners, maybe even handicapped, certainly over children (maybe just for their safety reasons) and therefore gives a 'decisive decision-making' priority over the slow and bothersome process of 'inclusive democracy', where everybody must be consulted before the elected representatives can formulate a compromise.

Without children, democracy is not inclusive. They are, for example, explicitly excluded from the right to vote. This fact alone must not necessarily present a tragedy for children, as long as they are fully consulted in their healthy families and as long as their parents or other care-givers genuinely represent children's interests in public affairs. However, just in case all this does not work so ideally, it seems wise to invent some other channels to be used by children when they want to communicate something to somebody in charge outside their immediate family (or the school, for that matter), or when they simply want to communicate their point of view on some significant issue. We all, in our different roles, can often profit more from having access to some civil pressure-groups who advocate our interests, and to the media, than from merely relying on our power to give our vote away every four years to a political party who can turn out not to have our benefit at heart at all. Yet, we are not willing to give our right to vote away, are we? Just as we realise that our vote is not sufficient, we can use all the means we can invent to control the people in power. Even having some of them available, it does not work perfectly, but a better system is still to be invented. Children also need to get access to as many modalities or means of participation as possible – if democracy is to be an inclusive myth.

CHILDRENS' PARLIAMENT IN SLOVENIA

I think it is a very promising sign for the future of democracy in Slovenia that the Children's Parliament started in the same year as the 'big' one, the first multi-party State Assembly, in 1990. I like to think that it happened because the people in power shared the same inclusive notion of democracy with the people who actually initiated the Children's Parliament, the organisation called 'Association of the Friends of Youth of Slovenia' (AFYS). They shared the conviction that everybody's intelligence was needed and that the children definitely must have their opinion on the significant public issues heard. The Association was very serious about all that from the beginning; it is hard to say whether the politicians, the hosts of the Children's Parliament, were equally serious. If they were not, they certainly did not show it.

To be quite frank, I was rather sceptical about the whole idea in the beginning. I thought that the adults were trying to use just another gimmick for making themselves look good and feel good about themselves while manipulating children into thinking that they were able to influence something and even make some decisions but all the time concealing the actual lack of power of children as a social group. Even if my concerns had been quite adequate, the process in the following years outgrew them.

The children we are talking about are students of the higher classes of the eight-year elementary school, 13 to 15 years old, but there are always also some younger than that, and some middle school students as well.

So there they were on 19 October 1990, 105 child representatives of 44 (out of 65) municipalities in Slovenia, discussing environmental issues with the president of the adult parliament, prime minister, ministers for education and for social affairs, 'Green' and several other parliament members and a number of other officials. In the beginning, it was not even called 'Parliament'. It was 'a meeting' of children and high political officials. It was actually because of what had happened the first time that the term Parliament was attached to the process.

It must be mentioned at this point that the session in the building of the Slovenian Parliament (State Assembly) represents only the final act, although, of course, the most solemn part of a much longer process. It starts at the school level where children first accumulate relevant knowledge about the given problem and then become involved in a discussion based on the theory and, of course, on the empirical evidence as they experience it in their everyday lives. It would not make much sense to chose a theme for the Parliament that would bear no significance to children's everyday experience. A couple of students are chosen to represent the school at the Parliament on the municipality level; there, a couple of students are elected to represent the municipality at the State level.

1990: ENVIRONMENT

In 1990, the theme of the Parliament process was 'Healthy and Safe Environment for Children'. Children displayed a considerable level of awareness and understanding of serious ecological problems threatening our planet, as well as of concrete ecological 'bombs' in their own community; indeed, they composed a pretty comprehensive list of the main ecological problem areas in Slovenia! Another sub-topic was really unsafe road traffic in Slovenia, which takes regularly about 500 lives yearly (per 2 million inhabitants). About 50 of those are children. Two classes, every year. They also spoke about the school as their living environment and pointed out how neglected and poor many of these environments were, and they also tackled a number of related issues from which they, at the end, chose a topic for the next Parliament.

The overall atmosphere was not too optimistic, it was rather depressing and accusing – accusing adults, of course, for such a state of affairs. They demanded serious changes, but they were not able to see themselves as competent agents of change. When they were invited to participate at sessions of some political bodies which would discuss their demands, a girl said explicitly that they had no intention of attending some tiresome meetings; they formulated their requests and expected politicians to do their job and to report to the next Children's Parliament! The adult politicians present were discussing and replying in a friendly and frank, although somewhat sweet and over-flattering, tone; they also made promises – not just because of the presence of the media, I believe...

The proceedings (a full transcription of the tape recording of the meeting) of the Parliament was published by the AFYS, accompanied by twelve short scholarly papers by adult experts, on pollution related health hazards, on the child in the road traffic, and on the school related stress of children.

I think 'environment' as a subject of the first Parliament was a very good choice. As children are our positive future, pollution is our negative future. Although we adults often seem to think that 'we'll be well dead before it really hits', we do care for our children and the future of the planet just enough to make pollution we create also our problem to solve. Children's basic message at the Parliament seems to have been: 'We want to have a future, but we do not seem to have any!' The adult reply seems to have been: 'We hear and understand what you are saying. We accept our responsibility and promise to take care of it'. Which was a kind of inter-generational alliance for the future, a sound basis for the development of the second Parliament in 1991. It was decided to be on the 'free' or 'leisure time' of children and youth, which is a really traumatic issue of a modern world. In a way, environmental issues are easy to discuss. It is a real problem; yet so complex that when nothing improves it is hard to point a finger to the 'guilty' party. Even a whole international community seems to be rather helpless! But if children and youth are not happy and constructive when they have the opportunity – in their leisure, free time – the cause must be somewhere really close; it must be caused by the way we communicate with each other, how we live our lives, what we, old and young, do to each other. It is about the 'health status' of the society. Therefore, an inter-generational discussion on the subject must be a real test of how meaningful their endeavour is.

1991: LEISURE TIME

Many things happened between the two Parliaments. Although environmental issues are a way to ask about your future, it was not the top 'future' issue at that time in our country. In 1990, the former federation of Yugoslavia was already in deep trouble and the future of it, of its federal parts and of all of us was tremendously uncertain. A girl at the first Children's Parliament actually challenged the president of the (adult) Parliament about his personal attitude regarding Slovenia as an independent state. After he had offered a very fair and honest reply (saying that we must create such a homeland for ourselves in which we would be the masters of our own destiny, but we must be aware that in the modern world nobody is alone, everybody must co-operate with their neigh-bours in a co-dependent world), the subject did not return.

At the time, very few seriously considered a possibility of a real war. Yet, in 1991, it happened. First in Slovenia (after the Declaration of Independence), very soon it moved to Croatia and then it blasted into Bosnia and Herzegovina in the Spring of 1992; three years later we still see no end nor solution to it. Hundreds of thousands of refugees moved in the reverse direction, from the war areas to the safe areas of Croatia, to Slovenia and further west, and also out of Europe. This was all beyond our worst nightmare that we had had just months earlier. The memories and vicinity of on-going war, plus all the economic and other difficulties a young country needs to face, caused a lot of anxieties among people; children were not spared from it. Child welfare organisations got involved in the work with refugees, adult Parliament was preoccupied with the new Constitution of the Republic of Slovenia, which was finally adopted by the end of 1991. Children's Parliament had to wait. But it was not forgotten; commitments were there, and a wish to continue, so it was actually held on 28 February 1992. That is another good sign for the future of democracy in Slovenia; children were not put aside, they were invited for further consultations, even in the most hard times (just a little later than planned!)

One would not expect such a thing as Children's Parliament to develop in time, because the majority of the actors change from one to another. But, social processes seem to have this ability of actually developing – even when all the actors change in a rather short time, as is the case with the members of the social group 'children'.

The second Parliament was actually a step further. For one thing, the government actually provided a report on the realisation of the commitments to the first Parliament. It was able to present only a few actual accomplishments in that short and hard time, but it was ensuring that the government was taking seriously all the children's requests and was intensively preparing further measures for improvements.

It was just the second Parliament, so it was still not completely certain how real it was and to what extent it was just 'make believe'. At that moment, I think, children decided to test their power. There was a vote on the government's effectiveness. *Nobody* thought the government had been very successful, but only a few assessed it as unsuccessful. The majority opted just for moderately 'successful'.

There was a separate report on the specific progress in the area of ecology (by a member of the 'Green' party, at the time also a member of the collective presidency of the Republic), which was quite optimistic, and did not provoke much discussion. And then, there was the report of the Minister of Education on the efforts of the government in the area of schooling. For whatever reason, his report was faced with discontent. Children felt that the minister was not replying to their questions. Speaker after speaker requested *concrete* answers.

Children, reflecting the general anxious state of society, came to the Parliament to complain, and they used the opportunity well. They had the power to choose, and they chose to be unsatisfied and also to show it. Talking about the trauma of leisure time, they mainly attacked schools for not fulfilling their tasks. They expressed their feeling that everything was actually better a couple of years earlier, that schools were cutting out extra-curricular activities, that there were too few facilities (like gyms and pools) and existing ones were in a poor shape, that the teachers were just about to start striking because of their poor salaries. Also that, overall, schools were not efficient and were taking much more of the students' time and energy than necessary. There were very few constructive suggestions for improvement. It seems to me that the children just wanted to see whether they would be heard and accepted if they were just angry, anxious and unsatisfied. And the good thing is, they were. Not an easy job for a Minister of Education, though. The Children's Parliament became quite serious. If the basic message of the first Parliament had been 'We want to have a future', the message of the second was, I feel: 'Take care of us. We are entitled'.

Through their complaints they were really saying to adults 'You promised so many things, yet you have let us down. Many of us feel lonely, and many of us are not self-sufficient, not even (or maybe the least) in our "free" time. This society devotes too little time, money and attention to our needs and does not provide sufficient assistance to our development'. Again, the good thing was, the adults did not reply 'That is not true, you ungrateful, selfish little brats'. They really said 'We hear what you are saying; we thought we were doing our best, but we will try to do better; but you need to be patient, our resources are limited, we cannot make it overnight'. Children were heard and accepted for their negative feelings and complaints in a fair parliamentary discussion. The adults argued their point of view honestly, showed personal feelings and concern, and the Parliament was a success. It created very solid ground for further development, and it also created a list of demands for the government to fulfil in the following year(s). Not surprisingly, the children decided to devote their next Parliament to 'the school'.

AFYS published the tape transcript of the meeting, accompanied by fifteen scholarly papers on the problems of the 'free' time of children and youth. Several public debates on the subject were organised in the following months.

1992: FRIENDLY SCHOOL

Following the third Parliament (held on time in December 1992) AFYS again published the tape transcript, but this time not accompanied by scholarly contribution but by the translation of the UN Convention on the Rights of the Child, the report of the organisation on its activities in 1992 and its plans for 1993.

The president of the AFYS, in the introduction to this publication, summarised several qualities of the third Parliament in a brief yet significant manner. The following sentences relate a good deal of the 'behind-the-curtain' process:

> The Association of the Friends of Youth of Slovenia is particularly pleased by the ever improving co-operation of the local authorities at the local Parliaments (presidents of municipal governments and parliaments). Accepting an initiative of AFYS, parliaments were even organised in some municipalities where we do not have our committees any longer. In some places, parliaments motivated revival of our branch. We estimate that we have overcome fears and prejudices that with this activity AFYS wants to continue a political manipulation of children, following this or that ideology. A conviction is firmly established now that AFYS is just a non-governmental and non-partisan organisation of people with different world views and aspects, joined by the common interest of acting for the welfare of children and youth. (Zbornik Otrokom Prijazno Solo (Friendly School to Children) 1993 Introduction (by the president Ludvik Harvat) p.1)

In the beginning, it was not completely clear whether the Parliament was or was not a manipulation of children, even to the organisation that was standing behind it. There was a lot of discussion going on in the organisation about that. The focus was on the 'big event'; the organisation did not have that much influence on the process of preparation at the lower levels and was not sure to what extent children were actually representing children's interests and to what extent they would just read a message that was written by some school or community related adult who wanted to send a message to the capital through the children's mouth. But, after two quite successful attempts, it became much clearer that the Parliament really had the powerful potential of opening a dialogue between the authorities and the authentic voice of children, even when we take into account the fact that children at this age need adult assistance in all stages of the process and that they still carry written (adult-assisted) notes with them to Ljubljana. There was a new confidence that the children's voice does come through.

Adults on many levels started taking the whole process more seriously; the organisation noticed the improved co-operation of the local authorities. The starting points of the process gained in importance, and consequently the role of mentors at the school level as well. AFYS started organising seminars for mentors (teachers or school counselling staff) to prepare them for the role of mediators, involving experts in the subject matter of the particular Parliament.

These changes were reflected immediately in the work of the third Parliament. One of the most important features was in the children who, being previously accepted even when they were not pleasing the adults, became much more co-operative and realistic in their discussions and demands. They had much better insight into which issues could and should be dealt with at the school level; which they needed to discuss with the local authorities; and which they really needed to address to the State level politicians. They gained in self-confidence and in the feeling that the Parliament may bear some concrete fruit, after all. Of course, not everything worked perfectly all of a sudden. About one third of municipalities still did not have a representative at the 'big' one; regarding the co-operation of local authorities, one girl at the Parliament said that they were there only as long as there were representatives of the media present, then they left them to talk to themselves.

In his Introduction, the president of AFYS also wrote:

> All of us who follow the work of the Parliament from the very beginning, appreciate continuing growth of the quality of young representatives' discussions. The third Parliament particularly excelled with the spontaneous performances of the representatives, who did not read texts written by their mentors. Which did not mean that these performances were not carefully prepared and thoughtful. (*ibid*, p.1)

The children also gained in their sense of power. A girl said at the third Parliament, with a nice touch of humour:

> We had elections in Slovenia.[3] Therefore, the old parliament has gone, while the new one has not started working yet. Our, Children's Parliament, which has a session today in the building of a Slovenian State Assembly, is at the moment the highest body of the Republic Slovenia, composed by representatives, elected by children all around Slovenia!

The third Children's Parliament worked under the title 'Friendly School to Children'. Children spoke about the material standards of schooling, but even more about the interpersonal relations in the school and about the quality of the curriculum. They had a lot of concrete suggestions. Instead of complaining, they were describing difficulties in a more matter-of-fact manner, and pleaded for the faster modernisation of the school (there was a lot of talk about computers). While asking adults (teachers) to be fair, they were quite willing to recognise their own role in making the school 'friendly', their obligation to behave correctly and to do their part of the job. One of them said: 'We too often misunderstand democracy as anarchy'. Several 'integrative' subjects were re-occurring repeatedly: suggestions for a tolerant dialogue, for better communication between the school and parents. Words like 'independent work', 'co-operation', 'solidarity with less affluence', 'relaxed atmosphere', were not uncommon. The children would themselves ask speakers not to repeat what they had already been told.

---

3   It was just after the second multi-party elections to the State Assembly.

As already mentioned, they often clearly expressed their understanding of which issues could be resolved at the school level, even when they mentioned them at the Parliament, while they addressed appropriate requests to the State officials. They included requests for more money to be invested in the younger generation, but also for more rational curriculum and more effective teaching methods, with more field work, modern equipment, etc.

The Minister of Education and his team replied very clearly and efficiently to the children's questions and discussions. There was no conflict. The minister was not the same one as a year earlier; maybe the new one was a better communicator, but the children were certainly more ready to listen because they had acquired the confidence that they would be heard. Even more: the children themselves often expressed optimism, they had noticed things 'to be moving' and they were quite satisfied with some of these 'moves', although the majority of the schools were just the same poor old ones, while there were only a few new schools with nice gyms opened in the meantime.

As regards the mental state of our society and the role of the Children's Parliament in it, I must say I do not find it surprising that the person who moderated the third Parliament exclaimed enthusiastically at one point: 'I must admit that I am surprised by the profoundness and vision displayed by the young representatives. I think this country has a truly great future!'

Looking for the 'basic message' of the third Parliament, I think it is: 'If you are fair, we can do our part. We can live together well'. The climate had obviously considerably changed, but I think the messages from the first two Parliaments should not be forgotten. They requested a future for themselves and they wanted to be taken care of before they agreed to co-operate.

Encouraged by the level of dialogue, while being quite critical regarding their own conduct, they were very concerned about bullying, smoking and drinking. They decided to address these particularly difficult issues at their next Parliament.

1993: FOR FRIENDSHIP WITHOUT VIOLENCE

Why should these issues be particularly difficult?

The Parliament started in 1990 by establishing a coalition between children and adults against a 'common enemy': deadly pollution and dangerous road traffic. Next the children felt free to put the adults on the 'other side' and address their complaints whilst offering co-operation. Now, with violence as a main subject of the oncoming session, titled 'For Friendship – Without Violence', they had to face the fact that 'they', the children, were not a homogenous group of people; they were about to divide themselves into 'good' and 'bad' kids.

At that time the adult community was also quite alarmed by the cases of violence against peers in and out of our schools, and still is. The school became the focus of public attention, while the school itself felt rather helpless. The police were specially concerned about the first appearances of organised groups, led from behind by young adults, intimidating younger children for money. A big auditorium, where AFYS organised a public panel discussion on the subject, as a part of the preparation of the mentors, was overcrowded. Although I never considered myself to be an expert in bullying (or any other form of deviancy of children and youth, for that matter), I was, as a researcher at the Institute of Criminology, invited to chair that panel. After the event, a number of schools from Ljubljana and vicinity invited me to visit them and have a talk with the teachers and parents. Their concerns were genuine and these evening talks were very interesting.

One school invited me to help them conduct their school Parliament. That was, unfortunately, my first 'first hand' experience with this process at the school level, and the only one, so far. I was, as could be expected, pleasantly surprised. Some students read very well prepared reports on the subject as a theoretical framework for the discussion. And there was a lot of open discussion; the teachers, some parents and a member of the local authority co-operated nicely. Some of the children tried to simplify the issue; some of them suggested the 'bad' children really needed some kind of help; the others would like them punished or somehow excluded. But some other children did their best to keep both sides of the story in balance, which was painful, because the children obviously needed to be protected from the bully, who was one of them. Talking about bullying with an adult does not only mean overcoming the humiliation of the victim, but also betrayal of the peer. The children quickly became aware of the dilemma (even if they had not had any bad experiences themselves) and did not look very convinced when they were told to consult a teacher or a school counsellor if they were attacked or pressed for money; for the reasons of their own safety and because of the fact that it is easier to help a bully if he is stopped early.

It was impossible not to notice that the 'bad' children were not at the school Parliament. They probably self-excluded themselves at the very beginning of the whole process. There were some children outside throwing snowballs at the window. Maybe they were just younger children amusing themselves. But, more likely, they were of the same age as those inside but they did not 'belong' to this nice, smart co-operative crowd.

At the 'big' Parliament in December 1993, the difficulty became even more clear. Many blamed society for the violence, smoking, drinking and drug abuse among youth, the culture of alcohol and violent movies and bad adult models (even drinking and smoking teachers were mentioned). Many were discussing family reasons for deviant behaviour, but many were also simply blaming it on the 'bad children', just that nobody knew exactly what to do about them. To be fair, there were many proposals regarding prevention. They called the families to devote more attention to children; they wanted the school to be a positive experience for everybody, so that nobody would need to seek affirmation in a negative way; some described good experiences, like class excursions, which helped to integrate the class better and lower the level of violence; most of all, they wanted more co-operation between students and teachers; they also demanded more control, in the school, and by the police. At this Parliament the children actually exposed their vulnerability. I think the basic message was: 'Protect us'. But it was not just 'You, good people, protect us, good children, from the bullies, drugs and alcohol'. It also meant: 'Protect us, good and bad children, from yourselves. Change your ways'.

I am not sure whether this message came through to the adult ears. It only occurred to me after reading the tape transcript over and over again and remembering the atmosphere in the assembly hall. But maybe the children have found their own way to make it come through, eventually, and to help adults to change. At the end they had to decide on the subject for the next session. There were several proposals, among them one that sounded really attractive: love. What are the things that make our life easier and help us to cope? That would be something very different from hard thinking about the dark sides of life. But they explicitly refused it and decided to talk about the relations and the communication between students and teachers, plus the students' school related stress. I think they did that because they wanted to create another opportunity to do a little bit of complaining, but also an opportunity to make some real impact. Maybe they will talk about love some other time; now they want to improve adults.

I feel it to be a good judgement. The subject of violence made them face their vulnerability and powerlessness. They had to call on adults for help. That is fair. Violence, drug abuse and drinking are issues beyond their power; they definitely demand very active and firm adult approach. Here they can play their part and co-operate if the adults change. They can try to help them change. I think they are right. A good school Parliament with a lot of open communication may be just the right thing to help integrate the school. In fact, I think it is already happening.

The adult State officials again made very valuable contributions, and displayed a sincere and honest attitude. The President of the State Assembly addressed the children in the beginning; the President of the Republic sent a message and apologised for his absence; the Minister of Education presented a realistic report on the progress of the 'friendly school' project from the last session and together with his team, answered many questions during the debate. They ensured that the kind of school that the ministry envisions will also greatly reduce tension and, consequently, violence as well. The Minister of Interior Affairs assured the young representatives that the police were concerned about the violence among youth and also very active. They both called the children to co-operate actively with the school in fighting the undesired conduct of their peers. This session left me in a reflective mood.

Some kids are more co-operative than others. Some are more rebellious than others. It may be their inborn character, but it certainly is a different kind of experience they have with adults that must be held accountable for this diversity. The process of the Children's Parliament attracts the more co-operative ones. (At least at this age. Later, in middle school, they are much more capable of organising themselves independently from adult assistance). Is it possible that we are actually doing a disservice to these 'good' children by involving them in the adult way of resolving problems? We often hear from experts that some kind of rebellion against the previous generation is necessary for the formation of one's individual identity. Are we not making it even harder for the 'good' children if we teach them that everything can be nicely 'talked out'? They will find it hard to rebel anyway. Should we pull them even further from their naughty peers? The naughty ones are going to have a lot of fun in their youth. The majority of them will mature to become good and responsible people, but will retain the capacity for fun and will understand children and youth. Well, the majority of the good ones will find some reason to rebel eventually, and get even with the bad ones, but, paradoxically, the good experience of the Children's Parliament may not perhaps help them in their development.

On the other hand, if the adults want to hear the authentic voice of children, they should not listen only to the good ones and pretend that they hear all. As we all know, some children are very hard to reach. Yet we must try. Not just because of the Parliament, of course. But if the school takes care that everybody is 'in' and belonging safely to the school community, it will be easy to include everybody's point of view in a discussion on important matters – important for children, that is. To reach more difficult children we may need to use some different methods; sitting and talking may be too much hard work for some of them. Whatever we can do to include them, we must do. Articulation of children's point of view is not valid as long as we exclude some or many of them, or they self-exclude themselves. A more integrated process may help the good and the bad equally.

People in power who sincerely want to learn from children, should not just wait for them to come and articulate their problems in a mature parliamentary manner. They should come at least half-way down to children and learn in the children's natural environment and re-learn some of the 'childish' ways of conveying messages; which at least some of them already do, but that is already a quite different story, not the story about the Parliament. Still, even the Parliament itself could profit from some non-verbal means of communication, drawings, posters, dramatisations of the topics.

Something else has been bothering me: when we finally sort out all the problems and everybody is well integrated in a perfect world, what will children then rebel against? And if there is nothing to rebel against, how will they form their identity? Have no fears, I hear everybody saying, there will never be a perfect world. Then why are we working so hard? Why don't we go have some fun – with children?

WHILE LOOKING FORWARD TO THE SESSION ON 'COMMUNICATION BETWEEN STUDENTS AND TEACHERS'...

In four years the process of the Children's Parliament has firmly established itself and has become a good tradition. Of course, there is still work to be done. It has not reached all schools in Slovenia, not even all municipalities. In the schools, it has not reached all students of the higher grades.

I have discussed already why I think it should reach all students. But why should it reach all schools?

When the focus of the process was on the Parliament on the State level and everything leading to it was a preparation for the 'real' event, a sample of children was sufficient to convey their message to the people in power. However, the focus has been gradually shifting. With the improving co-operation of the local authorities, children have been becoming more aware of the 'school issues', 'municipality issues' and the 'state issues'. With the new subject of communication between students and teachers the focus has definitely shifted to the school level, where the main part of the Parliament will be taking place this year. There is no reason why some schools, children and staff equally, should benefit from such a useful discussion leaving the other schools behind.

That does not mean that the rest of the process is no longer necessary. Very probably the discussion in the schools will reveal certain structural problems which may make improvements of communication difficult (although I hope that the adults will not be excusing themselves on the 'real world' too much). They can address such issues with the municipal authorities, who are responsible for schools. There they will be told which problems can be helped at the local level and which are out of their powers. Again, a voyage to the capital will be quite necessary.

After all, they also have to review the work of the government in the last year. What has it done about violence, alcohol and drugs? They will certainly want to hear about progress made regarding the 'friendly school', ecology, road traffic, and opportunities for spending a quality leisure time, as well. And they will discover new issues to talk about in the years to come.

Reading the transcripts of the first four Parliaments[4] and writing about them, I tried to present them as a social process in progress. I tried to read between the lines a lot to find the underlying emotional message of children

---

4   At the time of going to press the proceedings of the 1994 Parliament have not yet been published.

to adults, and their replies. I believe a different interpretation than mine is quite possible, because it is a very complex process and many messages were actually sent, some more effectively than others. According to my understanding, the children were saying 'we want a future', 'take care of us', 'we can do our part' and 'adults, change!'. I am looking forward to seeing what the change will be this year. It may easily happen to be: 'You see, we can help you and teach you something!'

REFERENCES

Otrokom varno in zdravo okolje. Zbornkik. *Informacije* (1990) Zveza prijateljev mladine Slovenije, Ljubljana, Novermber 1990, p.132. (*Safe and Healthy Environment for Children.* Thematic issue. *Information 1990*, Association of Friends of Youth of Slovenia, Ljubljana, Novermber 1990. p.132)

Prosti cas mladih. Zbornik. *Informacije* (1992) Zveza prijateljev mladine Slovenije. Ljubljana, junij 1992. p.160. (*Leisure Time of Youth*). Thematic issue. *Information 1992,* Association of Friends of Youth of Slovenia. Ljubljana, June 1990. p.160).

Otrokom prijazno solo. Zbornik. *Informacije* (1993) Zveza prijateljev mladine Slovenije. Ljubljana, April 1993. p.102 (*Friendly School to Children.* Thematix issue. *Information 2/1993*, Association of Friends of Youth of Slovenia. Ljubljana, April 1993. p.132).

Skynner, R. and Cleese, J. (1994) *LIFE and how to Survive it.* London: Mandarin (First published by Methuen, London, 1993).

CHAPTER SEVEN

Too Many Rights Don't Make a Wrong
The Work of the Devon Youth Council

Penny Townsend

INTRODUCTION – RIGHTS AND RESPONSIBILITIES

'Age is not reflective of responsibility but that responsibility is the product of experience and understanding, two areas that tend to develop with time.' This is an argument that Youth Councillors regularly use when faced with adults sceptical about whether young people can be responsible and whether they can have rights without contingent responsibilities.

The Youth Council experience, both as an organisation and as individual young people, is of adults confronting young people with a choice between rights, presented as freedom, and responsibility, presented as hard work for little reward. In fact, undertaking an appropriate level of responsibility within an individuals capabilities, whatever their age and without compromising their fundamental rights, remains an important freedom.

Devon Youth Council is an organisation which has managed both to change the policy and practice of local authorities and to retain a structure responsive to the needs of young people. This has been achieved through an understanding of the responsibilities associated with representing our peers, and the power we have as an organised 'voice'. In order to be relevant, both to the county's young people and to the local authority, Devon Youth Council has prioritised the development of long-term initiatives and policies. Devon Youth Council has also demonstrated responsibility through an approach which promotes compromise rather than aggression in lobbying techniques. The Youth Council has studied and used (often to advantage) existing political and organisational structures rather than alienating itself from traditional processes.

Children are the largest minority population in today's Britain and the only minority without the responsibility of participating in democratic government elections. However much some might debate its value and relevance in modern British society, the right to vote is a fundamental power which is denied our young people. In the view of Devon Youth Council, the fact that children have little participation in, or ownership of, the decisions that affect their lives is a clear argument for a co-ordinated children's rights movement.

DEVON YOUTH COUNCIL[1]

Background; the local context

The County of Devon is the third largest Shire county in England with a population of just over a million. It is a largely rural county with an economy dependent on fishing, farming and tourism. As an institution of local government the County Council is there to ensure that national legislation is implemented and to manage a decentralised budget which allows for a distribution of resources within the County in response to perceived local needs.

Young people clearly lack both political and economic influence. Reflecting national trends young people are disproportionately over-represented in the County's unemployment statistics. 26 per cent of unemployed persons in Devon are aged between 16 and 25 whilst this group forms only 16 per cent of the local population. Even if young people as a group were to be politically pro-active there are not enough of them to be elected as members of the County Council to make any significant impact which is why Devon Youth Council, the 'voice' of young people in Devon, is so important. The Youth Council works in a similar way to the elected County Council in terms of its democratic function. It is there to influence the distribution of resources, representing the 'purchaser' rather than the 'provider'.

The origins of Devon Youth Council

Roger Hart's (1992) model 'The Ladder of Participation' based on work reviewing young people's activities in many countries is helpful here in reflecting on the participative process in the establishment and role of Devon Youth Council. Hart suggests that there are a number of activities which are essentially non-participatory but are thought to be about 'involving' young people. Many people he points out have it in their power to assist children in having a voice but, unwittingly or not, trivialise their involvement. He describes a hierarchy or ladder with 'manipulation' being the least participatory activity, 'decoration' the next and 'tokenism' the third. Young people have all been viewed in these ways. More genuinely participatory activities are identified in relative degrees with participation, in its fullest and most significant form (the

---

1   Further Information about Devon Youth Council can be obtained from Mike Parker, Devon Youth Council, Room 106, County Hall, Topsham Road, Exeter, EX2 4QG.

top of the ladder), being seen in activities initiated by young people with their decisions being shared with adults.

The nature of children as a largely powerless minority group is such that any grass roots activity concerning their own rights requires initiation by an empowered and informed group. During the establishment of Devon Youth Council such guidance came through the sensitive and appropriate involvement of the County Youth Service. The setting up of Devon Youth Council was thus at the lower level of participation as judged by Hart's model, namely young people were consulted and helped shape an idea that had originated and was facilitated by adults but was rapidly appreciated by young people and moved to the full participation of young people initiating shared decisions with adults and directing activities. This participation has resulted in the perhaps ironic establishment within the Youth Council of an adult advisory panel!

Young people, therefore, had eagerly grasped an opportunity that was offered by adults and have used this as a catalyst for developing a large number of activities of their own and consolidating as a force to be reckoned with within the County Council.

The structure of Devon Youth Council

1991 was 'Devon Year for Youth', a county-wide celebration of the activities and achievements of young people. Incorporated into the programme of events was a 'Youth Awareness Day'. Schools, colleges and employers were invited to send parties of young people to County Hall, on a school day, to learn about the role of their local authority.

The day included a 'question time' session in which it became clear that, although highly influential to the lives of young people, the County Council was significantly remote from their concerns and values. A group of youth workers proposed the establishment of a Junior County Council – a proposal which was received enthusiastically by both the County Council and the young people. A working party comprising of young delegates from the Youth Awareness Day spent the following 18 months devising the constitution and role of the Youth Council. This work was funded and supported by the Community Education (incorporating youth) service. In March 1993 the Youth Council was officially launched with a day of debate between young people and adults in County Hall, this formed the early agenda of the Youth Council and initiated the affiliated (voting) membership.

The current affiliated membership of the Youth Council stands at approximately 150; 50 are individual affiliates, the remainder being affiliated organisations ranging from individual youth clubs to schools and county organisations such as the Devon Guides. Any organisation or individual may affiliate to the Youth Council but only those young people aged 14–25 and resident in Devon are eligible to stand for office and vote in elections. The Youth Council is now the recognised authority on the views of young people locally and is the first stop for those seeking the perspective and experiences of children. Such enquiries have included local councils, the police, health authorities, academics, students and many others. The fact that Devon Youth Council is in constant demand from other groups both within Britain and internationally underlines the positive reputation it has gained from its work and the high regard in which it is held.

Resourcing the Youth Council

Funding and support are the main measures by which the performance, independence and influence of the Youth Council has to be judged. Without support reflective of its needs, the Youth Council becomes impotent and irrelevant. It is in the area of resourcing that Devon Youth Council has been both fortunate and successful in pursuing funds. The budget for maintaining the basic running costs of the Youth Council is approximately £20,000 including:

- the salary and support of a co-ordinator
- operational costs (IT equipment, telephone, office space, etc.)
- travel costs for Youth Councillors
- development opportunities for Youth Councillors.

These funds are obtained entirely from Devon County Council, most significantly from the Education Department, although efforts are currently being made to allocate the costs across all departments. The Youth Council has also gained funding in the form of grants from within the County Council and external sources for identified specific projects.

An example of the sensitive and insightful resourcing made available to the Youth Council is the appointment, in 1993, of a Youth Council Co-ordinator – initially for a three month period and paid an honorarium. This post was later extended to a full-time 12 month contract and there is now a commitment to funding such a post permanently which must be held by a member of the Youth Council aged under 25. The postholder receives the following significant support:

- a Youth Council facilitator: a senior youth worker appointed to support the development and training of Youth Council members
- a County Council lease car and mobile phone: vital for work with rural young people and maintaining a national profile
- an office base in County Hall with support available from all departments.

The funding of the Youth Council and employment of the co-ordinator demonstrate the degree to which the concept of empowering young people has been upheld. The organisation's needs to achieve representation through participation have been appropriately and imaginatively supported and resourced by key decision makers in the county.

Devon Youth Council in a broader context

The very nature of the international children's rights movement is such that it is hard to make comparisons between differing models. This is due to a range of factors including: lack of research, local and national priorities, the political environment, disorganisation and a genuine lack of resources. In this section an attempt will be made to identify some of the varying models for children's democratic participation and highlight European trends as perceived by Devon Youth Council.

Given the situation described above it would be fair to argue that Devon Youth Council is unique in its support and resourcing. That said, across both the UK and Europe there are many examples of similar organisations and a whole range of youth fora at municipal and regional levels. The numbers of these have grown in recent years as the Council of Europe and other bodies have demonstrated clear support for the democratic participation of children in their communities. Broadly speaking, Devon Youth Council recognises two distinct approaches to involving children: Youth Fora and Youth Councils.

In the experience of the Youth Council, youth fora provide a general arena for discussion between adults and children in a small town or region centering around issues of direct impact on young people. These may result in joint statements, community actions, or an agreement to take the matter to an authority. The distinction between youth fora and youth councils is that youth councils have some authority and are made up of, and organised by, young people who are the democratic representatives of a youth electorate and have direct access to decision makers.

In the experience of Devon Youth Council the 'youth councils' in France actually fit our definition of youth fora as they are service rather than politically orientated. The Devon Youth Council Co-ordinator attended a conference of European Youth Councils organised by ANACEJ, the French National Assembly of Youth Councils, during which the absence of political lobbying within the French Youth Councils was discussed. The French young people felt this was to do with continental society and that many French Youth Councils were traditionally reluctant to see themselves as agents for change, although they were beginning to use the methods of the pressure group to articulate their beliefs. This model was mirrored in the work of young people in the majority of Southern European countries attending the conference.

The activities of young people in North European countries generally took quite a different approach. The Norwegian experiences and the Danish Youth Houses were examples of 'Youth Enquiry Services', offering young people independent and confidential advice and support in order to facilitate informed decisions by young people in all aspects of their lives including the political dimension. But the northern countries still lacked an organised politicised force of young people.

It is interesting that examples of Youth Councils closest to Devon Youth Council were to be found in the new European Countries from the East. The Municipal Youth Councils in Poland and Hungary seemed to share similar structures and objectives to Devon Youth Council and the example from Krakow, Poland, indicated a similar level of achievement in political activism.

It would appear that youth organisations face similar problems to their adult counterparts. Where there are traditional practices and ideologies working, change and development are slow to develop. This would explain the reluctance of French youth councils to become politically motivated and the inability for groups of young people to grow into a youth forum and then develop into a youth council. Where the initiatives are new, as in the case of Devon Youth Council (launched 1993) and the East European countries, the organisations are in general much more politics- and rights-centred. The lack of growth among similar organisations is also an indication of the lack of organisation among the children's rights movement as models of good practice are rarely promoted nor ideas shared. This is partly due to the importance of a local identity for children's rights groups and partly because the children's rights movement as an organised force has only recently begun to be recognised.

Exercising our rights responsibly

Devon Youth Council works to the premise that participation by young people in an organisation is the key to success. However, the Youth Council is realistic in assessing the difficulties and long-term commitments required to enable young people to participate. Through direct consultation, Devon Youth Council has identified a number of areas that are obstacles to the participation of young people in political processes. These include:

- The ageing of society: demographic transformations arising from the combination of low birth rates and rising life expectancy has led to a decreasing share of children and an increasing share of adult and elderly persons in the total population.

- The increasing poverty of children and young people: the numbers of children living in one parent families and families living in difficult circumstances has raised common questions about taxation, social and family policies. Recent figures demonstrate a change in the make-up of the unemployed in Britain. While headline figures are stagnant or falling, the figures for the unemployed aged under 25 continue to grow significantly.

- Young people's scepticism of traditional politics: it is the assessment of Devon Youth Council that children and young people are rejecting traditional party politics in favour of issue-based 'Pressure Group' politics. Young People rarely trust politicians and feel alienated by the new 'purchaser/provider' models.

Devon Youth Council has undertaken a high level of responsibility for ensuring these problems are overcome in order to ensure that young people are fully able to participate. The Youth Council has undertaken work in areas of concern to young people and has developed both political and project-based initiatives and has aimed to make solid achievements in both the short and long term. Two examples of good practice of promoted by the Youth Council are its 'Bullying' leaflet and 'Partners Against Crime'.

The first of these demonstrates the Youth Council undertaking a process of research, response and evaluation in a highly professional and appropriate manner. Bullying was an issue discussed at the inaugural meeting of the Youth Council. It was agreed that this topic of common concern would be investigated in discussion with academics, education professionals, representatives from social services and young people themselves. The action the Youth Council chose to follow was the publication of a peer education leaflet containing information about bullies, being a victim, and possible responses from the victim's point of view and, in a broader social context, it also included contact points and highlighted the responsibilities of schools. The leaflet was aimed at children aged 10–14, the text was written entirely by young people and a 17-year-old student was commissioned to design the graphics. Copies of the leaflet were then distributed to every secondary school in the county and responses collated before a second print run was produced. The Youth Council is now investigating how to use the leaflet with primary school children and what further responses can be made to the problem of bullying.

'Partners Against Crime' is another example of the Youth Council taking responsibility for responding to a problem facing all communities and not solely young people. It demonstrates the process by which an initiative is developed. 'Partners Against Crime' began as a county Conference in July 1994. The Youth Council, supported by the police, led a day of debate on issues of young people and crime involving young representatives from schools, youth clubs, and the affiliated membership. All the sessions were convened by Youth Councillors but also included Police Youth Affairs officers and adult representatives from other organisations. The Conference feedback was then written up as a report and published in September 1994. One of the outcomes was the need to have similar debates locally. This the Youth Council followed up with local conferences in North and East Devon. A second and more targeted conference was held in July 1995 at which direct actions were decided upon for the Police, County Council and Youth Council to follow up. It is planned to hold another county conference in the summer of 1996 to report back on the action taken the previous year and reflect further on the problems and achievements of 'Partners Against Crime'

The process of organising and managing the Youth Council has involved the highest degree of management control by the Youth Council including monitoring the budget, identifying priorities and exercising restraint in spending. This level of control is unique to Devon Youth Council, but the Youth Council has not been left to stand or fall on its own. Appropriate expert help and skills training to adopt the responsibility has been provided by the County Council. A further element of this relationship of mutual support between the Youth Council and County Council are requests for the Youth Council to take responsibility for County Council initiatives. An example of this is the working party for the UN Convention on the Rights of The Child. This is an official part of the County Council committee structure linked to the Policy Committee. It sets a precedent in being chaired and convened by the Youth Council which supports both the Youth Council's aspirations to see the Convention implemented and reduces the time required by hard-pressed County Councillors and officers. A paper agreed at the last meeting was that all departments of the County Council produce a report detailing their implementation of the Convention and related areas of special interest. It will be the responsibility of the Youth Council to write a paper to the working party based on the reports received from departments that will give the direction, for the next eighteen months to two years, on steps the local authority must undertake to ensure the implementation of the Convention. It is quite clear that however much the County Council values the Youth Council and aims to take the views of the young into consideration, this function has been delegated to the Youth Council because it is able to exercise this power appropriately.

In addition to taking direct action on issues of concern to young people, Devon Youth Council has also responded by generating external sources of income to support projects for Devon's young people. A good example of this work is the SCODA: Young People at Risk from Drugs, Grants Programme. This programme is the first funding response by the Department of Health to the government white paper 'Tackling Drugs Together' and is aimed at innovative projects that reduce the numbers of young people using drugs in a harmful way. Devon Youth Council has it on its agenda to see peer-led work used more frequently, and on a wider range of topics, and so approached a range of agencies in Devon dealing with young people and drugs to form a partnership. This group, named 'The Devon Consortium', then entered a bid to SCODA focused on peer-led work around drugs issues. The Devon Consortium comprises of two Health Authorities, Devon and Cornwall Constabulary, The Youth Trust (a registered charity), Devon County Council and a range of other specialist agencies. Devon Youth Council wrote the bid and devised the budget in the name of all these agencies and is responsible for maintaining communication between the consortium and convening and chairing meetings of the group. The Devon Consortium bid was successful in securing a grant of £22,000 funding for a seven-month project. This funding will go into the training and employment of young people as peer-led workers on drugs issues in their own communities. The programme follows a process of 'outcome funding' and the Youth Council therefore has to ensure the project meets identified targets and is monitored and evaluated effectively. It is the Youth Council, in consultation with the consortium group, which holds the responsibility for the final decisions regarding the project and is the main project contact for the Department of Health.

From this section it is clear that as well as advocating rights and securing power for young people, Devon Youth Council is also a body exercising a high degree of responsibility and professionalism in its work and that by being seen to work in this manner earns the respect that enables it to be independent. However, whilst accepting rights and responsibilities in equal measure, Youth Councillors also have a role to inform and undertake consciousness-raising with their peers. A recent example of this aspect of the Youth Councils work is the 'Next Generation Project'.

The Next Generation Project uses the arts as an educational medium for the themes of peace, the future, and international responsibility through citizenship. The aim of the project is to demonstrate to children that the sacrifices made during World War Two and illustrated in the recent VE Day Celebrations are just as important and relevant today in the context of the environmental problems we now face. The project will motivate young people to be active in creating an Agenda 21 for Devon so that this new understanding results in positive and relevant action for the future. It is hoped that these aims will result in the personal growth and understanding of Devon's children and also in documented tangible work. It is also hoped that the project will enable young people to become actively involved in community environmental projects. In addition to the social and educational aspects of this project, the opportunity for the child participants to express themselves is given equal value – an aspect that sets the Next Generation Project apart from similar initiatives organised by adults. The use of the arts enables the children to express themselves in entirely their own manner and a further opportunity for debate will be created in the 'Celebration Day'. The climax to the project will, it is hoped, in effect demonstrate young people's vision of the future and their place within it. The afternoon will comprise a question-time session where the children involved in the project will have the opportunity to interrogate those directly involved in environmental policy and practice – such as representatives from the environment department, the Youth Council and environmental activists.

WHERE DO WE GO FROM HERE?

A frustration shared by all youth organisations, particularly those with a political focus, is that children grow up. So just as young people have developed the skills and confidence to work effectively within the organisation their time is up ! However, this is to be looked upon as an achievement as those young people leaving are then able to take a responsible role in adult society and be effective advocates on behalf of children's rights.

The Youth Council has looked at sustaining an effective structure despite this regular turnover of members in two ways: first by targeting work and resources to children aged 5–13 (officially below our recognised membership) and second by trying to develop a more active affiliated membership.

Promoting the UN Convention on the Rights of The Child has been a useful mechanism in beginning work with younger children. The Youth Council is currently devising workshops explaining the Convention to primary schools across the county and has been invited to participate in Primary Headteachers conferences in 1996 which are on the theme of citizenship. The reason for work with younger children is to develop their knowledge and skills so that at the age of 14, children are able to take an effective role in the Youth Council more quickly, and that children who choose not to participate still have some information and skills regarding their rights.

Building a more pro-active affiliated membership is a process that will take time but this is now beginning to happen more quickly as Youth Councillors are now completing their term of office whilst still young enough and keen to participate. This is creating a situation where, in addition to the 20 elected representatives, there is a pool of active and experienced volunteers to undertake specific areas of work and to promote the Youth Council locally.

With a growing active membership and increasing relevance to the county, Devon Youth Council is now securing children's rights and the consideration of children in the development of policies by local authorities. The future for the Youth Council is to overcome the traditional cynicism of young people and involve them effectively in the political processes with established agencies within their local authority. This process of building trust and involving children in political processes on their own terms has already begun and can be witnessed in the way in which not only have members of Devon Youth Council been transformed in their belief in the system but also the way in which they have transformed that system itself.

REFERENCES

Hart, R. (1992) *Children's Participation from Tokenism to Citizenship. Innocenti Essays, No.4.* Florence: UNICEF, International Child Development Centre. Florence.

PART FIVE

A Voice of Our Own

CHAPTER EIGHT

Underground Power[1]

Jo Bird and Kunle Ibidun

INTRODUCTION

Underground Power is a Young People's liberation movement. It is the most exciting movement of the 1990s in that it represents the way that young people in the United Kingdom are now getting organised to make representations about their rights for themselves. 'Young' people are aged 21 years and under. We are not 'kids' or 'children' but young *people*. Why a 'liberation' movement? In a sense that is the sort of question that would only be asked by someone who is not 'young'. To be young is to experience economic oppression – that is most of us are absolutely 'skint'!![2] Money is not the only problem. Other problems are to do with the way that we are treated. We are rarely treated with respect and we are almost totally denied power of any kind. Our movement for liberation, however, is not just confined to us. Young people's liberation means everyone's liberation as it aims to remove the basis for all oppression. Specifically, our aims for all young people regardless of age or size are:

- the right to vote
- the end of sexual, physical and emotional abuse
- benefits, e.g. Income Support, Educational grants, housing benefits
- more say in how schools, colleges and universities are run
- complete and utter respect for young people.

---

1 For more information (membership, newsletter, leaflets etc.) contact Kunle or Jo on 0161–224 4846 Underground Power, 161, Hamilton Road, Longsight, Manchester, M13 OPQ, England.
2 In the UK, particularly in the North of England, 'skint' is used to mean very short of money.

If we look at the context within which we are pressing for this sort of recognition – which we regard as our right – it is worth remembering that half the world's population, yes, half, is under 22 years of age and 34 per cent of the world's population is under 15 years of age. It is interesting to speculate on why it is that, although we figure as such a large proportion of the world's population, we remain almost utterly powerless. Nevertheless, young people are treated with disrespect and denied basic human rights such as the vote. Underground Power aims to eliminate every form of humans harming humans by replacing the collapsing capitalist system with one which is built on *complete respect* for all people. In order to achieve this we have, in the first instance, encouraged everyone to start by respecting themselves and then all other young people. It is our belief that it is only then that we can work against our oppression. What has been clearly needed is a movement of young people for young people's rights which was why Underground Power was originally set up. The adult's role is crucial, however, in assisting young people to take themselves seriously and to really listen to what young people want. What young people see as young people's rights is often different to what adult's see such rights as, for example, the right to vote. Young people need to be involved in every stage of the process, indeed they need to be leading it and deciding how it is done. Adults can assist the transfer of resources and skills into the hands of young people and trust them to work out how best to use them.

In our publicity material we answer the question 'Why join Underground Power?' as follows:

- to take powerful steps towards the world we all deeply want to have
- to empower yourself to take action for young people's liberation
- to be in touch with smart, powerful people who think like you (you are not alone)
- to get and share information
- because it's cheap.

Since 1990, Underground Power has been leading the field as a national organisation campaigning for young people's rights. Led by young people, we have been actively involved with the Children's Rights Development Unit. We have been working hard over the past few years to consolidate Underground Power's membership and campaigning base. This has been undertaken in a number of ways. There have been three conferences. At the conference in 1994 the programme included consideration of the UN Convention on the Rights of the Child and some training sessions including empowerment training, media skills, goal planning sessions, leadership training and counselling skills. We also, at that conference, looked at the work we had done and could do with other organisations, and undertook a review and stocktaking of our progress and thought through future plans and strategies – and of course we had some fun with a talent show and culture sharing. By that time we had about 200 members of which about 50 were active. Not very many perhaps, but it was a beginning and we have, in the few years we have been operating, achieved considerable recognition and influence both locally and nationally.

Funding comes mostly from voluntary donations and traditional fund-raising sources, for example membership subscriptions, advertising, workshop fees and small grants.

CAMPAIGN TO LOWER THE VOTING AGE

Our campaign to lower the voting age has been a major focus since we started and we still put a lot of energy and feeling into activities connected with this. At the time of the last general election in 1992, we gained massive publicity on local and national radio with our demonstration 'Lower the Voting Age' in both Manchester and Southampton This was followed by two articles, one in the Guardian and one in 'Cavort', and interviews on local and national radio. This gave us a lot of encouragement and publicity !! Since then we have been campaigning to lower the voting age in relation to local councils and elections for the European Parliament. We have used brainstormings to bring out lots of ideas about ways of drawing attention to our views on the voting issue and would certainly like to follow these through – particularly the ideas about street theatre which we feel would be particularly effective. We also produced, for the first time in June 1993, our first Underground Power newsletter – *Uprising*. There have been two Underground Power conferences in Birkenhead. Channel 4 T.V. did an interview and there are weekly meetings in Manchester – so no-one could say that we are inert and inactive!!

NATIONAL RECOGNITION

We have begun to receive recognition as an important national pressure group by having been invited to be on the management committee of the Children's Rights Development Unit. In 1992, we decided to send some representatives to the World Conference on Research and Practice in Children's Rights at the University of Exeter as we were very interested in establishing what was going on as it had been clear to us that governments all over the world had agreed that young people should have the rights in the United Nations Convention of Rights of the Child. This Conference was based on this Convention. We had been interested as this conference was trying to take seriously one of the rights in that Convention – i.e. that young people have the right to have a say in matters which affect them – so young people had been invited to form an Evaluation Panel for the Conference and feed back their views on the presentations to everyone there. Whilst there, we met Gerison Lansdown who told us about the Children's Rights Development Unit – a small group of about seven adults who were paid to see to it that young people get the rights they should have. We were invited to help them do it by being on their management committee. Anil Gomes and Kunle Ibidun have been to their meetings in London and Nick Ward and Jo Bird have been a few times. This is important as, not only have we been undertaking all sorts of activities on our own to draw attention to our campaign to lower the voting age, but also we are now part of an official organisation looking at the UN Convention and putting in our view as to what needs to be done and what really affects us.

OUR CARNIVAL

In July 1995, Underground Power organised a successful Carnival for Young People's Rights in Greater Manchester.

Below we reproduce our Flyer which outlines what it is about:

About the Carnival...

Who is underground power?

Underground Power was formed four years ago to campaign for young people's rights in line with the United Nations Convention on the Rights of the Child – a document which this government signed in 1991 and has done practically nothing to implement. Underground Power works with both adults and young people to increase young people's participation in society.

Why did underground power organise the carnival?

Young people are often getting the blame for problems in society. Now they are getting together to organise a positive event and raise awareness of their own concerns at the same time. This Carnival has been organised by young people and adults working together.

What are the aims of underground power?

Some of Underground Power's aims are to raise awareness and educate people about:

Benefits for 16- and 17-year-olds; United Nations Convention on the Rights of the Child; education; smacking; prisons for 12- to 14-year-olds proposed by the Criminal Justice Act; the voting age.

You don't have to agree with what we say on these issues though we would like you to read our leaflets, find out what we think and talk about it.

What have people said?

Gerison Lansdown, Director of the London based Children's Rights Office said, 'The Carnival will provide a great opportunity to challenge the negative image of children and young people so frequently portrayed by the media and to promote the case for greater respect for children and young people's rights'.

One of the organisers, 15-year-old Ludmylla Seale-Anderson, said, 'We've organised the Carnival to raise awareness of young people's rights and to say that young people are just as important as adults and have the right to speak. I'm hoping the Carnival will bring young people, children and adults together and have fun at the same time'.

WHAT DO YOU SAY?

I say, ...

WHAT NEXT?

If you mostly agree with us, we'd like you to join Underground Power. Members receive regular updates on what is happening. We need more people to get involved. If you have an idea you can make it happen. What would you like to do to help?

HOW WE SEE SCHOOLS

We have work to do, however, in raising consciousness at the grass-roots level by operating in relation to matters which really affect many young people in their day to day lives – namely their life at school and the powerlessness most of them experience there. Our view is that young people have always been immensely powerful and intelligent people, especially before the invention of school. Taking a quick glimpse back at history, at the turn of the century we find that young people were the leading force in changing the capitalist system (A system that puts money in front of everything and is the main reason why oppression stays in place.) Young people were very well organised at this time and, with the threat of a revolution and change to socialist politics, we posed a great danger to the people in power. The owning classes were scared of losing their money and their hold (albeit a false hold) on power so they thought that if they could get these young activists off the streets, they could rid the country of this threat.

Schools were brought about to do this and, despite our protests, we were still dragged kicking and screaming into schools. At school we were constantly told how stupid we were and started to believe it, we lost respect for ourselves and the belief that we could change the world (or make it the wonderful place it is meant to be). This slowed down our liberation and was never any real benefit to anyone, even the people who caused it.

The threat to our liberation was never that we were going to learn things, it was that we were being force-fed misinformation about ourselves and our countries. We were told that the system in which we live is the fairest system for everyone and that there are no alternatives. We were kept pre-occupied with work that instead of stimulating our intelligence, suppressed it. We were stopped from thinking. The net effect of this was that we lost sight of our original goal and stopped campaigning for social change.

Now the Education system is justified with the lie that we are gaining an education to put us in good stead for later life. This excuse was thought up after the education system was already there. Another popular myth is that young people are excluded from pubs for the benefit of our health. It was, in fact, to stop young people passing on socialist ideas. Pubs were the places in which these ideas got passed on and where young people got themselves organised.

When we take the breakdown of the education system and analyse it, we realise that it is just keeping in place the system that oppresses the working classes (the majority of people and where everybody originally stemmed from), that is, about five per cent of the population of Britain go to Universities of which only seven per cent qualify for full grants. It is blatantly obvious how this system is biased against ordinary people and keeps class oppression and young people's oppression in place.

We are not saying that education is a bad thing. What we are saying is that we need to learn the truth. We need proper information about the world we live in and part of the job of education is to stimulate thought. It is no coincidence that politics and philosophy are rarely taught to younger young people. We strongly believe that were this the case, we would not justify the death of 500,000 children each year (a figure quoted by UNICEF on the basis of their research) due to factors relating to the profit motive. Nor would we believe that happiness derives from money. We would not destroy this planet and squander its resources for short-term financial gain. A fundamental mistake by all organisations trying to combat this system is that they have seen education as the way out; rather than ridding the world of this oppression, they are buying into the system and joining the oppressors.

Given that our members have had these really bad experiences in their schools, often they can't quite put a finger on what is wrong. We had a few brainstorming sessions to set about trying to think of ways in which we ourselves could do something to improve the situations. First we tried to summarise the actual problems. We thought there were three major areas – teachers, the subjects we study and exams. A major source of difficulty for us is, not surprisingly, the teachers. It is true there are good teachers but others are disrespectful, boring, treat young people badly and do not even teach!!! Young people feel that teachers have too much control and sometimes wonder if they are 'on some sort of power trip' or if 'they are getting revenge'. Another source of frustration comes from the subjects we have to study. We have no choice in which subjects we take in the lower years and a lot of the subjects we are forced to study are irrelevant to our future lives and jobs. We feel that this system suppresses people's talents. Exams are a source of pressure. If you don't do brilliantly you lose confidence and could get put back a year or two. Basically all you do learn is how to pass exams, and they are neither a proper nor fair way to assess people's ability.

We considered carefully what action young people could embark upon which would bring about some changes in their school. We very quickly came to the conclusion that a major source of difficulty was that young people don't have the opportunity to discuss their problems and that they have no chance to challenge or change incorrect decisions. We decided that a good way round this would be to form a School Student Union. Basically a School Student Union (SSU) is an organisation of young people who represent the students in their school and campaign to improve school-life for all students. Our advice as to how to go about setting up such a Union follows distinct steps:

1. Form a group of friends who agree with the idea and talk more about the idea and get support for it.

2. Pass the word around so that everyone has the chance to get involved.

3. Find two people from each class or each year to represent the views of their peers; a good way to do this is to have an election (the best way to make your SSU effective and representative is to include students from all groups, i.e. younger young people, black people, young girls, young boys, people at the bottom of the class, etc.)

4. Agree to meet regularly and discuss the things that you want to change.

5. In meetings, make sure that everyone has a chance to be heard (a way of doing this is to pass round a stick. The person with the stick gets to talk and everyone gets to hold the stick).

6. Form a list of things you want to get changed and campaign to change them, e.g. talking to teachers and other people in authority, by writing a petition, by writing to the press, by arranging a strike, etc.

Remember young people are always told that they are a lot less intelligent than they really are. This is because it is a good way to keep things the same. If you really want to change things you can and you will, so don't get discouraged! It is also worth keeping in mind the fact that the United Nations Convention on the Rights of the Child states the rights of young people around the world and has now been adopted by over 150 countries including the UK. Important in relation to setting up School Student Unions are the following three rights:

- The right to have a say in matters that affect your and your opinions *must* be taken into account (Article 12).

- The right to express what you think as long as you don't break the law (Article 13).

- The right to join organisations, take part in meetings and peaceful demonstrations as long as you don't break the law (Article 15).

IN CONCLUSION

Young people have always been aware of the way out and we are the ones who are going to change the world. We think that believing that by oppressing young people we are prevented from becoming what adults seem to fear – raving world-changing, arse-kicking revolutionaries – is a great mistake. The truth is that we are powerful NOW!! When at last we all really realise that, then we are going to kick ass, and sort this world out. Clearly we were on our way to doing this when another obstacle was put in our way. When we have finished dealing with this slight setback we will be back on course to reclaiming our freedom.

Young people are the most brilliant in the world and if anyone can sort this planet out it is us – so let's do it!

CHAPTER NINE

Running Our School

Olivia Croce, Bonnie Hill and Matthew Williams

PERSONAL COMMENTS

OLIVIA: I have just joined Sands School during my second year on GCSEs and from visiting the school for a week and spending camp with them all. I find the hardest thing to organise (not only at meetings) is to make the majority happy. I feel that this is because the students have such freedom in their own speech and that no teacher tries to influence your opinion or lead you the way you wish not to go. The teachers don't because they can't! Now from going to Sands School I feel that my particular secondary school rules out your self-originality, your own 'you' and that is a real shame because the kids who are missing out will only find out later about themselves, later in their lives. One thing I really like is that there are so many comparatively different people at Sands. There are lots of different sorts of people at state school too, but it's hard to find that out. At Sands people can behave quite differently from one day to the next. You don't have to act out a role consistently. No day is exactly the same – more life, more reality than at my last school. That's great.

BONNIE: I would say that the learning we do at Sands is more enjoyable than at state schools because of having the choice to go to lessons or not. Some lessons are more fun than others, not because the teacher 'makes' them fun; it comes partly from the kids – the lessons are what they make them. But if you have chosen to do exams (which practically all of the older students have) you have to do boring things as well. The major part of Sands for me is to do with learning how to be with other people, how to work things out. Although I'm 16

I have chosen not to do GCSEs this year; for me Sands is not just about passing exams – if that was what I wanted I would go to a further education college.

OLIVIA: There is such a range of different people there. There are at state school too, but you don't get to know much about the ones outside your immediate circle of friends. There is a good balance and a range of experience of life, and we get to know about it. You get more of a chance to find out about other people's problems.

BONNIE: Most of the time the atmosphere at the school is good, but sometimes it's horrible and stressful. I think this is OK because in school meetings and at other times we can look at what is causing the stress and what we can do to make the situation less stressful. It helps us to learn to deal with situations which are stressful. Some students think the school is ideal, but I don't, and I don't think it should be or can be.

INTRODUCTION

Sands is a fee-paying day school for boys and girls from about 11 to about 18 (starting and leaving ages are flexible). We all share responsibility for running the school, and this is done through the school meeting where all members of the school, teachers and pupils have a vote. The idea is that if pupils are given responsibility they become responsible; if they are trusted they become trust-worthy.

OLIVIA: The thing about being trusted doesn't always work – some people take the trust and abuse it, especially the ones who have not been trusted in the schools they were at before, or at home.

BONNIE: And some of the students try to make the teachers responsible for them.

MATTHEW: Some of the teachers try to become responsible for some of the students, others encourage the students to be responsible for themselves.

THE SCHOOL MEETING

Policies and decisions are made at the school meeting. We have no school uniform and only the rules that have been proposed and agreed to in meetings. The school has been run in this way since it started in 1987. Every school member has a right to attend meetings, and guests can attend if the school meeting has agreed. The chair of the meeting and the secretary of minutes are chosen at the beginning of each term. Usually they are students.

We have a school administrator whose job it is to make sure decisions made at the school meeting are carried out. You go to the administrator if you want something put on the agenda, which he puts together each week. We can put anything on that we want to discuss.

MATTHEW: Originally the administrator stuck a piece of paper on the board and people wrote what they wanted on the agenda. Then it became the chair's job to put the agenda together. Then the chair stopped doing that job so the administrator took it over. We haven't had a proper chair for about a year or so.

BONNIE: I don't understand what the administrator is supposed to do. I still don't understand what his role is. Is he really a head teacher with a different name?

OLIVIA: I think he could have a lot of power if he wanted to. Who makes sure he carries out the decisions, and what can you do if you think he isn't?

These are some of the things we decide at the meetings:

- Whether to accept pupils who have applied to join the school; if we think they won't fit in we discuss this and decide whether Sands would be a good place for them and vice-versa.

- The appointment of new teachers. The school meeting decides where to put adverts. We get a pile of applications. Some pupils volunteer to help the staff sift through these, then, when the short-list has been made, there are interviews. This is a boring job so not many people volunteer to do it, but we do get the opportunity to, and if we don't take that opportunity we can't blame other people if we don't agree with that choice. Whoever is about at the time interviews people. It used to be a committee doing this, but now it's not, which means you get a greater variety of people interviewing the teachers. When they have been interviewed, they teach a trial lesson. Those who have interviewed and/or been in the trial lesson report back to the school meeting and a decision is made in the usual way. There have been meetings about whether teachers should be sacked but in my experience it hasn't gone that far.

- Whether or not a student should be suspended or expelled if they break the rules. These are: no alcohol or drugs on the premises and smoking only in the summerhouse or at the far end of the garden. Another rule – more an expectation really – is that you are expected to take advantage of the school and not prevent other people taking advantage of what it has to offer.

The meeting is supposed to remind everyone regularly that the school really is ours and that we have the right to change it if we like, and that the changes we make can either make the school successful or create further problems.

BONNIE: That's a quote from something someone wrote about the school. I don't know who wrote it and I don't feel the school meeting really does this. It *sounds* as if it would work, but it doesn't because the meeting is really run by a set group of people who think the school is theirs, but some people sit there and think they can't say anything – so the school is not theirs. When I first went to the school a year ago I used to think I wouldn't say anything because I would get attacked by others. Now I have started saying things. Some of them are controversial and I get shouted down, but I still say them because I don't care what other people think now. This takes a long time, but I think it is a good thing to learn to do.

OLIVIA: Unfortunately once you have said what you think the majority of people there won't hear it, they will still be with the thing the louder and more powerful person has said before you.

BONNIE: The good thing, though, is that I find the meetings less intimidating now, and feel better when I've said what I think even if it is shouted down.

MATTHEW: That is a problem for the chair.

OLIVIA: Some kids are shy and scared to say how they feel and what they would like to see be done about the matter being discussed. It is very difficult when this happens because the problem becomes heavier to handle for both students and teachers.

If students are confident of the meeting they can use it but if they are not confident in the process they can't. Most of the organisational decisions are straightforward, like how to spend money, etc. Others are more difficult; like a decision we had to make recently about suspending or expelling some students who had broken the rule about drugs in school. We spent hours in this meeting and it was so stressful. In the end the vote was to suspend them for a week; we didn't just say you broke the rule so you must go, but listened to everyone's views and decided to give them a second chance. Sometimes the students are more sensitive than the teachers, sometimes vice-versa, or there can be a mix. Some of the students, and probably all of the teachers, think that the well being of the school and its image are the most important thing, others, usually the students, think that the problems of students who are being disruptive or breaking rules are the priority to discuss in meetings. So sometimes we have two camps of people, and after a difficult meeting everyone is exhausted, but it is also important to have all points of view heard and thoroughly discussed if a decision is going to affect someone's life; like a pupil or teacher being kicked out of the school. It's usually the kinder people who win on those issues, not the hard-liners who try to shout you down.

USEFUL WORK

We don't have staff to do cleaning and cooking. This is done by pupils and teachers. It is a constant source of friction, some people do less than their share and the ones who do more than their share get resentful. If you don't do your 'useful work' it can be brought up at meetings and you can be asked to do extra useful work at the end of the day. When things start to look more shoddy than usual we organise whole days when we clear up the mess to make the school look better and easier and more pleasant to be in. At the beginning of each term we do a lot of cleaning up, preparations, repairs and decorating. So we are encouraged to realise that we are responsible for the mess we make.

SPORT AND OTHER THINGS

Most outdoor pursuits, swimming and visits to local fitness centres will happen if there is enough enthusiasm for it. Other sports happen on the spot when enough people have free time. There is no organised sport other than regular swimming and fitness sessions in the winter. Every year at the end of the summer term we have a camp; to Cornwall, the Scillies or France. We climb and swim and walk. Sometimes we go canoeing. When it is hot we go and swim in the river. In the youngest group, if we are fidgety and restless in a lesson, the teacher will say 'Would you like to do games instead?' and we do running games, tramlines, football, basket ball and dodge-ball.

ACADEMIC WORK

In the school brochure it says that unless children feel valued and respected, their work is of little importance to them. This means that some children do better academically at Sands than they would at more conventional schools.

BONNIE: The point is, you have a choice about whether to do academic work or not. No pressure is put on you to do as many GCSEs as possible. There is no competition around academic work. If someone works hard and does well I feel pleased for them but if you don't do well, you don't feel like a failure. If a student wants to do well academically they will work, but if they don't, any number of lessons won't motivate them to work. The timetable is completely full of lessons because that was voted on by the majority of students. That is a democratic decision made before I came here. If we had a vote on it now I would vote for more free time. If we particularly want to do something which is not on the timetable or which the teachers at the school can't do, it is up to us to ask for it and the teachers will do their best to provide it.

OLIVIA: There should be more timetabling for free time. The teachers have meetings on how to organise the timetable, but I think the students should be involved in that too. Each student should write in how much time they would like for which subject.

MATTHEW: I think the academic side of Sands is very good at motivating me to do the work. The ideology of self-motivation works for about half the people so a counter-philosophy has grown in the rest of the school which is about wanting to learn but you don't have the motivation yourself so you enjoy being in lessons with people you enjoy being with, who are the teachers. I don't enjoy the self-motivation of having to get everything together for myself, because it means I don't have as much time for sitting around talking to people and moving around and socialising. I know where the academic work begins and ends because of the timetabled structure. But the atmosphere in the lessons is similar to the rest of the time at Sands.

COMMENTS BY THE YOUNG PEOPLE'S EVALUATION PANEL

I found the workshop 'Running Our School' by Sands School, very interesting. Their ideas are unique, but unfortunately a lot of people instinctively attack the school because it goes against the traditional style.

The pupil's education is extended, in my view, further than any other school as the pupils make all the necessary decisions at the school meeting. They cook, clean and are in charge of maintenance. This means that the person who breaks a window normally fixes it.

Pupils feel that they are friends with their teachers in lessons even though the teachers are in control. The pupils who have been to local comprehensives say that there is a much more relaxed atmosphere.

Finally, I'd like to say that Sands School is a light at the end of the tunnel for students who find the conventional way of school life difficult and uncompromising.

CHAPTER TEN

Piggy in the Middle
What Happens To You When Your Parents Separate

Sarnia Harrison

SYNOPSIS

My parents separated five years ago and, obviously, the problems which come along when your parents separate have taken up a lot of my time since then.

Although I never went out looking for a booklet to help me with my situation, I didn't even notice one, and I think that as my parents had separated I would have noticed a booklet if there was one around. Such a booklet should be easily available to children and placed somewhere that they can pick it up relatively unnoticed as they may well feel uncomfortable having to ask for it. So, to establish a need for my booklet, I looked around at what was already available in places like the library, doctors' surgeries, school counsellor, etc. I only found a couple of leaflets similar to mine, and they were not very effective or easily accessible to children. Therefore, I realised that there was definitely a need for my booklet.

As I was twelve when my parents separated, I felt that my audience shouldn't really be any younger then this as I wouldn't be able to empathise so easily. I also don't think a younger child could really benefit from such a booklet. I decided on an audience of 14- to 16-year-olds. By aiming at an audience in the middle of the teenage years this meant that teenagers older and younger can benefit from my booklet.

Before I actually started thinking about it, I hadn't realised the endless number of topics I could include in this booklet. Divorce is a very complicated area and the feelings and problems that the children have to overcome are even more complex. To help me decide on the most important things to include, I conducted four structured interviews and designed a questionnaire to give out aiming to find out which things came up as being most important to children going through the divorce of their parents.

My main aim was to produce a booklet to help children to overcome their feelings of isolation when going through the problems that their parent's separation may bring, and to make them see that good things can come out of it all.

THE BOOKLET

To the reader

Hi! My name's Sarnia and I'm 17 years old. About five years ago my parents separated because my mum had fallen in love with someone else, although they said that they were drifting apart anyway. At first I couldn't accept it at all, they'd never argued or fallen out about anything before.

I lived mainly with my dad for quite a while after they first separated and hardly saw my mum at all. This was mainly because I was angry at her for leaving, and also I felt sorry for my dad who was now on his own.

My parents encouraged both my sisters and I to talk to them about how we were feeling a lot. This was hard at first as I didn't want to hurt anyone's feelings, but after I got used to doing it, it got easier and helped me a lot.

My parents' divorce felt like it was going to be life-shattering at first but this feeling does go away. People said this to me when my parents first separated and I didn't believe them – but it DOES get better! After a while you accept it as how your life is going to be from now on.

I hope you can benefit from my story and also get some use from the rest of this booklet. Some of the advice is straight from me to you as I do know what it's like, and the rest is from people I've talked to and things I've read on the subject. Don't forget, your parents' separation doesn't have to be all bad – many good things can and will come out of it. It gave me a chance to get to know both my parents as individuals and improve my relationship with them. I have become much more independent and matured a lot through having to deal with the problems that my parents' separation has brought. You will find that as time goes on something positive will come out of your situation too.

Good Luck

Sarnia xxxx

It was like everything was a waste of time,
What's the point of trying to do something if you end up with nothing?

I cried for him, he still loved her,
I cried for me, I was losing her,
I cried for them, they were crying for us,
Crying for our pain, because it was all changing.

They said they still trusted each other,
That they still loved us,
But it didn't matter, because we knew that.

But we didn't know why,
Why it had to happen to us,
So I just cried.

Sarah, aged 12

What exactly is divorce?

Divorce is a legal term for the separation of a married couple. It simply means that they are no longer husband and wife and that their marriage is legally over. Your parents probably will have already separated before the legal separation (divorce) takes place as the process they will have to go through takes a long time. Although they will be separated as husband and wife this does not mean that they have separated as mother and father, they are still united as your mum and dad and nothing can change that.

Why are my parents getting a divorce?

There are many different reasons why your parents may be getting a divorce. Your parents should have explained to you exactly why they are separating, and if they haven't then you could ask them to explain their reasons to you. Understanding why your parents have separated is very important as it will help you to start dealing with this new situation.

Obviously I don't know exactly why your parents are separating but many parents do just fall out of love, but falling out of love with each other does not mean that they do not love you any more. You are the one thing which still connects your parents and the one thing they will always be a part of.

In other cases one parent may fall in love with someone else. Whatever the reason that your parents have for getting a divorce it is extremely important that you understand what it is. Ask your parents any questions that you want to, and don't feel bad about it, you have a right to know what's going on.

It is not your fault

When your parents first tell you they are separating it is often a great shock and one of the first things that may have come into your head is 'Maybe I did something to make them argue, and that's why they are splitting up'. This is a natural reaction but your parents break-up is not your fault. Your parents are the ones who have made the decision to separate and they have their own reasons for doing so. If you do feel that it is your fault then this is why it is so important that you talk to your parents and ask them exactly why they are separating. Once you understand the real reasons for your parents separation then this will help you to stop feeling guilty. On the other hand you may not feel a shred of guilt about your parents separation – this is brilliant!

After the shock of your parents break-up has sunk in you may naturally feel a bucket load of other feelings which feel like they will never go away.

All these feelings are perfectly natural so don't feel ashamed or guilty about any of them, and although it doesn't seem like it now, they will go away. Although you won't get rid of them by keeping them to yourself this will just make you feel worse. Tell someone how you are feeling. It doesn't have to be your parents, it can be anyone you feel comfortable talking to.

Don't feel bad about having any of these feelings, they are your feelings and you have every right to have them.

Anger

You may feel very angry at your parents for doing this to your family, after all if it wasn't for them then you wouldn't have to be going through all this mess. It can help to tell your parents how angry you are as this releases some of your anger at the right people, although I do know that this is a lot easier said than done.

Upset, hurt, annoyed

> I was confused and I was upset, obviously. I didn't really know I was just sort of upset and I didn't really know how to feel. – Sarah 12.

As Sarah says it is obvious that you will be upset, and no one would expect you not to be. These feelings are all a natural reaction to your parents separation, so don't try to hide them away. They need to come out so you can deal with them.

Confused, worried, scared

The best way to overcome these feelings is to ask your parents about anything which is worrying you. Once you really understand what is going on then you won't feel so confused and worried any more. If you are scared of what's going to happen in the future then ask your parents (although bear in mind that they may not know themselves, but even so they will be able to reassure you and answer any questions you need answering.)

You may also be worried about what seem like very little things, like who's going to come to your parents evening or pick you up from school, or who's going to give you your pocket money – don't feel like these things are too little to ask about, you aren't being selfish by thinking them. If they are important to you then they are worth asking about!

Alone, let down, embarrassed

When your parents separate you do feel like you are the only one in the world having to go through this. Even when you know that this can't possibly be true you still feel just as bad, and because you feel so alone you feel embarrassed to tell anyone what's happened and how you're feeling.

Once you talk to someone these feelings won't be so intense. It would help you a lot if you could talk to someone else who has been through what you're going through. If you have any brothers or sisters then it would help you a lot to talk to them, as you will probably find that they are experiencing a lot of the same kinds of feelings as you.

Also in a way your parents have let you down. The two people who you always counted on being around for you are splitting up. This is a natural reaction but it is important to realise that your parents believe that separating is the best thing for them to do, and even though they won't both be living in the same house as you they will still be there for you when you need them.

Relieved

You may very well feel upset and hurt by this whole situation but on the other hand you may feel extremely relieved that your parents have split up. They may have been arguing all the time and now at least you'll have some peace and quiet. It is perfectly okay to be relieved that your parents are separating. Every individual person reacts differently and so however you are feeling is just your natural response to an upsetting situation.

If there has been violence in your family leading up to the separation of your parents then these feelings of relief are even more understandable.

> We were both silent. After a couple of minutes I burst into tears. I just cried. Nothing else – didn't talk, didn't scream at mom or dad, didn't run out of the room. I just cried. After I could control myself I noticed

dad was crying too! I went over and hugged him, not for much of a reason but just because I loved him. – Sara 12*

Ask all the questions that you want to and don't be afraid to show your feelings, whatever they are! You shouldn't really be made to cope with this, it's your parents' mistake and fault, not yours! – Rebecca 13

Will my parents get back together?

…your parents have been together for the first eight years of your life, you can't imagine them just splitting up, and you think "no this can't be right they're just having a row and they'll be back together", but then I realised! – Nikki 14

A very common reaction to your parents' separation is to deny the whole thing and convince yourself that they will get back together. Your parents may well have tried to keep their marriage together before they decided to separate, and have failed, so it is unlikely that they will try again now they have decided to separate. I'm not going to say that your parents will not get back together as some do save their marriage, but I am afraid that it is quite unlikely that this will happen. Basically your natural reaction to being told that your parents are splitting up is one of shock, and, therefore, believing that they aren't really going to separate is a way of dealing with this shock. This is perfectly understandable, but unfortunately convincing yourself that your parents are going to get back together may only mean that you will get hurt again when you finally realise this is not going to happen.

But I could try and get them back together…

Trying to get your parents back together may also come into your mind. This is a perfectly natural reaction but I'm afraid that the harsh reality is that it will probably not work.

Hoping and wishing that your parents would get back together and that everything could go back to normal is a normal reaction and you may well feel like this for quite a long time after your parents separate, but along with all the other feelings it does go away as you begin to accept the situation. You may feel by trying to get your parents back together you are doing yourself and your family a favour, but the reality is that you may well be actually causing more pain. Especially to yourself as in the long run you will realise that your parents

---

*   To help me write this booklet I looked at a number of different books one of which was extremely good and featured many different childrens' stories of what they went through when their parents separated. The quotes which I have starred are taken from this book – HOW IT FEELS WHEN PARENTS DIVORCE, by Jill Krementz.

aren't going to get back together, and this will hurt a lot as you will have put so much effort into trying to re-unite them.

> You shouldn't try and stop your parents getting a divorce, but let them know if you're upset... – Nikki 14

> I never thought that my parents would get back together but when my mum's 'bloke' left her I thought they were going to get back together – but they never did. – Sarah 12

Accepting the fact that your parents have separated and are not going to get back together is extremely hard, as you can't imagine how your life can be normal when your parents are living apart. So when you realise that they aren't going to get back together then you have taken a big step towards accepting the divorce of your parents – and this will happen however unlikely it seems!

Where will I live?

> ...to start with I just lived with mum but after a while she had a chat with me and said that if I wanted to I could go and live with dad, but I didn't want to so I stayed with my mum. – Nikki 14

One of the worrying things when your parents separate is what's going to happen to you? This is naturally one of the first things that comes into your head, and unless your parents have decided for you who you are going to live with then you have a very hard decision to make. It is almost impossible to make this decision, as you think that it isn't fair to make you choose between two people who you love equally and want to see all the time. You're right to think this, as it isn't fair! The one thing to remember is that you have to do what feels right for you as hard as this is. Don't let your parents pressure you in any way as who you live with affects you and your life and it's important that you feel as happy as possible.

> It would be nice if there was a special house for divorced families. It would be like two houses, side by side, with a place in the middle where the kids could live. – Heather 11*

I used to say to my parents that they should buy me and my sisters a house, and they should come and visit us seeing as they were the ones who decided to separate in the first place. Unfortunately this just wouldn't be possible so you have to try to get on with things the way they are.

Although this is difficult, and I know it is easier said than done, you must try not to please everyone. Don't go to live somewhere that is going to make you unhappy because you are trying to please your parents and make things easier. The first person you should think about pleasing is yourself. If you explain the reasons for your decision to both your parents then they will understand. Whichever one you don't see so much is going to be hurt but they will accept it. When your parents made the decision to separate they would have realised that they may not see you as much as they'd like to and will already be prepared for this to happen.

Your parents may be getting a Judge to decide where you are going to live, in which case they will send someone to talk to you and ask you what you want. The court will then decide what they feel is best for you, taking into consideration your comments and your parents'. In this case you should still make sure that you make it clear what you want to happen.

> I move from one house to another. During the summer we alternate every six weeks, and we always spend Christmas with my father and Easter with my mother. On our birthdays it's whoever we're with and then the other parent calls. – Roberta 14*

A new living arrangement is not going to be easy whatever it is, and at first everything may seem really unorganised and hectic. There is no easy solution to this problem but speaking from experience I would try to make a base with one of your parents where you can live most of the time – don't try to live in two houses! Even though this is a hard thing to do, and you will naturally miss your other parent, it will make things a lot easier for you.

There are good things about having two houses:

- You get to spend more time with each of your parents on their own. Even though you will want to see the parent who you aren't living with more, try to look on the time that you do get to spend with them as being even more special because it is only a small amount. Remember it is quality not quantity that matters!

- You get two bedrooms! In fact you get two of almost everything which can be quite nice.

- You've always got somewhere to retreat to if you need to. If things get too much for you at whichever house you are in then you can always go to the other one just to get away from it for a while.

> It's kind of nice the way it is because whenever I want to see my other parent I can, and if I have a fight with one of them, instead of having to take off and stay with friends, I can just go eat at my mum's house or my dad's, whatever the case may be and I think that's good. – Zach 13*

Coming to terms with your parent's new partner

> One of the first things that really bothered me about him was that he tried to kind of gain our affections by buying us stuff, and that really pissed me off 'cos, you know, I knew what he was doing. – Joy 17

To gain my respect he needs to earn it...he makes me feel pushed out in my own home – Emily 17

He's a bastard! – Nathan 19

Having a new person around is very hard to get used to and will take some time to accept. No-one will expect you to get on with them straight away as, after all, you may feel that if it wasn't for them your parents would still be together now. It will be difficult to see your parent with someone else and you may well feel jealous of the time that they spend with each other – which will give you another reason to dislike this new person. These are perfectly understandable feelings, but don't keep them to yourself. Make sure someone knows how you're feeling and then at least you don't have to cope with it alone.

> There are times when I get jealous of my dad's new wife because she's getting a lot of attention I used to get, but I'm happier when she's around than when she's not. I tried to explain to my dad that I could love her and still feel jealous and that I wasn't going to try to compete with her, but of course he wants everything to be perfect. – Nancy 15

One thing that your parent's new partner does do is make your parent happy, so there must be something good about them. The main reason that you may dislike your parent's new partner is because of where they are, not who they are. It is natural to feel jealousy, anger or even hatred towards this person, but you shouldn't let these feelings stop you from getting to know someone who could actually be okay. If you get to know them and you still don't like them then fair enough!

> ...with my parents' current partners it's like having extra parents. They all think about me in the same way... – Nikki 14

Although it might not seem like it now, your parents new partner(s) could turn out to be very special. It can kind of be like having extra parents, although I know this may be hard to imagine right now.

The most important thing is that you tell someone how you're feeling. If you feel like your parent's partner is trying to replace your mum/dad then tell them that (if you can). If you think that your mum/dad is spending more time with their new partner than you, then tell them. There is nothing wrong with feeling like this but I know you'd feel a lot better if you could just get rid of some of the emotions inside you.

> ...my dad's wife – there's not really much you can dislike about her actually. I get on really well with her now, she's kind of like a second mum/aunt kind of person, which is really nice – Joy 17

Coming to terms with stepbrothers/sisters

Your parent's partner may have children of their own in which case you may have to live with even more new people. You may even have to share your room which could be extremely annoying. You may naturally not like these children very much. Really you'd like them all to go away and let you get your life back to normal.

One thing to remember is that, like you, these children probably aren't too happy about this situation either. They have new people to get used to as well. You may even find that if you talk to them about how you're feeling then they might be able to help, as they will know exactly what you're going through.

You may also feel jealous of the attention that your mum/dad is giving these children. Your mum/dad may well be trying extra hard to make their partner's children like them, but this is only because they want everything to be right and want everyone to get along. Nothing will ever change the fact that your mum is your mum or your dad is your dad and if you really feel left out then tell them, as they won't be able to do anything about it until you do.

> …I got on okay with her but she was…she caused a lot of stress to the rest of my family. She was very argumentative and she really upset them. So on the one hand I quite liked her as a person but she was really upsetting all my family. – Nikki 14

Money!

When your parents first separate your lifestyle may change. One of your parents will have to find somewhere else to live and therefore a lot of their money will have to go into that. One or both of your parents may well be having to cope on their own now and there just won't be so much to go around as there used to be. Also if either of your parents has other people living with them, then it will cost a lot more for them to support everyone. This may make you feel quite annoyed at first but given time you will accept it as the way things are going to be.

I know it's really hard to see how everything is going to be alright when it all seems such a mess now. All you probably want to hear now is that, yes, your parents are horrible for doing this to you, your parent's new partner is a monster, and it isn't fair that you shouldn't have so much pocket money just because your parents have separated! This is fair enough and you are quite right to feel miserable and no one likes change very much, but the only reason I'm telling you that it will get better is because it does. Honest!!

> …it's weird 'cos I'm stuck in the middle. If I need like five pounds for something then mum wants me to get it off dad, and it's easier for her to say that, because it's hard for me to go and ask. I can't walk down

> there and say 'oh could I just have some money please' 'cos it seems like I've just gone down for the money. – Josie 16

You may often find yourself stuck in the middle of your parents' arguments about money. There are constantly things that you will need money for, like school trips, new clothes, etc, and it is difficult to know who to ask. Sometimes you will ask one parent and they'll tell you to ask the other one and this just carries on going round and round. Don't try to sort this out yourself. If your parents are sending you round in circles then simply tell them to sort it out between themselves and state that you aren't going to have anything to do with it! It may very well be that neither of your parents can afford what you're asking for but the important thing for you is not to get involved. It is up to your parents to sort out.

Be aware of your parents' feelings – but don't get too involved in them!

> …My mum was quite upset after she split up with my dad, so I spent most of my time looking after my mum. – Nikki 14

> At first my mother and father didn't spend too much time with me because they were both like little kids themselves after the divorce. – Daryl 10*

When your parents first separate it is hard on them too. You may think, well they decided to split up in the first place it shouldn't really upset them, but they may well be going through a great deal of pain themselves:

- They may be having to cope on their own for the first time in a very long while.
- They could be having a hard time getting used to having their partner's children around.
- They may be upset because they have just been left by their husband/wife.

It could be any number of things, but they may well be feeling too sorry for themselves to notice what you're going through.

Talking to your parents can help both of you to sort things out in your heads, but whatever you do don't let your parents lean on you too much. They are big enough to look after themselves and will have people to talk to if they need to. So you shouldn't get too caught up in their problems as you may neglect your own.

Make sure your parents know how you're feeling and what you're worried about – it helps them as well as you, as they obviously can't read your mind!

TALK TO SOMEONE!

"...talk to people cos I never did and sometimes I wish I had and in the end I had to go and talk to someone. And I became really claustrophobic and stuff...just go and talk to someone."
- Josie 17

"...I talked to other people who's parents had divorced and a lot of them had done a lot worse as far as their parents were concerned. Like one of their parents had gone away and they never saw them again,and I realised that I was pretty lucky. So that did help me!" - Nikki 14

I can't stress enough how important it is for you to get all these feelings out of you,and the only way to do this is to tell someone about it. It could be anyone...

MUM DAD TEACHER
BROTHER
SISTER AUNT COUNSELLOR
GRANDPARENT FRIEND CAT
UNCLE DOG
STEPDAD
STEPSISTER TEDDY STEPBROTHER

One of the best people to talk to is someone who has already been through this and will be able to tell you that it's okay to feel the way you are. When you realise you aren't the only one to feel this bad then you feel a lot more positive about everything.

An extract from Sarnia Harrison's booklet

Why are my parents changing?

You may notice little changes in your parents after they've separated. Maybe just little things in their behaviour that you might notice or they might let loose and take up some strange hobby they've been dying to to do for years. This is just one of their reactions to separating from their husband/wife. It may upset and confuse you at first. As everything is changing the last thing you need are your parents changing too. Don't worry too much. It doesn't have to be a bad thing, change can be really good. It will give you a chance to find out what your parents are really like!

> ...fathers are a right doss when they're on their own... Let me tell you something about fathers. They always take you out for fish and chips and things like that 'cos they can't be bothered to cook anything...and if you stop at the service station they always buy you chocolate and they let you do whatever you want to do... – Nikki 14

Talk to someone! [1]

> ...talk to people 'cos I never did and sometimes I wish I had and in the end I had to go and talk to someone. And I became really claustrophobic and stuff...just go and talk to someone. – Josie 17

> ...I talked to other people whose parents had divorced and a lot of them had done a lot worse as far as their parents were concerned. Like one of their parents had gone away and they never saw them again, and I realised that I was pretty lucky. So that did help me! – Nikki 14

I can't stress enough how important it is for you to get all these feelings out of you, and the only way to do this is to tell someone about it. It could be anyone. One of the best people to talk to is someone who has already been through this and will be able to tell you that it's okay to feel the way you are. When you realise you aren't the only one to feel this bad then you feel a lot more positive about everything. On the other hand in some cases it can be helpful to talk to someone who is totally removed from your situation.

> If you want to talk to someone just to moan about your situation it would be better to talk to someone like a counsellor because you know that they aren't going to say anything to anyone. If you have a problem which you think should be sorted out, it is best to tell your parents or a relative. In any case it doesn't really matter who you talk to, as long as you do talk. – Rebecca 13

---

1   See extract opposite.

Talking to your parents can be very hard as you don't want to hurt their feelings, but it can be good to tell them what's going through your mind. If they know then they can try and help you. Make sure you ask them anything that is worrying you – however insignificant it seems. The more you understand about your parents' divorce and what's going to happen the easier it is for you to accept things. Not knowing is the worst thing – so find out!

> ...I didn't know if I was saying the right thing. I didn't want to say something that would upset them. – Sarah 12

If you feel that you just can't talk to your parents then find the person you feel most comfortable talking to and talk to them about what you're going through. Don't be ashamed or embarrassed to go to a counsellor either. They will be very understanding and helpful and your parents won't have to know if you don't want them to.

> ...it helped me sort things out in my head a lot and put things into perspective...I think it mostly made me feel like I wasn't alone.
> – Joy 17

What happens to me if my parents are going through the courts?

In my experience and the experiences of other people I have talked to, the parents have managed to sort out where the children are going to live between themselves. However, not all parents can do this without disagreeing and therefore they need someone to decide for them – which is where the court comes in.

If your parents are asking the court to decide where you are going to live then there may be an order placed by the court which will affect you.

It may be any one of these:

- A Residence Order which says where you should live and with whom.

- A Contact Order which says who can visit or stay with overnight or who can visit you or who can write to you or who can talk to you on the telephone.

- A Prohibited Steps Order which stops a named person from doing a particular thing unless they have asked the court first.

- A Specific Issues Order which lets the court decide about something which you and/or your parents can not agree about.

Your parents will ask for one of these orders to be carried out by the courts and if you don't agree with the one they've put forward then you have the right to ask for one of these orders yourself. But the court has to be sure that you understand what's involved, so make sure your parents explain everything to you.

Even if you live with one parent rather than the other as a result of what the court decides, both your parents will usually carry on having responsibility for you while you are a child.

Will anything good come out of my parents' separation?

> I've become a lot more independent…I was the strongest out of me and my sisters. I had to support a lot of people really, which sounds like a bit of a burden but I think it helped me at the same time. – Joy 17

> I think the way I am is quite good, but I don't know if that's 'cos of my parents or not, 'cos you can't really tell. I think that my mum and dad have been able to express themselves better…especially my mum definitely has been able to express herself, and like the way she is better. I mean only recently but still through the break up; and me and my sisters get on better! – Sarah 12

> I gained two more parents and I think my mum was more confident in a way…she actually stopped her teaching job because she really wasn't enjoying it and she went for a different job and got it. So I think it made her think 'no this isn't the only option, I can do something else if I want to'…and I moved around a lot, which in some ways is a bad thing, but…you get to know different areas and start making friends. – Nikki 14

> I get to go surfing more and I can get away with being slack – Ben 17

> You get more money on Birthdays and Christmas. – Jasmine 18

> I now see my parents as two whole people with individual views, etc. Instead of two people agreeing for the sake of argument. – Rebecca 13

> I don't mind, I'm quite happy with it as it is now…I spent a lot of the last five years trying to please everyone and see everyone at the same time…but I've got my own life to sort out now and I can't spend it trying to keep everyone else happy. – Joy 17

> I've gotten used to things the way they are and now I'd have a hard time living with two parents at the same time. I can do things with my mother that I can't do with my father and vice versa. – Roberta 14*

So your parents divorce doesn't have to be all bad, there are many good things that will come out of it. You will grow up and change and the pain of your parents separation will lessen as time goes on. Just make sure you talk to someone as this is the only way to overcome the feelings you are going through.

Although your parents are not living together any more this doesn't mean that they don't love you – nothing can change the fact that they are your parents. The fact that they aren't living together now can be a good thing as you will now get the chance to build separate and hopefully good relationships with both your parents as individuals.

Remember you are not alone even though it may feel like it now, the best advice I can give you is to talk to someone – anyone. I can't tell you enough how important this is and how much it will help you to get through the separation of your parents.

FURTHER READING

Berman, C. (1980) *What Am I Doing In A Stepfamily?* London: Angus and Robertson.

Blume, J. (1994) *It's Not The End Of The World.* London: Pan Piper.

Fine, A. (1989) *Madame Doubtfire.* London: Puffin.

Hogan, P. (1981) *Mum, Will Dad Ever Come Home?* Oxford: Blackwell Raintree.

Krementz, J. (1984) *How It Feels When Parents Divorce.* New York: Knope.

Leeson, R. (1981) *It's My Life.* London: Fontana.

Mayle, P. (1979) *Divorce Can Happen To The Nicest People.* New York: MacMillan.

Mitchell, A. (1986) *When Parents Split Up.* Edinburgh: Chambers.

Tugendhat, J. (1990) *What Teenagers Can Tell Us About Divorce and Stepfamilies.* London: Bloomsbury.

Wallerstein, J.S. and Kelly, J.B. (1980) *Surviving The Breakup...* London: Grant McIntyre.

PART SIX

Using Our Voices

CHAPTER ELEVEN

The Child-to-Child Trust

Ella Young

Child-to-Child is a new approach to health education and primary health care. The key to this approach is the recognition that empowered children are able to take responsibility for their own health, and that of their families and communities.

The Trust was set up in 1978 in preparation for The International Year of the Child at the Institutes of Education and of Health at London University. Three staff support education and health workers by producing copyright-free materials, facilitating training courses and by networking in over seventy countries.

Primary health care seeks to involve communities in making decisions and taking action to improve their own health. The Child-to-Child approach involves children in this task in three ways:

- through helping to care for their younger brothers and sisters and other young children in their family group, and working with parents to improve the health of the whole family

- through assisting children in their own age group, including those who do not go to school and disabled children

- through working together to spread health ideas and improve health practices in the school and community as well as in the home.

The scope of Child-to-Child activities is very wide as health is seen in its broadest sense. The latest set of Activity Sheets is to help children in difficult circumstances, such as those living on the streets, in institutions, and those who experience war, conflict and bereavement.

Cultural expectations may diminish and marginalise children. In some countries children are not expected to initiate conversations with adults. The 'welfare state mentality' expects the government to do all the health care providing, without any input or effort by the people themselves.

Raising self esteem is an important part of working with people; self-esteem is about feelings, which play a vital part in the way people behave. Child-to-Child projects aim to raise self-esteem, increase empowerment and facilitate action. This is achieved by encouraging children to take an active part in what they are learning, and put health ideas into practice. Children are also able to make decisions and feel important because they are being listened to. This new empowerment often has a positive effect on all of their school work. The knowledge and enthusiasm of children is communicated to adults who are catalysed into joining the action for better health.

Here are some examples of Child-to-Child in action:

- **Bangladesh:** 1000 schools are running Child-to-Child activities. One of the key activities is for children to weigh and measure babies, monitoring their growth carefully for signs of malnutrition. By spotting deficiencies early on, the children help mothers improve the babies' diets so that they grow well. UNICEF is working with the National Curriculum Centre to make Child-to-Child activities an important part of school life.

- **Romania:** In a Saturday Club in Bucharest, health messengers aged 5–14 years are trained to organise and run Child-to-Child action groups. The 'press office group's' reports on conservation, dental health and care for the aged have been broadcast on the radio and press.

- **Britain:** Primary school children in Knowsley identified drugs, litter and dog-dirt as health issues which concerned them. They planned and carried out research and action in the community on these topics.

- **Brazil:** At health workshops, street children learn about AIDS, skin diseases and first aid. They pass this information on to others.

- **India:** Ten-year-old 'Health Scouts' in a slum area of Bombay adopt two families each, and teach them about anaemia, scabies, diarrhoea and other health topics they learn at school. So far, 4000 families have been reached, making a significant impact both on the health of the community, and on the academic achievements of the scouts. The following leaflet about what the Health Scouts do is illustrative of some of the work of Child-to-Child.

CHILD-to-child PROGRAMME

International Year of the Child 1979

c/o Institute of Child Health
30 Guilford Street
London WC1N 1EH

HEALTH SCOUTS

THE IDEA

A healthy community is a strong and a happy one. A community is healthy when the people who live in it:

- understand what they need to be healthy;
- know what services are available and how to use them well; and
- care about the health of everyone else.

Children can help in making their community a better place to live in and this activity sheet shows some ways in which children can do this, for instance by:

- finding out about the health care resources in their own community;
- passing on to their families and others important health information;
- caring about the health of others, particularly children who live near them, by helping their families make the best use of available health services.

WHO COULD INTRODUCE THE ACTIVITY TO CHILDREN?

- teachers of children in the upper classes of primary schools;
- youth leaders, who can also make use of health badges in organisations that have badge schemes, such as the Boy Scouts;
- health workers and others working in community health programmes.

Teachers and health workers can plan this activity together. Parents should be told what their children are doing and why.

THE ACTIVITY

Finding out about the health needs of the community

Surveys or 'find out' projects give the children practice in collecting health information and making good use of it. Children can find out about the health conditions of babies and young children in their community.

Illness and deaths from diseases like tuberculosis, diphtheria, whooping cough, tetanus, poliomyelitis and measles can be prevented if babies and young children are immunised. An important survey that children can make is to find out which children in their community have been immunised against these diseases.

Before carrying out the survey discuss with the children

- the reasons for immunisation;
- which immunisations are common in your area?
- who provides them?

Perhaps a health worker could be invited to discuss this with the children.

To carry out the survey the children could make a record chart for babies and young children near them, with symbols for each of the most commonly given immunisations, e.g.

BCG — which protects against tuberculosis

DPT — which protects against diphtheria, whooping cough and tetanus

Polio — which protects against poliomyelitis

Measles — which protects against measles.

WHO has been IMMUNISED ? Names	▲	■	●	◆
1 Arthur SSÓNKO	✓	✓	✓	
2 James KIWANUKA		✓		
3 Helen KIBIRIGE	✓	✓		
4 Sunday MUKAAMA	✓	✓		
5 Fayce NAAMA				

▲ BCG protects against TUBERCULOSIS
■ DPT protects against DIPHTHERIA PERTUSSIS [whooping Cough] TETANUS
● Polio protects against POLIOMYELITIS
◆ Measles protects against MEASLES

Children can find out about children in their own families and can be made responsible for several households near them. They will need to ask parents what immunisations the children have had.

From this survey the children will have found out which babies and young children need to be immunised. Older children can tell mothers about immunisation clinics and they can tell the health worker which babies need to be immunised.

Finding out about the health services available to the community

Often in a community there are many people with different kinds of health knowledge:

- some people know how to make herb teas;
- there are women who help at childbirth;
- often someone knows about first aid;
- the various trained health workers.

Where can we get help quickly and which of these people is the best one to help? This information is very useful for all of us but often we do not have it.

Children can find out about all the people in their community with some special health knowledge;

- where they can be found;
- what their special health knowledge is;
- who is the best person to go to.

Discuss these things with the children and let them make a list of all the people in their community who have some special health knowledge: eg clinic sister, midwife, herbalist.

Figure 11.1

CHILDREN MAKE IT HAPPEN

How Child-to-Child Activities are Saving and Improving Lives all over the World

NUTRITION

Many young children suffer from malnutrition not because of the lack of available food but because they do not eat often enough. Older children help their mothers feed young children small meals throughout the day.

New research reveals that vitamin A deficiency not only causes blindness but also affects immunity to disease and mental development. Children help each other and their families to grow and eat vegetables and fruit.

PREVENTING AND TREATING DISEASE

Although immunisation is now available to most people, many do not bring their children to be immunised. Children help spread the messages of immunisation.

Pneumonia kills babies quickly. Danger signs are easy to recognise. Children learn to observe, count and measure breathing rates and warn parents that they must get medical help speedily.

Children with a high fever must be kept cool and given plenty to drink. Many customs worldwide concentrate on "sweating out a fever" which can cause brain damage or death. Children learn to nurse sick brothers and sisters safely and effectively.

Malaria kills more people that AIDS. Young children are particularly at risk. Older children help stop mosquitoes biting and breeding.

HYGIENE

Little children's stools are eight times more infectious than adult ones. Older children who often care for little ones can help prevent infection of the whole family by helping to keep younger ones clean and washing hands.

Diarrhoea leads to dehydration which kills millions of children. Children learn to prevent it by better hygiene and how to make and administer rehydration drinks when children suffer from diarrhoea. They can even save lives in cholera epidemics by rehydrating children until they can be taken to hospital.

Figure 11.2

FURTHER INFORMATION FROM

The Child-to-Child Trust, c/o Centre for International Child Health, The Institute of Child Health, 30, Guilford Street, LONDON WC1N 1EH, UK.

For a publication list and to order Child-to-Child publications, please write to

Teaching Aids at Low Cost, P.O.Box 49, St Albans, Herts ALI 4AX, UK.

CHAPTER TWELVE

The Power to be Me

Alex Mellanby, Fran Phelps and John Tripp

INTRODUCTION

The 'A PAUSE' (Adding Power And Understanding to Sex Education) programme was established to determine the potential for medical and teaching
professionals working together with teenagers to develop a sex education
programme. If successful, the programme should have both educational value
and benefit the health of teenagers. A major component of this programme was
to be delivered by the teenagers themselves – the sessions referred to as 'The
Power to be Me'. The strategies used in the programme and its objectives
derived from a review of research literature and visits to projects in North
America. The main theoretical framework is of Social Learning Theory (Bandura 1977). The objectives mirror those suggested by the Sex Education Forum,
a multi-disciplinary body including education, health and religious institutions;
they are listed below:

A PAUSE

Objectives of the intervention:

1. Improving tolerance, respect and mutual understanding.

2. Improving knowledge of risks and counteracting myths.

3. Improving effective contraceptive use by teenagers already sexually
    active.

4. Providing effective skills for those who wish to resist unwelcome
    pressure.

Background

Sexual activity for young teenagers is usually unplanned, unprotected, often
unwanted, and on the increase. The trends are similar in Britain to those in

North America and other countries (Johnson *et al.* 1994). The outcome is a high incidence of sexually transmitted diseases (Donovan 1990), nearly one-third of females pregnant in their teenage years (Bury 1984), and a long-lasting deleterious effect on life style (Lee 1983).

While many sexually transmitted diseases are showing a decrease in incidence, this decrease has had little effect on those diseases primarily affecting the young, particularly women. Chlamydia, producing a possible 20 per cent incidence of salpingitis and infertility, is still one of the most common presenting conditions at genito-urinary clinics. Moreover, the human Papillomavirus is on the increase amongst women and several studies have linked this condition with carcinoma of the cervix. This may partially account for the relationship between cervical cancer and sexual intercourse at an early age. Nearly one-third of girls in this country have a teenage pregnancy; for those under 18 nearly all are unplanned and the majority unwanted (Curtis 1989b). Less than half use contraception at first intercourse (Royal College of Obstetricians (RCOG) 1991), and contraception is often not used effectively on a regular basis. There are around 30–40 thousand abortions to teenagers each year, nearly one-third of the pregnancies in this age-group.

The unplanned and unprotected aspects of young teenage sexual behaviour suggest that there are problems in communication and making decisions. Teenagers may be confused about expectations of their behaviour and this may not just be from their partner; teenagers often receive confusing, ambivalent and sometimes hypocritical messages from adults. As Kisker (1985) writes: 'American teenagers are beset with confusion. The resulting ambivalence permits adolescent women to be swept away by sexual passion, but not to admit that passion leads to coitus' (p.89).

Teenagers are certainly exposed to sexual activity. Estimates suggest that the average teenager in Chicago would expect to see some 9000 scenes of suggested intercourse in a year's television viewing and the sex portrayed is generally between unmarried individuals who experience none of the adverse outcomes. Despite this supposed freedom of sexual expression the individual teenager is likely to meet with embarrassment, hostility (Lee 1983), legal conflict, and duplicity in regard to their own sexuality. As one mother of a pregnant teenager said, while at the same time complaining that her daughter had been 'sleeping with all the boys': 'but she's the best stacked 15-year-old I've ever seen' (Perkins *et al.* 1978, p.185).

It is no wonder that the teenager discovers the necessity for regarding sexual experience as a covert operation. As Bell (1966) notes: 'For many parents and their children, the conflict about premarital sex will continue to be characterised by the parent's playing ostrich and burying his head in the sand, and the youth's efforts to keep the sand from blowing away' (p.44).

This inhibition of communication is likely to infect the teenager's early relationships. Kisker found when interviewing adolescents that most would regard discussion of sexual matters with a new partner as difficult and best avoided, and planned contraception would infer possibly unwelcome preconceptions in a new relationship.

Evidence for earlier maturation (Bury 1984) may provide a biological factor for increasing teenage sexual intercourse. Menarche below 12 years of age is associated with increased sexual experience and pregnancy amongst under 16-year-olds. This group may have reached sexual maturity before even gender identity has been fully established. In addition to the biological and romantic pressures on teenagers to undertake sexual experience, pressure from peers and partners may be intense. Schulz *et al.* (1977) have shown a linear relationship between personal sexual experience and the number of close friends with experience. Curtis (1989b) has shown that sexually experienced teenagers associate with similarly experienced friends. Spanier points to the pressure from partners: 'Individuals may change their sexual behaviour in a brief period of time if the opportunity exists. Thus a partner who is willing to advance or who insists on advancing to greater levels of intimacy will take precedence over, or negate, all other past sexualising influences' (Spanier 1975, p.39).

Lack of either parental supervision or imposition of curfews may reduce resistance to peer pressure and increase the incidence of teenage sexual intercourse (Curtis, Lawrence and Tripp 1988a). Generally teenagers will experience a conflict of ideology between their parents and their friends, and the outcome will depend on the nature of the parental relationship.

Unfortunately, young teenagers may not have reached a stage of formal operation in their cognitive development to allow themselves to think ahead. Associated with this is the teenagers' propensity towards risk-taking activity and lack of appreciation of risks associated with sexual experience. This may partially account for Curtis *et al.*'s findings (1988b) that younger teenagers accord more significance to shorter relationships, and, if they do progress to intercourse, do so after a shorter time than their older counterparts and take more risks (Mellanby, Phelps and Tripp 1993a)

In the sexual arena the male teenager has a severe problem establishing his identity. Despite their expressed wish for information they often receive the least (Curtis *et al.* 1988b). Beset with emotions they have the least outlets for expressing these feelings (Lee 1983). Society and peers exert pressure for them to develop their physical sexual experience. Research workers find difficulty recruiting them (Curtis *et al.* 1988b), or their fathers. So it is, perhaps, not surprising that they are often dismissed with a statement such as Cvetkovich *et al.* (1978) make: 'Briefly, it seems that 16- and 17-year-old males have had intercourse unless they are opposed to premarital sex for reasons of morality or family background, or have been unable to find a willing partner' (p.232).

Indeed, some research workers have suggested that there is not sufficient information to suggest that males should be involved in sex education at all. Whether a teenager will or will not submit to pressure will depend on the effectiveness of their social skills to defend themselves. Despite this, loneliness and isolation, conflicting parental role models, poor life expectations and deprivation may confound the best intentions of any newly sexually awakening teenager.

There has been world-wide recognition of the problems related to early teenage sexual intercourse. Attempts to intervene in this area have ranged from authoritarian direction on abstinence to the provision of contraception in schools. The role of education has generally been poorly defined, and met with considerable hostility. The prime expressed cause for concern has been that education on sexual matters might promote an increase in sexual activity.

Promotion of pre-marital abstinence in isolation, and without recourse to the nature of teenage relationships, has placed teachers from many countries in an untenable situation. However, reliance on this technique still continues, for example, in many North American states.

The effectiveness and methodology of school-based sex education continues to be the subject of debate and criticism (Oakley et al. 1995). Multiple studies in America have shown that instructional sex education will increase knowledge of sexual matters. The majority indicated that sexual activity amongst teenagers is not altered by school sex education (Kirby 1984; Wellings 1995). Reviewing the findings in 1989, Stout and Rivara (1989) concluded: '...that the existing data suggests that a classroom course alone cannot be expected to change sexual behaviour in a direction that is in opposition to the adolescents sexual world as moulded by the television, motion pictures, music, and advertising industries, as well as peer group and adult role models.' (p.377).

There have been exceptions with some programmes increasing teenagers' acceptance of premarital sex, partially increasing willingness to have sex, or actually increasing sexual activity within certain groups (see Kirby et al. 1994). The results from other health interventions would certainly suggest that unwelcome behaviour has been produced by certain strategies used in these interventions (Rundall and Bruvold 1988). Four previous studies have been associated with potential health gain; two including delay in first intercourse and one a reduction in teenage pregnancy. Small sample sizes, inconsistencies within groups and reversal of effects in later evaluation has not assisted in the definition of effective methods. However, we concluded from our literature review (Mellanby, Phelps and Tripp 1992b) that there were potentially effective methodological strategies to propose an experimental school-based sex education programme to investigate reductions in sexual risk behaviour.

A major component of our programme, and other newer programmes, has been peer-led education (taken to apply to education led by same-age or slightly older teenagers). The effect of the peer group on teenage sexual behaviour appears well documented. Teenagers' trek through adolescence sees them moving away from parental influence to peer conformity (Utech and Hoving 1969) and this may start quite young (Hartup 1983). Teenagers' views on sex appear to more closely mirror their friends than their parents; their contraceptive decisions involve either parents or friends but not both; their sexual behaviour is considerably influenced by their peer group. Females, it appears, pay greater emotional costs in order to maintain peer relationships.

Peers have been used in a wide variety of health related initiatives (Baldwin 1978; Davis, Weener and Schute 1977; Vriend 1969) and while their efforts are welcomed and appreciated their effects are infrequently evaluated. The evidence from other areas of health education, such as alcohol, suggested that peer leaders could be more effective than adults; peer education has been considered an 'essential element' in smoking education (Glynn 1989); a meta-analysis of substance abuse suggested that programmes involving a peer component were more successful than purely adult-led programmes (Rundall and Bruvold 1988); and sex education courses involving peer leaders decreased unwanted pregnancies (Vincent, Clearie and Schluchter 1987) and postponed first intercourse (Howard, Blamey and McCabe 1990). It is not necessarily that peer education is by itself better than adult education, especially in communicating factual information; adult-led education can influence sexual behaviour (Kirby *et al.* 1991).

We believed that, despite the required effort, peer education should be a component of the programme, and that improving skills appears to be the clearest theoretical basis for including peer education. We also concluded that the effective peer-led sessions were controlled, often scripted, and that the peer leaders were well trained (Howard, Blamey and McCabe 1990; Vincent, Cleanie and Schluchter 1987).

The A PAUSE Peer-led sessions

The project and the derivation of teaching strategies and material has evolved over a five-year period. Our involvement in schools has required frequent meetings with staff, parents and governors. A large range of novel teaching content has been derived. The peer-led sessions have been based on the work by Marion Howard in Atlanta, and it has been with her permission that we have adapted and developed the strategies for selection, training, and delivery of these sessions. The peer-led component is only one of the strategies used in the A PAUSE programme. It has never been our intention that younger teenagers should be able to provide all sex education. The whole programme provides sex education throughout a student's secondary school career with sessions delivered by teachers within the schools, medical and teaching staff from outside the school, and the peer-led sessions.

The peer leaders are aged between 17 and 19. The selection and training procedure is designed to ensure that they are confident and competent to deliver sessions to normal class groups of 13 to 14-year-olds. The content is designed to maximise the 'peer effect'; all activities, including small group and class discussions and role-plays, take place within an agreed and pre-determined framework which includes the maintenance of ground-rules.

To select students, the schools use criteria which stress the importance of role models with 'street credibility', reliability, expected empathy for the project's aims and potential for leading group work. They are volunteers and, before any involvement, meet with ourselves and previous peer leaders to discuss their possible involvement.

The training aims to enable the peer leaders to:

- work with others to improve their knowledge and presentation skills
- refine (in teams) the scripts on which the lessons are based
- learn how to establish and maintain 'ground rules'
- address their concerns and develop individual and team 'coping' strategies such as managing personal comments concerning themselves or others.

The training sessions are formalised; they require rehearsal and presentation of material; they include exercises to improve knowledge of risks; and practice methodologies to promote students' involvement.

The first session establishes ground rules, examines the risks and myths associated with sex. The establishment and maintenance of the ground-rules ensures their safe passage through the remaining sessions, when the novelty factor has worn off. In the first exercise they ask groups to consider the reasons that young teenagers start having sex (sexual intercourse). Their answers have been collected, grouped, and are presented in the pie chart (see Figure 12.1). A large proportion relate to pressure: pressure from friends and partners. Few mentioned a long-term relationship and 'love' was a surprisingly infrequent term. In the next session media pressure, particularly from advertising, different types of relationship and setting physical limits within these are discussed. The class looks at the pressures that the media use to make individuals buy products, how adverts can make people, especially teenagers, feel inadequate about their bodies and their appearance. The peer leaders use the image of a 'Stick person' to ridicule the pressures and to value individual difference. They expose myths about the prevalence of teenage sexual behaviour – including the myth that most teenagers are having sex. Before the peer sessions, over half the students' responses (60%) indicated that they erroneously believed most teenagers are sexually active before they are 16. After the peer sessions, this is reduced to about a quarter (27%). The same change was noted the following year but it was noted that the answers at the pre-test were higher, a possible indicator of a general change in attitudes within the programme schools. During the same session the peer leaders look at setting limits for physical expression in relationships. They ask the 13 to 14-year-olds to write anonymously on paper where, if anywhere, they think teenagers of their age should stop. The results from the collected answers are shown in the bar chart (see Figure 12.2). The

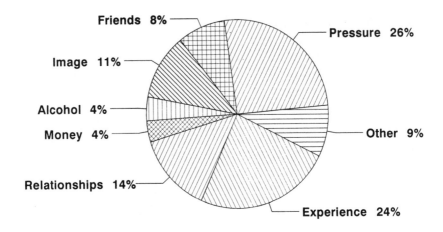

N = approx. 435/4 (students working in small groups)

Figure 12.1 Why do young teenagers start having sex? Responses from 13–14 year olds obtained during peer led sessions

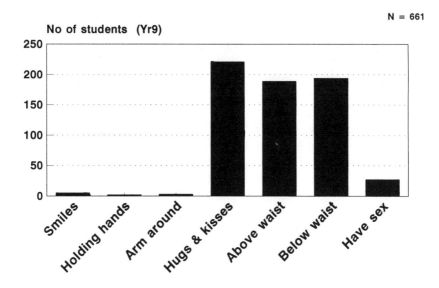

A PAUSE Peer Sessions, 1992/3

Figure 12.2 Setting physical limits in relationships for 13–15 year olds

results indicate a surprisingly low number who consider intercourse to be appropriate at their age. The proportion who respond 'sex' approximates to the prevalence of sexual intercourse at their age. The third and fourth sessions focus on the students recognising pressure lines and learning assertiveness techniques effectively to counteract the pressure. The peer leaders demonstrate, and then involve the students who model these techniques in role-play situations which they help to develop. This is not a 'say no' component, but the learning, practising and demonstration of techniques which allow a pressurised individual to regain control. The points below are taken from the lesson and illustrate some of those skills:

The Power to be Me:

1. State your position clearly and firmly and keep repeating it.

2,. Do not allow yourself to be made to feel guilty or intimidated by threats.

3. You may agree with some of the things the other person is saying but keep repeating your position.

4. Do not give any reasons or excuses.

THE PEER LEADERS' VIEWS

More than two thirds of the peers acknowledged that the training had improved their knowledge of a variety of sexual issues including the possible consequences of sexual activity in young teenagers (78%) and had considerable impact on their own skills development (93%) and self-confidence (98%). That did not mean they were not concerned or anxious about delivering the sessions – 'nerves' were mentioned by nearly all the peer leaders but their free responses and spontaneous comments have all indicated a very positive attitude to the experience: 'I was worried, but only about how I would cope if the class misbehaved. Talking about sex was like those discussions you have among friends of your own age'; 'The thought of not knowing what the kids would come up with made me sweat a bit. When I got into the flow of things I felt great, the kids were great. I didn't run dry on things and generally relaxed'.

THE TEACHERS' VIEWS

At the outset some teachers were inevitably concerned for both the peer leaders and their classes. Students were encouraged to discuss their training with tutors and other teachers as well as their parents. The comments from all these groups have only been positive since the actual sessions started, and these comments have included specifically positive remarks about the effects on peer leaders' achievements – subsequent to the programme.

Two of the observing teachers expressed reservations about these lessons before they began but all were enthusiastic afterwards. All twelve teachers who had observed the sessions said the classes responded well, for example: 'very positive, after initial embarrassment, students were able to involve themselves fully. They obviously enjoyed these sessions and made worthwhile contributions'.

YEAR 9 STUDENTS' VIEWS

The students were asked to complete anonymous questionnaires about the programme. Responses indicate that the programme positively affected the students' own perception in gaining information, 95 per cent said they had learned 'something' or 'a lot'. The majority of the students (98%), including those with low self-esteem or special needs, participated in discussion (90%) and role plays (83%), and nearly nine out of ten had talked about the programme (specifically about the role plays – with friends: 66 per cent; parents: 24%). Demonstrating in front of their peers caused embarrassment for some: 'a lot' (3%), 'sometimes' (39%), 'very little' (40%) and 'never' (17%). Their reported level of embarrassment was not associated with how much they said they had learnt, nor with their participation in discussion or role plays, nor with the post-test scores for the 'knowledge' questions. The questionnaire included space for free responses. The vast majority were very positive: 'the lessons were fun', 'more interesting than normal lessons', 'good that there were young people teaching', 'made me feel more open about sex'. One male student wrote: 'I realise that I do not have the right to pressure anyone into doing something they don't want to do' and another: 'It helped me say to a girl who asked me to have sex, no and if you really care for me you would leave me alone'. A few students responded that they felt 'embarrassed', 'scared' when they were asked to take part in the role plays but often they said that after the experience they were 'pleased', or 'proud' that they had managed to act out the scenes.

Comparative evaluation

Evaluation of the complete A PAUSE programme has been conducted with a questionnaire in Year 11 (students aged 15/16 years). This questionnaire has been used in the schools which have received the programme and control schools from around England which have continued to receive their own sex education programmes. The A PAUSE programme implemented and delivered over a five-year period to students in their secondary school years has shown, at the end of this process, significantly different attitudes, knowledge of risk and a decrease in sexual activity amongst those teenagers who had the programme, compared to the control population (Mellanby et al. 1995). Not only have we observed these changes and been supported by the schools in the delivery of the project, but the students have given us their support and approval – both subjectively and in controlled questionnaires, they have said that they enjoyed the programme.

Discussion

The programme has been delivered during a climate of major change in education and school administration. Since the inception of this project there have also been changes to the objectives and policies of sex education. The policy changes have culminated in the Education Act 1993 redefining the role of parents and the position of sex education outside the National Curriculum. The practice of sex education has seen a change away from a wish to promote informed choice to one of expected health benefit. Behavioural evaluation has moved from a peripheral position to become central in the promotion of sex education (Wellings *et al.* 1995). There have been calls for the liberalisation of sex education, citing Holland as the best example of good practice with its low rates of unwanted pregnancies; interestingly the Dutch have noted that their teenagers, as well as having low rates of pregnancy, start sexual activity, on average, at an older age than other Western teenagers and they consider this to have a causal link with sex education (Van Lunsen 1994). There have been calls for the restriction of sex education and the promotion of abstinence programmes with titles such as 'sex respect' (Hafner 1991) perhaps implying those who dispute the programme's worth are somehow 'disrespectful'; but we have found no good evidence to support any behavioural effects from these programmes. There have been calls for a charter, reviews of practice, working groups (RCOG), ministerial pronouncements, rows and chastisement of those teaching sex education, and the setting of health targets. The findings from our repeated years of questioning teenagers in our 'control' schools, have indicated that over the same period teenagers have not become more informed, do not consider that they have had any better sex education, and have become significantly more likely to have had sexual intercourse. Although successful methodologies have been identified we are unaware of any project other than our own that has included behavioural evaluation in this country, let alone successful effects. Our discussions with others involved in sex education have indicated that projects have found difficulties in establishment, continuing support, and evaluation. We are aware that our project does not cover every aspect of human sexuality; it is a focused experiment and as such will need some revision before promoting the extension of its use to a wider audience. We do believe that the support we have received, and have sought through consultation and positive responses to sensibilities, has been a crucial component of this project. We are certain that no matter what effect is required from sex education, or any other health education, it can only be achieved with the support of those concerned – teachers, parents, governors, education authorities, health professionals, and most importantly the teenagers.

The behavioural change we evaluated was the timing of first intercourse and additionally we have indicated that we will continue to collect information on other health related contacts (pregnancies, etc.) over the next year. Although a decrease in the prevalence of sexual intercourse amongst those under sixteen is consistent with the current legal position in this country and would cause a decrease in pregnancies to this group (a Health of the Nation Target) it is perhaps not clear why a reduction in sexual activity is a valid target for a medical intervention. The justification derived from the current research indicate that the promotion of good contraceptive practice by young teenagers is difficult to achieve and variable in outcome, even when directly promoting services (Allen 1991; Kirby *et al.* 1993), that young, under sixteen, teenagers appear much more likely to take risks in relationships than older teenagers. Curtis, Lawrence and Tripp (1988a) found that those sexually active under 16 went on to have more sexual partners, more partners per year and started sexual intercourse sooner in subsequent relationships than older teenagers. We found that this extended to poor contraceptive use and risks from sexually transmitted diseases (Mellanby, Phelps and Tripp 1993a) and our most recent survey of 17–19-year-olds indicates that it also applies to pregnancy and contracting sexually transmitted diseases. These factors have received substantiation from the retrospective data in the National Survey of Sexual Attitudes and Lifestyles (Johnson *et al.* 1994). A possible conclusion is that poor contraceptive use and risk of sexually transmitted diseases are linked to the circumstances of young teenagers' sexual experiences. Young teenagers indicate that intercourse is often related to pressure, that it is often regretted, and, in our study, over 90 per cent answered that they felt it was not appropriate for 13–15-year-olds to start having sexual intercourse.

We considered that the best chance of reducing some of the medical problems associated with young teenage sexual activity would be associated with a reduction in the numbers having sexual intercourse while still of school age. This has been achieved in this study, not by directive messages which are almost certainly ineffectual (Christopher and Roosa 1991), but through providing skills which teenagers feel able to use and have modelled their use in a controlled environment, together with an associated change in attitude amongst their peer group. The substantiation of our results with medical data is essential and this will be collected during 1995/6. The final justification for using sexual activity as the primary behavioural evaluator in this programme relates to the acceptance of data collection in school. The method of determining sexual activity (Tripp *et al.* 1994) has been acceptable to a wide range of schools and personnel. Furthermore, we believe that this method provides a more reliable estimate of sexual activity than direct questioning. We would not have achieved the same level of acceptance, nor the low rate of parental withdrawal from the questionnaire sessions, had we asked direct questions about contraceptive practice and exposure to sexually transmitted diseases. Students in school are not volunteers, and despite the emphasis on the voluntary nature of the questionnaire and the questions, students may not always feel that they have sufficient power to be able to make their concerns known. The low level of missing data (under 2%), the very small number of unusable questionnaires (about 15 from 8000) and the high level of those volunteering to answer postal questionnaires one year later (around 75%) suggests that the questionnaire retains the interest and co-operation of the students and is therefore a successful tool in evaluating the programme. We believe that we would not have achieved the same degree of student or school support with a more personally invasive questionnaire.

The review and observation of research programmes conducted at the start of our programme indicated the methodologies which had potential for achieving the successes which we have demonstrated. We have not evaluated each individual component to determine which has been most effective in being associated with the decrease in sexual activity. We have evaluated, as part of the development of the teaching material, the gains in knowledge achieved by each component of the programme, and have observed the changes in teenagers' perceptions of the prevalence of sexual activity brought about by the peer-led sessions but not by the adult sessions. However, we have not attempted to dissect the programme for its essential components. This has not been done because, although we considered that there was a potential for success, this had not previously been achieved, and the results from other health interventions in this country did not produce encouraging results (Nutbeam *et al.* 1993). We thus felt it best to include all 'good practice' we could identify to determine whether the results could be achieved at all rather than how. Our review of peer-led education and the results we have from this project (Phelps *et al.* 1994) indicated that peer-led education may well have greater effects on teenagers, especially when dealing with negotiations in relationships. The peer component in this programme is one of many types of education that have been grouped together because they are delivered by someone who appears closer in age or experience to the subject than the persons more usually delivering education. The term 'peer education' has been applied to such a wide variety of methodologies, from individual counselling to drama delivery to whole schools, and to many different target groups, such as to student nurses, members of youth groups, within drop in centres, schools, prisons, etc, that it is unlikely there will be a unifying measurable component demonstrated by all these interventions. The peer sessions we have used are given by trained individuals who deliver a uniform and supervised programme to Year 9 students. We would neither suggest that programmes which do not deliver in this way are not effective nor would we advocate the use of unsupervised peer-led group discussions with 13-year-olds.

The A PAUSE programme is an expensive research programme which has demonstrated a potential for health benefit from sex education. This raises the questions of generalisation to a wider population, extension of the techniques to other health areas, and funding. We are currently extending the intervention to other local schools. In doing this we are using nursing staff rather than doctors but continuing to employ teaching staff to work alongside them. The nurses involved have a wide experience in delivering sex education in schools and we consider that they will be able to implement the programme successfully, although this will require evaluation. Thus the service model from this research project should be less costly. To determine cost effectiveness requires a larger population than we have yet evaluated, although this process is now underway. We and observers of the project consider that the techniques used do have potential for use in other health education areas. Marion Howard has already extended her peer sessions to drug education in Atlanta, and this work is being widely used in California. If the process is to be promoted as a model for health intervention there will need to be some attention to the educational implications.

The current programme has taken components from successful programmes and has thus been 'results based' rather than 'theory based', the effects attesting to the success of this process. Previously used models, such as the Health Belief Model, fit closer with our educational system than the Social Learning Model with its greater emphasis on skills and modelling. In the long term it will be necessary for a successful programme to have an acceptable theoretical basis and this will be an important concern in the funding of work in health education. Despite the Health of The Nation targets and the emphasis on education in achieving these targets, health education is not a core subject and is squeezed in the busy curriculum. Perhaps there is a cogent argument to suggest that health education should take a more central and examined role. Possibly medical professionals have failed to make health an understandable issue for education. From the medical side it is sometimes surprising to hear educationalists extolling the necessity of genuine educational aims in health education but at the same time embracing some of the least well substantiated medical theories such as those relating to diet. Health and its effects on the individual are rarely simplistic and therefore educationalists might be encouraged to see it as a real challenge for the school curriculum. Health benefits would have an impact on the health budget and we are currently investigating methods to evaluate the costs of the medical problems associated with some teenage behaviour. Social benefits, and cost reductions to yet another budget, would accrue from reductions in teenage pregnancies. Each of these budgets are attached to differing working principles. The challenge this programme raises is can we afford not to have successful health education?

REFERENCES

Allen I. Family Planning and Pregnancy Counselling Project for Young People. Policy Studies Institute Publishing, London 1991.

Baldwin, B.A. (1978) 'Moving from drugs to sex: new directions for youth-oriented peer counselling.' *Journal of American College Health Association 27*, 75–78.

Bandura, A. (1977) *Social Learning Theory.* Englewood Cliffs: Prentice Hall Inc.

Bell, R.R. (1966) 'Parent–child conflict in sexual values.' *Journal of Social Issues 22*, 34–44.

Bury, J. (1984) *Teenage Pregnancy in Britain.* London: Birth Control Trust.

Christopher, F.S. and Roosa, M.W. (1991) 'An evaluation of an adolescent pregnancy prevention program: Is "just say no" enough?' *Family Relations 39*, 68–72.

Curtis, H.A., Lawrence, C.J. and Tripp, J.H. (1988a) 'Teenage sexual intercourse and pregnancy.' *Archives of Disease in Childhood 63*, 373–379.

Curtis, H.A., Tripp, J.H., Lawrence, C. and Clarke, W.L. (1988b) 'Teenage relationships and sex education.' *Archives of Disease in Childhood 63*, 935–941.

Curtis, H. (1986B) *Teenage Sexuality: A Study on the Relationships and the Factors Surrounding Teenage Pregnancy.* MD thesis, University of Wales.

Cvetkovich, G., Grote, B., Lieberman, E.J. and Miller, W. (1978) 'Sex role development and teenage fertility-related behaviour.' *Adolescence 13*, 50;231–236.

Davis, A.K., Weener, J.M. and Shute, R.E. (1977) 'Positive peer influence: school-based prevention.' *Health Education 8*, 20–22.

Donovan, C. (1990) 'Adolescent sexuality.' *British Medical Journal 300*, 1026–7.

Glynn, T.J. (1989) 'Essential elements of school based smoking prevention programs.' *Journal of School Health 59*, 5, 181–188.

Hafner, D. (1991) 'Promoting a charter for sex education: the American experience.' Paper delivered at the Family Planning Association conference: *Sex education for All.*

Hartup, W.W. (1983) *Peer Interaction and the Behavioral Development of the Individual Child. Social and Personality Development: Essays on the Growth of the Child.* New York: Norton.

Herz, E.J., Reis, J.S. and Barbera-Stein, L. (1986) 'Family life education for young teens: an assessment of three interventions.' *Health Education Quarterly 13*, 2, 201–221.

Howard, M., Blamey, J.A. and McCabe, J. (1990) 'Helping teenagers postpone sexual involvement.' *Family Planning Perspectives 22*, 1, 21–26.

Johnson, A.M., Wadsworth, J., Wellings, K. and Field, J. (1994) *Sexual Attitudes and Lifestyles.* Oxford: Blackwell scientific publications.

Kirby, D., Barth, R.P., Leland, N. and Fetro, J.V. (1991) 'Reducing the risk: impact of a new curriculum on sexual risk-taking.' *Family Planning Perspectives 23*, 6, 253–263.

Kirby, D., Resnick, M.D., Downes, B., Kocher. T., Gunderson, P., Pottoff, S., Zelterman, D. and Blum, R.D. (1993) 'The effects of school-based health clinics in St.Paul on school-wide birthrates.' *Family Planning Perspectives 25*, 12, 12–16.

Kirby, D. (1984) *Sexuality Education: An Evaluation of Programs and Their Effects.* Santa Cruz: Network Publication.

Kirby, D., Short, L., Collins, J., Rugg, D., Kolbe, L., Howard, M., Miller, B., Sonenstein, F. and Zabin, L.S. (1994) 'School-based programs to reduce sexual risk behaviors: a review of effectiveness.' *Public Health Reports 109*, 3, 339–359.

Kisker, E.E. (1985) 'Teenagers talk about sex, pregnancy and contraception.' *Family Planning Perspective 17*, 83–90.

Lee, C. (1983) *The Ostrich Position*. London: Unwin Paperbacks.

Mellanby, A., Phelps, F., Lawrence, J. and Trip, J. (1992a) 'Teenagers and the risks of sexually transmitted disease: a need for the provision of balanced information.' *Genitourinary Medicine 68*, 4, 241–244.

Mellanby, A., Phelps, F. and Tripp, J. (1992b) 'Sex education: more is not enough.' *Journal of Adolescence 15*, 449–466.

Mellanby, A., Phelps, F. and Tripp, J. (1993a) 'Teenagers, sex, and risk taking.' *British Medical Journal 307*, 25.

Mellanby, A.R., Phelps, F.A., Crichton, N.J. and Tripp, J.H. (1995) 'School sex education: an experimental programme with educational and medical benefit.' *British Medical Journal 311*, 414–417.

Mellanby, A.R., Phelps, F.A., Crichton, N.J. and Tripp, J.H. (1993b) The use of self generated identity codes to collect anonymous data from teenagers and their parents, (submitted for publication 1993).

Nathanson, C.A. and Becker, M.H. (1986) 'Family and peer influence on obtaining a method of contraception.' *Journal of Marriage and the Family 48*, 513–525.

Nutbeam, D., Macaskill, P., Smith, C., Simpson, J.M. and Catford, J. (1993) 'Evaluation of two school smoking education programmes under normal classroom conditions.' *British Medical Journal 306*, 102–107.

Oakley, A., Fullerton, D., Holland, J., Arnold, S., France-Dawson, M., Kelley, P. and McGrellis, S. (1995) 'Sexual health education interventions for young people: a methodological review.' *British Medical Journal 310*, 158–162.

Perkins, R.P., Nakashima, I.I., Mullin, M., Dubansky, L.S. and Chin, M.L. (1978) 'Intensive care in adolescent pregnancy.' *Obstetrics and Gynaecology 52*, 2, 179–188.

Phelps, F.A., Mellanby, A.R., Crichton, N.J. and Tripp, J.H. (1994) 'Sex education: the effect of a peer programme on pupils (aged 13–14 years) and their peer leaders.' *Health Education Journal 53*, 127–139.

Loudon, J., Turnbull, A., Bury, J., Edington, P., Kenmir, B., Macfarlane, S., Massey, D., Paintin, D., Reader, F. and Tacchi, D. (1991) Royal College of Obstetrics Gynaecology Working Party on Unplanned Pregnancy Report.

Rundall, T.G. and Bruvold, W.H. (1988) 'A meta-analysis of school-based smoking and alcohol use prevention programs.' *Health Education Quarterly 15*, 3, 317–334.

Schulz, B., Bohrnstedt, G.W., Borgatta, E.F. and Evans, R.R. (1977) 'Explaining premarital sexual intercourse among college students: a causal model.' *Social Forces 56*, 1, 148–165.

Spanier, G.B. (1975) 'Sexualisation and premarital sexual behaviour.' *The Family Coordinator 24*, 1, 33–41.

Stout, J.W. and Rivara, F.P. (1989) 'Schools and sex education: does it work? *Pediatrics 83*, 3, 375–379.

Tripp, J.H., Mellanby, A.R., Phelps F., Curtis, H.A. and Crichton, N.J. (1994) 'A method of determining rates of sexual activity in schoolchildren.' *AIDS Care 6*, 4, 453–457.

Utech, D.A. and Hoving, K.L. (1969) 'Parents and peers as competing influences in the decisions of children of differing ages.' *The Journal of Social Psychology 78.* 267–274.

Van Lunsen, R. (1994) *Sexuality – Problems and Solutions.* Presented to Third Congress of the European Society of Contraception, Dublin.

Vincent, M.L., Clearie, A.F. and Schluchter, M.D. (1987) 'Reducing adolescent pregnancy through school and community based education.' *JAMA 257*, 24, 3382–3386.

Vriend, T.J. (1969) 'High-performing inner-city adolescents assist low-performing peers in counselling groups.' *Personnel Guidance Journal 48*, 897–904.

Wellings, K., Wadsworth, J., Johnson, A.M., Field, J., Whitaker, L. and Field, B. (1995) 'Provision of sex education and early sexual experience: the relation examined.' *BMS 311*, 417–20.

CHAPTER THIRTEEN

Children and the Right to Play
Lessons from Peru[1]

Elsa Dawson

THE RIGHT TO PLAY

This chapter looks at the experience of Ayni, a Peruvian non-governmental organisation, in bringing play to children in a deprived neighbourhood of Lima, the Peruvian capital. It asks whether this initiative is supported by the literature on play and its role in child development, and examines whether any judgement can be made about the impact of Ayni's work on the children targeted by their project. The project was funded by the Save the Children Fund, for whom the author worked as Field Director in Peru from 1983 to 1991.

In 1944, the Dutch philosopher Huizinga published his influential work postulating the close links between play and the development of civilisation. His study 'Homo Ludens', in tracing the history of European and Asian civilisation, highlights the play element in such adult 'games' and social contests as religious ritual, philosophical debates, lawsuits and artistic creation. Play is depicted as creating order in an imperfect world, and as the first phase in the development of culture. Once the play-rules are broken, 'a society falls into barbarism and chaos'.

Piaget (1951) developed a theory of cognitive development which linked the development of play with that of intelligence (Silva and Lunt 1982). Winnicott (1971) developed the idea that play promotes creativity, it being the 'creative apperception more than anything that makes an individual feel that life is worth living.' This he contrasts with 'a relationship to external reality

---

1 This work was presented at the World Conference on Research and Practice in Children's Rights at the University of Exeter in September 1992 and later published in *International Journal of Children's Rights 1*, 33–48,1993. Reprinted with kind permission of Kluwer Academic Publishers, the Netherlands.

which is one of compliance' which 'carries with it a sense of futility' and 'that life is not worth living'.

On the basis of such theories, it is now widely advocated that children should be endowed with an essential right to play. The United Nations Convention on the Rights of the Child, Article 31, declares that 'State Parties recognise the right of the child to rest and leisure, to engage in play and recreational activities appropriate to the age of the child and to participate freely in cultural life and the arts'. Article 29 also states that 'the education of the child shall be directed to…the development of the child's personality, talents and mental and physical abilities to their fullest potential'. Since writers such as Piaget and Winnicott argue that play is essential to the development of the child's fullest potential, its central place as a child's right can be seen as firmly established by the Convention.

The existence of the International Association for the Child's Right to Play with consultative status with UNESCO and UNICEF, and their triennial international conferences, is further evidence of a growing belief in the child's right to play. In an inaugural address to the 1983 conference, RP Khosla, Secretary to the Government of India, Ministry of Social Welfare, emphasised the particular importance of play for children growing up in the fast-growing, over-crowded cities of developing countries 'where space is barely adequate for a family to sit and sleep, space for play is an unheard-of luxury…and the atmosphere of tension…is hardly conducive to the proper development of the child.' He goes on to point out that 'small neighbourhood areas where children can play are rarely provided by urban planners, as a result of which children are driven to using the streets for their games.' Since it is, as he says, 'unlikely that the flow of population to the cities will be checked in the foreseeable future', it is urgent to find ways to stem this erosion of play opportunities for children.

A document produced by UNESCO (1980), to encourage the use of play as a pedagogical technique in different socio-cultural contexts, states that 'it would seem only natural that play should have its place in the classroom', and laments the lack of recognition of this fact by education authorities. YS Toureh is quoted as criticising the aversion of many adults to children's play and that they 'even try to repress it, as though it were a waste of time and energy when there are more urgent and serious things to do'. This applies particularly to parents in 'poorer socio-economic environments, in which the age for play is cut short or done away with altogether, so as to turn the child into a miniature adult, expected to engage in subsistence activities before he has even really learnt to play'.

In Peru, this position is reiterated by a specialist in the theme of children's play, Carmela Izaguirre, writing in the same volume. She describes how the 'massive exodus of indigenous peoples to the capital' of Peru have produced a Lima where 'children no longer have anywhere to play'. She also laments the loss of traditional Peruvian games, which she relates to the 'far-reaching deculturation (sic.) of the most underprivileged social strata in Peru, and especially the peoples of Indian origin.'

However, she does note that in Peru before the Spanish colonialisation, evidence shows that 'children were integrated into working life from an early age and...had proper tasks to perform within the community which probably left them no time for play.' Also 'the games played by the Indian child nearly always took on the form of a sort of training for his future occupations as an adult.' Feitelson (1977) draws the distinction between 'imitative behaviour', and play as 'serious preparation for adult work' and 'representational play', where 'a certain imaginative play is the mainspring of activity.' Her thesis is that it is 'representational play' which tends to occur in 'technologically creative civilisations', and whose 'beneficial effect on children in Western societies has been extensively documented and does not need further corroboration'.

A psychoanalytic study of an underprivileged group in a Lima shanty-town by Rodriguez Rabanal (1989), claims that this early incorporation into adulthood means that the child's specific needs are left unattended, and the value of his/her play is denigrated. This he sees as leading to the violent behaviour characteristic of children in such poor sectors of Peruvian society, since it is impossible for children to have the internal and external space they need for their healthy mental development.

THE ASSOCIATION FOR INTEGRATED CHILD DEVELOPMENT (AYNI)

Ayni was therefore not alone in believing in the importance of providing children in deprived sectors of Lima with increased opportunities for play and creativity. This was the basic motivation for the setting up of the association by a small group of teachers and psychologists in 1986. Their central objective was 'to promote child rights within and from within the school, by means of developing children's identity through play'.

In this way, they hoped to contribute to the fuller development of human potential in Peru, and particularly to the creation of a more humane society in a country suffering from prolonged internal strife, in which the child itself would help improve social relations. All through the 1980s, the country's situation deteriorated in every sense – an estimated 25,000 died in a bitter conflict between the Shining Path guerilla movement and government forces that spread from the Andes to the shanty-towns of Lima which became crowded with refugees from the violence in the country-side. Meanwhile inflation soared to five figures and economic growth ground to a halt, adding fuel to the social conflict.

Ayni's associates aimed to address what they saw as a denial of childhood and play in Peru by supporting the development of children's freedom of expression, creative imagination, and capacity for experimentation and invention. They criticised the authoritarian attitudes of state school teachers, who repress children's creativity, spontaneity and playfulness, instead of recognising these as essential elements in the development of children's full potential. Ayni saw such attitudes as producing passive and uncritical adults incapable of removing the barriers to their country's development. They also saw the general lack of respect for play as inhibiting the child's development of a clear sense of cultural identity. Such a sense is seen by many Peruvians to be essential to overcoming the problems of under-development and civil war.

These objectives were carried out via the following activities:

- Training pre-school-, primary- and secondary-level teaching staff.

- The proposal and implementation of curricular modifications for primary and secondary schools, and for teacher-training, which more closely reflected the reality of poor Peruvian children than the curriculum currently in force.

- The organisation of art and communications sessions for primary and secondary school pupils, and groups of children in the community.

- Research into play and its implications for child identity development.

- Publications on Ayni's institutional themes.

- Encouragement of greater levels of participation and representation of parent associations in the educational process.

- The organisation of events, co-ordination and centralisation of neighbourhood organisations at the local, district, regional and national levels around the defence of child rights.

Two slight confusions will be noted here:

1. That Ayni professed to promote child rights in general, but was really only concerned with certain educational, social and psychological rights, particularly those related to play and creativity. They were not concerned with rights to adequate diets, clothing and housing, nor with campaigning or broadly-based advocacy in favour of child rights.

2. The assumption that parent associations would automatically support the pursuit of their own institutional objectives.

These contradictions explain some of problems the Children's Rights in Schools Project later came to have.

THE CHILDREN'S RIGHTS IN SCHOOLS PROJECT

This was Ayni's first project, funded almost entirely by Save the Children. It was located in Mount San Pedro, one of Lima's most overcrowded and impoverished inner-city slums. Several such hills exist in El Augustino District, close to the city centre, where families live in dwellings clinging precariously to the steep rocky slopes. Around 2000 families live in Mount San Pedro, and average population density is approximately 2500 per hectare. The steep slopes make the construction of adequate water provision and sewage systems especially difficult, and many homes are reliant on buying water from lorries by the jerry can.

These slums suffer a high rate of violent crime, widespread prostitution, drug-addiction and -trafficking, and Mount San Pedro is widely known as a refuge for petty criminals and terrorists. The police station located half-way up the hill was abandoned in the mid-1980s after successive attacks by terrorists and delinquents.

Such slums have grown up in and around Lima in the last forty years, their populations swollen by those escaping the violence and frequent droughts in the Andean provinces. Inhabitants are employed mainly in services, street-vending, small trading establishments, and mechanical repair shops. Fifty-eight per cent of the district's population are employed in the informal sector, and thus lack stable incomes.

The children of Mount San Pedro grow up in an atmosphere of violence and deprivation with consequent negative effects on their healthy development. Their behaviour tends to be aggressive, exhibiting low self-esteem, limited capacity for self-expression, and a great need for affection. Ayni's concern was to find low-cost ways of addressing their problems: physical and sexual abuse, exploitation as workers in family businesses, and early involvement in crime and drugs.

It occurred to them that the pupils of the local secondary school, run by a Catholic congregation of nuns, the Madre Admirable School, could provide the answer. As part of their weekly routine, they were supposed to carry out some kind of service for the community. Why not train them to support the children of Mount San Pedro? It was from this initial idea that the Children's Rights in Schools Project evolved, Ayni deciding to designate the pupils they began to train as 'Children's Rights Promoters'.

In 1990, Save the Children approved a year's budget of £10,000 to set up a pilot scheme in the School, to train 15- and 16-year-old pupils as children's rights promoters. This amount would cover salaries for two teachers and a project co-ordinator, educational and publicity materials and administrative costs. It was hoped that once its functioning had been consolidated in the original school, the scheme could then be replicated in state schools in similar slums.

Ayni drew up the following objectives for their original pilot scheme:

- The development and socialisation of children contacted by the project, helping them gain critical and creative skills and evolve attitudes of solidarity and respect for life and human dignity.

- To guide the secondary school pupils towards a commitment to defending children's rights and solving community problems.

- To generate more awareness and commitment amongst teachers with respect to attending to pupils' real needs and basic rights.

These general objectives were to be achieved via the following specific activities:

- Setting up permanent art, play and recreation workshops in Mount San Pedro aimed at helping children develop their potential, fraternal relationships and respect for life and human dignity.

- Training fourth- and fifth-grade secondary school pupils as community child rights promoters.

- The commitment of neighbourhood organisations to creating a child rights defence committee for Mount San Pedro.

- The incorporation of school teaching staff into the venture by developing their awareness of possible child rights abuses which could occur both within the classroom and in the wider community.

- The publicising of the most relevant aspects of the UN Convention on Child Rights, particularly stressing the right to play, recreation, artistic and cultural creativity, and to an education directed towards the development of basic skills.

- The drawing up of curricular proposals for the state school system aimed at the formation of a constructive relationship between the community and the school it serves, based on the strategy of school child rights promoters.

As the project developed, a confusion showed up in its basic focus: was it aimed primarily at assisting the children of the Mount San Pedro community, or at improving the situation of school children in relation to their rights by means of modifications in the attitudes and teaching practices of school staff.

Ayni resolved this confusion by re-writing the project's main objectives, and developing a renewed concept of the project. The new objectives concentrated on the creation of an alliance between the school and the community aimed at defending child rights, both in their education and the organisation of teachers and pupils in favour of child rights.

They also added a new objective, that of contributing to curricular innovations at a national level. Such innovations aimed to transform the Peruvian educational process making the child and his needs, the development of his personal identity and the promotion of his rights its point of departure.

Activities and Project Results

Ayni organised, stimulated and accompanied three parallel educational activities which took place: the training and motivation of Madre Admirable School teaching staff; the training by teachers, accompanied by Ayni, of fourth and fifth graders; activities with the children of Mount San Pedro carried out by these pupils (see Figure 13.1).

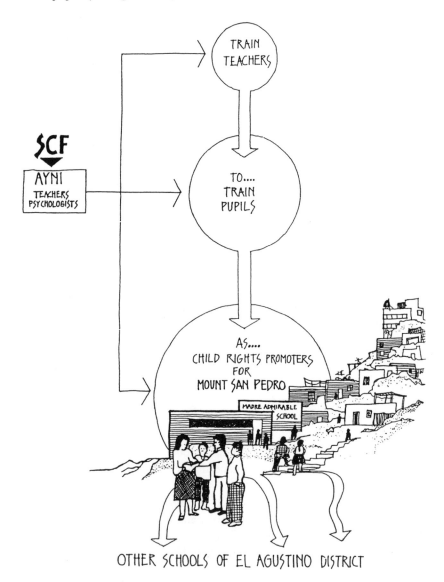

Figure 13.1 Ayni's project in El Augustino District, Lima

The interest of the teaching staff in incorporating child rights into their classes was so great that, at times, Ayni's small team was unable to respond to all of them. However, the teachers were also involved in other projects the school had taken on and therefore had less time than Ayni had hoped so less activities in the community were carried out than planned. Save the Children had furthermore approved funding for the project before the school-year started. To have delayed the project for another year would have wasted Ayni's voluntary efforts which had considerably motivated staff in the year leading up to the project. This meant that the project began with uncertainty as to whether it would receive funding so Ayni could not undertake all the commitments planned.

The teachers were assisted in the production of materials and helped to re-design their classes for three of the standard school subjects: psychology, civic education and art. Ayni trained them to adapt the courses in the following ways:

> Psychology: the theme of self-esteem was developed, and the recuperation of the adolescent's childhood by taking pride in the body, greater understanding of sexuality, and improving self-perception in general. Techniques were borrowed from theatrical education and the literature of the gestalt school. Materials were written and duplicated for teachers to use with their pupils to help them understand the problems of adolescence, recall the spontaneity of their childhoods and criticise any repression suffered. In this way, it was hoped to create an empathy between the pupils and the children of the community based on mutual identification.

> Civic education: pupils were helped to see the contrast between the real conditions suffered by Peruvian children, especially in slums like Mount San Pedro, and those claimed for children by the UN Convention on Rights of the Child. They were then encouraged to help the community organise around child rights as a practical activity.

> Art (music, theatre, drawing and painting): the play activities to be carried out with the children of San Pedro Mount were prepared. The team emphasised the role played by art in the development of children's creativity, powers of expression, movement, spontaneity and playfulness.

One hundred and sixty fourth- and fifth-grade pupils were trained as child rights promoters in the first year of the project. The psychology course was voted the most popular with its invitation to develop greater self-knowledge as well as a way of addressing the needs of Mount San Pedro children. Pupils acclaimed the course as a significant event in their lives.

Ayni's project team noted significant changes in the pupils following on their work, such as:

- The freedom and personal interaction encouraged led to the development of greater self-confidence, enabling the pupils to express their ideas and feelings about themselves more openly.

- Re-discovering their own childhoods meant they were able to gain greater self-knowledge and enrich their sense of personal identity and self-worth.

- Timidity, apathy and anarchical behaviour gradually gave way to constructive leadership attitudes.

The pupils carried out the activities with the Mount San Pedro Children with great enthusiasm. They went out into the community once a week during the session specified by the school as 'Educational Community Practice' (Promoçion Educativa Comunal). They organised creativity workshops, street processions, theatre sessions, and game and arts festivals. In particular, they provided support for the eight pre-school playgroups which were operating under a government scheme in the area. The community workers in charge of the playgroups co-operated with Ayni by evaluating the pupils' work, and Ayni provided them with training in using play to support child development. The workers noted that children began to lose their timidity, show greater trust in adults, be less violent towards each other and be more ready to share with other children.

Ayni observed that the pupils were also generating greater respect in the community for children, promoting the idea that it was possible to place greater trust in a child's intelligence. However, they were not able to give enough time to working through these themes with parents so such respect may not have reached all homes.

Replicating the original pilot scheme

As a first stage in seeking the scheme's replication, Ayni decided to analyse their experience in detail, in order to evaluate the methodology they had followed and its results. Had they achieved their objectives? They focused their review on the question of to what extent the play methodology employed had made it possible for pupils to develop greater self-esteem and empathy with the children of their community. This question was the basic one they needed to analyse in order to judge the results of their methodology. Their lack of self-esteem was seen to be based in problems the adolescent pupils had experienced as children. Therefore, if they could understand and come to terms with such experiences, they would empathise more easily with children in the community.

They identified a variety of changes observable in the pupils' behaviour which apparently demonstrated their strategy's success, such as overcoming fears of talking about themselves in front of their classmates, exposing themselves to possible ridicule. They also noted certain indications that the pupils were developing leadership characteristics and motivation for community service as they gained confidence in their own capacity to stimulate a community initiative, to organise group activities, to freely express their opinions, and to listen to those of others. When working in the community, they noted the following developments in their relationship with the children: more patience, shows of affection, concern for and interest in their welfare and opinions.

But these phenomena were not measured in any scientific way, except to say, for example, that 'three-quarters of the pupils managed to achieve greater self-expression and overcome inhibitions'. They give examples of this, and of the results of various techniques they used. Thirty per cent ceased to be apathetic members of the community and began to show visible signs of firm leadership.

Ayni then tried to relate these changes to their work in raising pupils' self-esteem. For example, their increased capacity for tolerance could be explained by the greater levels of self-confidence achieved. They attribute the greater levels of concern and interest in children demonstrated by the pupils to their work in re-awakening what Freud terms 'childhood amnesia', the memories of pleasure and liberty repressed by a society which disparages such experiences as signs of immaturity. The changes in behaviour are also seen as a reflection of new attitudes produced in the Madre Admirable School teachers towards their pupils – attitudes of encouragement and congratulation, concern for their pupils' personal lives, and physical gestures of affection. These characteristics are seen by Ayni as evidence of a more democratic relationship between teachers and pupils.

More evidence would be required to show that the methodology really had an impact. But, can one expect more from a small, newly-formed NGO, on a minimal budget? SCF provided an extra £400 for bibliographic material and general support for the writing up of the project, but the project team lacked time to carry out the discussions and writing required.

Nevertheless, their contribution to Ministry of Education pre-school playgroups earned Ayni the appreciation of the local education authority for El Augustino District, who consequently showed interest in supporting their project. An agreement was signed whereby Ayni would oversee the setting up of similar schemes in all the schools in El Augustino, helping pupils all over the district to support government pre-school playgroups.

A survey of 15 per cent of third- and fourth-year pupils of the district was carried out to determine their attitudes to working with children and their general interest and opinions. Information was collected regarding family and neighbourhood contexts so that their preparation as child rights promoters could be carried out with their real living conditions and interests as a starting point. The team would then know what particular attitudes and aspects of their understanding would require influencing for them to become successful child rights promoters.

They were accepted, particularly by the pupils, in all the schools bar one, which had been taken over by the Shining Path guerrilla movement. The pupils in the state schools actually showed more enthusiasm than those of the Madre Admirable School, since for them such a project was a novelty, while the pupils of Madre Admirable had experienced many different projects concerned with community service.

Courses were held with a selection of teachers who showed interest in taking on the scheme in their schools. The training was carried out in a less intense form than in the Madre Admirable School focusing on the training of child rights promoters and the materials developed by Ayni.

The El Augustino District Council also showed interest in supporting the pupils by supplying premises for activities with children, sound equipment and banners, and the neighbouring district's educational authority (La Victoria) was considering adopting Ayni's scheme.

Ideas resulting from the project and experience gained by Ayni via its implementation were used by its Director in 1990 when he was invited by President Fujimori's first Minister of Education, Gloria Helfer, to help develop an action plan for the Ministry. Helfer was anxious to find ways of incorporating the principles outlined in the Child Rights Convention into the educational system, and to create awareness of problems suffered by children amongst teaching staff. She hoped to develop state schools as centres of integrated attention for children, rather than places where they were merely treated as recipients of knowledge, and judged according to their ability to assimilate it. At the same time, she tried to build ways in which communities could become more actively involved in running schools by setting up school community councils. Problems associated with the embargo on public expenditure imposed by Fujimori to resolve the country's deficit problems meant she was unable to continue in office, and therefore few of Ayni's ideas were in the event disseminated via the Ministry of Education.

Difficulties encountered

The project failed to establish the preparation of fourth- and fifth-grade pupils as child rights promoters as a norm in Madre Admirable School due to delays caused by teachers' strikes and Save the Children's approval of the project. Activities started in the community may have therefore lacked continuity.

Ayni also realised in retrospect that they lacked adequate experience and technical capacity in curricular proposals and planning school teaching pro- grammes, despite their background in teaching and child psychology. They saw it as a mistake to have tried to combine the community activities with the design of curricular modifications. It would have been better to restrict their interven- tion to proposals for general strategies and educational guidelines in line with the child rights thesis. In future, they would agree general objectives and activities with teachers during the year, and allow teachers themselves to programme the exact content of their classes.

There was also a need to examine whether it was justifiable to combine the wider children's rights issue with the personal development of pupils and children. This combination possibly led to confusion amongst the project participants and beneficiaries which inhibited their identification with the project.

The confusion could have contributed to this failure to motivate the community of Mount San Pedro to set up a children's rights defence committee to guarantee continuity for activities conducted with the community's children. If more effort had been dedicated to work with parents on the importance of devoting resources to their children's healthy development, and sufficient connection made between the Child Rights Convention and their lives, this objective could, perhaps, have been achieved.

However, the small team primarily focused its time and energy on Madre Admirable School, and on preparing pupils as child rights promoters. Despite the fact that the problems they identified as affecting children mainly originated with adults (parents, teachers, other adults in the community, exploiting or abusing children in different ways), their work was concentrated on the relationships amongst children and adolescents. Their over-riding concern with school pupils also meant that the project failed to concentrate on the most disadvantaged children of San Pedro, normally those unable to attend school.

Finally, they were unable to measure impact in a sufficiently scientific manner as has already been described.

IS THE IMPORTANCE OF PLAY OVER-STRESSED?

Was Ayni merely trying to impose a good idea on the people of Mount San Pedro, without developing and implementing a solution together with them? Judith Tendler (1982), in her critique of private voluntary organisations and their projects, points out that this is often the case, despite their rhetoric of involving the active participation of the communities with whom they work. This begs the wider question of whether such activities are democratic, since non-governmental organisations are, by definition, unelected and depend on their close relationship with the community for their democratic legitimacy.

The failures of this project indiate a need to question the assumptions which lay behind its conception, in particular the importance of play to children's development in Peru. Barbara Tizard (1977) noted that the widespread enthusiasm for play was not based on a solid basis of research findings, and that the whole idea of free play was 'likely to appeal to people who may not have any knowledge of psychological theories but who have a strong belief in the importance of individuality, autonomy, creativity and intrinsic motivation' and that such people tend to be rich and to have the luxury of working, not so much to earn money, but 'for the enjoyment of the job'. As she points out, for such people as the slum dwellers of Mount San Pedro, 'autonomy and creativity are not part of their working lives and are not necessarily valued'. Such people are liable to be somewhat 'puzzled' at teachers' enthusiasm for their children's paintings, for example. Her comments could explain the community's lack of involvement in Ayni's project and justify the kind of adults, described by Y. S. Toureh in the UNESCO document, who repress children's play.

Peter Smith and Helen Cowie (1988) reviewed the main play theorists and corroborate Tizard's opinion that the case for play had still to be proved since 'the evidence for strong cognitive benefits...is not convincing'. That for 'social competence' was better, but had been studied less thoroughly, 'while the postulated benefits of play for emotional release and catharsis have scarcely received any well-controlled experimental study at all.' They point out the emergence of an alternative view from studies of both animal and human play, that 'while play is likely to have benefits, it is unlikely that they are essential', since these benefits could be achieved through other means.

Nevertheless, Kathy Silva in a keynote address to the 1983 Afro-Asian Conference of the International Association for the Child's Right to Play, expressed the hope that such cynicism could be averted by the work of David Weikart (1978). Weikart developed a 'cognitively oriented nursery curriculum...based on the theories of Jean Piaget', based on guided play rather than free play:

> Children are helped to make deliberate choices concerning their play, to carry out their own plans, and then to discuss the outcome with adults and peers. The aim of the programme is to instill cognitive skills (for example, concentration, problem solving and novel ways of doing things) and the awareness that one has mastered them.

The results have been carefully monitored over the years of the programme's implementation in the United States and have shown that it can help children from poor homes to 'dramatically improve their chances in life'. Children who had experienced the pre-school curriculum showed better rates for completing their schooling, for gaining employment, and in avoiding delinquency and teenage pregnancies. Individual children interviewed showed a striking belief in their own capacities.

CONCLUSION

Undoubtedly the discussion on the importance of play for child development will go on for many years. This article has not been able to cover all the various facets of the argument to date. The undemocratic nature of private voluntary organisations such as Ayni whose associates have not been elected by the community they serve makes this discussion all the more urgent in the evaluation of their work.

Further research is obviously required with regard to the importance of play to the kind of child development most appropriate to developing country realities and felt to be most relevant by members of low-income sectors. Related to this is the need for Peruvians to decide more clearly the role children should play in their society and, therefore, how much priority they wish to lend to the development of individuality, autonomy, creativity and the kinds of qualities play seems to be most useful for.

Also, more thought needs to be given to what kind of play is most relevant. It would seem, for example, from the studies mentioned in western societies that representational play and guided play are most beneficial with regard to developing children's potential. How do these theories translate into the contexts of developing countries?

Finally, it must be said, as Smith and Cowie (1988) note that no-one can deny the sheer enjoyment of play, and this itself gives it an 'enduring value'. This is especially true in the face of the kind of difficulties currently being experienced by Peruvians. At the very least, Ayni's project contributed to the happiness of the children of Mount San Pedro and of El Augustino District. And at the most, if Huizinga's proposition of the importance of play for civilisation is taken at face value, they may have contributed to the vital struggle for a more humane society in Peru.

REFERENCES

Feitelson, D. (1977) 'Cross-cultural studies of representational play.' In B. Tizard and D. Harvet (ed) *The Biology of Play*. London: Heinemann Medical Books.

Huizinga, J. (1949) *Homo Ludens: A Study of the Play-Element in Culture*. London: Routledge and Kegan Paul.

Izaguirre, C. (1980) 'Play and teaching in the underprivileged socio-cultural strata in Peru.' In *The Child and Play: Theoretical Approaches and Teaching Application*. Paris: UNESCO (Compiled by Juliette Raabe).

Otter, M.E. (ed) (1984) *Afro-Asian Conference on the Role of Play in Child Development: Report from IPA*. International Association for the Child's Right to Play.

Piaget, J. (1951) *Play, Dreams and Imitation in Childhood*. London: Heinemann.

Rodriguez Rabanal, C. (1989) *Cicatrices de la Pobreza: Un Estudio Psicoanalitico*. Caracas: Editorial Nueva Sociedad.

Sylva, K. (1984) 'Keynote address 1 – nurturing play in a cold economic environment.' In M.E. Otter (ed) *Afro-Asian Conference on the Role of Play in Child Development: Report from IPA*. International Association for the Child's Right to

ACKNOWLEDGEMENT

In writing this chapter I am indebted to my friends at Ayni, particularly Luis Guerrero, both for the opportunity to work with them, and for the information they have provided. I am also grateful to Jo Boyden for her helpful comments on initial drafts of this case study, and to Save the Children for facilitating my work in Peru and my subsequent research.

Play, The Indian International Centre, New Delhi, India, 14th–18th November 1983. Sheffield: IPA.

Sylva, K. and Lunt, I. (1982) *Child Development: A First Course.* Oxford: Blackwell.

Smith, P.K. and Cowie, H. (1988) *Understanding Children's Development.* Oxford: Blackwell.

Tendler, J. (1982) 'Turning private voluntary organisations into development agencies: questions for evaluation.' *USAID Programme Discussion Paper No 12,* Washington DC: Office of Program and Management Support, Bureau of Food and Voluntary Assistance, and Office of Evaluation, Bureau for Program and Policy Coordination, US Agency for International Development.

Tizard, B. (1977) 'Play: the child's way of learning?' In B. Tizard and D. Harvey *The Biology of Play.* London: Heinemann Medical Books.

Toureh, Y.S. (1980) 'Guide peer l'étude et l'utilisation en pedagogie des activites indiques.' In *The Child and Play: Theoretical Approaches and Teaching Applications.* Paris: UNESCO.

Weikart, D., Epstein, A.S., Schweinhart, L. and Bond, J.T. (1984) 'The Ypsilanti preschool curriculum demonstration project.' In M.E. Otter (ed) *Afro-Asian Conference on the Role of Play in Child Development: Report for IPA.*

Winnicott, D.W. (1971) *Playing and Reality.* London: Tavistock Publications.

PART SEVEN

The Roots of Personal Powers?

CHAPTER FOURTEEN

Empowerment and Autonomy from Babyhood

The Perspective of 'Early Years' Research

Jacqui Cousins

INTRODUCTION

It is intended that this chapter heightens awareness about how very early the infant begins to experience personal power and independence and how simply they can develop given encouragement. It is hoped it raises questions for consideration in the same way that its preparation has been done for a number of young people who have worked with me on the preparation of this contribution. I wish to start by thanking those young people for their help and for the sensitive way in which they have questioned and challenged my words.

The Convention on the Rights of the Child came into force world-wide on 2 September 1990. Here we look at what Articles 12 and 13 mean in practice. We focus on how these apply to babies and young children under eight years of age and those who care for them. This age group is referred to in Britain as the 'Early Years'.

What follows addresses how young children begin to express themselves. This is an area of early communication which many young people said they were curious about. It provoked many questions about how soon in childhood self-expression begins and how it can be recognised and encouraged. My young collaborators wanted to know more about how children's talking develops. Many of them already recognised the importance of the role of the listener. Learning how to listen to children has always been important but has become increasingly emphasised by those who work in the early years, not least because they are usually the first people called to support families when situations have reached a stage of crisis and children are in a state of shock or confusion.

SETTING THE SCENE

Recent conferences on children's rights have typically included a variety of workshops or discussions in which young people and adults worked together. Most of these have begun with a short introduction by a speaker who has told the audience what their sessions were going to be about. Many of the people who were speaking were completely unused to the presence of young people in their sessions. One such speaker began: 'Accessibility of knowledge and information is a crucial ingredient in the dissemination of...'. At this point there were mutterings from the group and a young voice piped up: 'Excuse me, but I don't understand what you mean!' (You will see resonances of this in the commentary on Rudi's chapter which follows.) There was a long, a *very* long pause for thought. It was an uncomfortable moment for everyone and translating her words from 'jargon' into plain English proved to be very difficult for that speaker (Manchester Conference 1994). That young person brought home strongly the point that where their rights are concerned, young people need to be able to understand what we say to them and write for them.

In the likely event that there is any misunderstanding of the intended meanings in my title, both words refer to encouraging freedom of expression in practice and how and when this can be achieved. Empowerment means, in my view, to *give* power or to enable or to allow freedom of expression. Autonomy means to have personal freedom of choice and it includes being allowed to exercise such choices.

There were other words and ideas at the conferences which the young people also found puzzling simply because they (and others) didn't know about the world of child care and education in Britain, a world which has developed its own professional language. Explanations of some terms and ideas follow. The term 'family' for example is taken to include all possible variations of people with whom the babies and young people live. In this way the needs of those who do not live with their natural parents or who live in various institutions are not seen differently or separately. The term 'carers' include early years educators who are all concerned with quality day-time provision for babies and young children.

The process of empowerment is not restricted to any one context of people with whom children mix in their lives. In the earliest years it is usually the family who are agents of their empowerment and it is the family as their initial educators who encourage and facilitate their children's early choices or autonomy. My young co-writers also pointed out that children also empower each other and give each other confidence and encouragement. They also help each other to make sense of puzzling situations. Other children can also be a source of oppression. In the cases of children who have been bullied, the feeling of personal power or a positive self-image and confidence can quickly be eroded or taken away. This is a point stressed by young people who had themselves suffered.

As children become part of the broader social scene of child care and education outside their homes (such as at playgroup, nursery or school), to empower children becomes even more a shared responsibility. The idea of sharing includes the sharing of knowledge about young children's development. The predominant view of the young people at the conferences I attended was that our record in this respect has been very poor. Some adults felt that the reason for this was because we are too used to working in isolation and find it difficult to trust each other. We feel threatened and territorial. Others felt that it was because the system which is designed to care for children is itself too cumbersome and concerned with its own powerful hierarchy. The children complained particularly about the length of time it had taken them in the past to get help or to be listened to seriously (a point which Richard Kinsey substantiates in Chapter 18).

At the International Early Years Conference, 1994, a large group of inner city children spoke from their own experiences of a Britain where they perceived a lot of 'social class' snobbery and other forms of prejudice. They felt that this had stopped people listening to them seriously in the past, because they were young people from poor areas. Many said that collaboration between adults and children and the forming of networks or groups who could share interest and knowledge was becoming even more important because of the area of child protection. They spoke about their own efforts in workshops to find ways to help young children gain positive and balanced views of themselves and to be confident enough to express themselves freely and honestly and, therefore, seek help if they needed it. That is using early years jargon to be assertive.

Many people who work in the early years believe that in order to empower and enable young children's choices, a need is for children to learn about trusting relationships and about assertiveness. The professionals feel that this needs to be practised positively and regularly in groups where children do feel safe and secure. They also come to know, through that practice, that words, and in particular talking, are more powerful tools for their views or feelings than aggressive behaviour.

An explanation of the Convention's term 'freedom of expression' and how this worked in practice for young children was something my young co-writers wanted to know more about. The word 'expression', as used here, is not limited only to talking. Other opportunities for self-expression need to be explored and used, amongst which all art forms are of particular importance. This point is recognised by people who care for young children and by anybody who works with those who have been very frightened or who are angry or upset. They often need to work in ways which allow feelings to be expressed safely, not necessarily in words. At times they need to encourage gentleness and work with materials which are soft and comforting. We all have a lot to learn about this from colleagues in the area of therapy and special education. They frequently use materials which appeal particularly to the senses or can be used in such a way as to discharge anger and facilitate self-expression and 'finding a voice'.

The complex challenge to us as professionals working in child-centred ways with children is not only to accept these young voices but to find ways to interpret the youngest children's meanings however these are expressed. We have to be creative in finding ways to talk to them in a language which is plain yet not patronisingly simple. Because this is an intricate and time consuming area of communication, there is the danger that many adults will dodge the issue altogether and assume that the youngest group are not capable of expressing themselves at all. Articles 12 and 13 of the Convention do not distinguish between age groups because it is intended that the youngest children will be included in everything which has been written.

The realisation of these Articles in the early years of a child's life calls for greater understanding of early communication. Adults need to give time to listening and taking notice of what such young children have to 'say'. This calls, particularly, for adults to find ways to encourage young children to express themselves confidently and, for their part, for the adults to find ways of understanding and accepting the meanings of those expressions.

Young people at that conference (Manchester 1994) repeatedly returned to how, in practical terms, we put the words of Articles 12 and 13 into practice where the very young were concerned. Early years representatives have spent a great deal of time in trying to convince people about most young children's capabilities where language itself was concerned. There was a conviction that many young people in our society are not able to express themselves at all. Such children were traditionally seen to be the children of 'problem families'. This was repeated by a large group of young people who themselves had been fostered or 'in care' and who felt that their limited fluency was used as an excuse for ignoring their views. As their young spokesperson said:

> Even here today we've talked about children and their rights as if they begin somewhere around 12 and only then if they come from certain groups in society. Children's Rights are for *all* children and we have to keep reminding ourselves that childhood starts at birth, not when babies become old enough to say things for themselves. Babies and young children speak to us in all sorts of ways and it's up to us to give them time to express themselves. When they can talk we've got to learn to listen to them and to act on what they're telling us! (Participant in the Manchester Conference 1994).

CHILDREN FINDING THEIR VOICES

It is impossible to provide a complete insight on communication in a brief article. Young people have certainly raised some very important issues about general ignorance on that subject and referred to some popular misconceptions which affect how we listen to very young children.

In recent years we have witnessed an acceleration in studies from around the world which have focused attention on the observation of the young. Some of this research has been carried out within families and some in nurseries or other institutions. There has been a distinct move away from research of the 1960s and 1970s which studied babies and children as individuals isolated from others rather than as part of a social group. Much current research has made good use of the increased sophistication of recording equipment and video recorders. With all this specialist study and the possibility of complex observations of whole families themselves in such work, there is an increasing realisation that the majority of babies are much more competent communicators and capable beings than was previously believed. We now have first-hand evidence that conversations and other forms of dialogue take place with babies often being included actively, and with meaning being given to their baby 'babbles' long before they can actually speak in words. They learn many of the social rules such as taking turns or how to interrupt by being treated as partners and being involved in 'conversations'. A great many of these rules have become second nature in our culture, so much so that we are hardly conscious that they take place, let alone that they have been learnt.

Within our multi-ethnic and multi-cultural society in Britain there are people who positively include their young babies in their own social group from the beginning of their lives. There are cultural norms in rules of talking and within these are many of the attitudes which people have about not only listening to people (including children) but in taking action based on what they say. In Britain when we examine the aims of our National Curriculum on Speaking and Listening, we find that they support the view that language is a powerful tool in bringing about change and are guiding young people towards reasoned argument, logical debate and their eventual public use of speech.

EARLY YEARS LANGUAGE PROJECT

To ensure that I have really grasped the words and the meanings of the children, in this part I have spent a lot of time checking my interpretations with children themselves.

My own research into young children's talking 'Early Years Language Project' was focused on a subject which had cropped up again at young people's conferences; that is young children's ability to talk and to express themselves. Broadly, my study was carried out in an area of Britain where all the children who took part spoke English as their first language. It was an investigation of the concern felt by many people that young children of four year of age were not able to express themselves or, in simple terms, to talk when they first started school. The majority of those concerned also believed that this related to their social class or home situation.

James and Thomas my twin grandsons, now aged eleven, were just beginning to talk when the project began and lived through that research with me. They certainly both show a remarkable interest and skill in listening to some of the tape recordings and transcriptions of them in recent years. They have given me invaluable help because of their ability to identify with and to expand on what has been said. I call this help their 'I know what he (she) means!' In simple terms they are natural sense makers; in technical terms they are my negotiators or mediators of meaning. They have used their spoken language to build a bridge which links the points of view and realities of children and the points of view and realities of adults.

CHILDREN TALKING: ADULTS LISTENING

There are certainly other young talkers who have been able to shed a lot of light on the way that young children see things. One of the most exceptional of these for me in recent years has been a child of five called Sonnyboy. He belongs to a group of traditional Travellers and within their culture, talking and questioning the sense of things is of great importance. Like James and Thomas, Sonnyboy is surrounded by people of all generations who not only talk a great deal in front of him but also encourage him to have views and to express them. He knows too the clear cultural rules which relate to talking and the strong value placed on the family by his own people. This includes knowing how to listen with respect to what others say but not being afraid to hold or express a different point of view. He had a strong sense of 'fairness' and a lot of self confidence. If he wasn't entertaining the other children with his outstanding yarns and stories he was challenging his long suffering teacher with 'That don't make no sense, Mrs A!'. He wasn't being cheeky. He simply couldn't understand many of the rituals which either went on, or were talked about in his class. His teacher knew a great deal about Sonnyboy's Travellers' culture and she had the humility and humour as well as considerable patience to go back over what had been said so that it would eventually make sense to him. She found this very worthwhile because she discovered that there were many other children who were equally confused but who hadn't liked to say.

For Sonnyboy's calm teacher, listening to children was one of her own priorities but a group of young people at a recent conference on children's rights in Manchester (organised by Underground Power as outlined in Chapter 8 by Bird and Ibidun) made us all sit up and take notice when they spoke about 'listening'. They saw the majority of adults clearly as 'people without time to listen'! They faced us with their own reality which was that they had seldom been listened to seriously in the past and certainly not when they were in their early years – except by their infant teachers. One young man said that this situation had become worse recently because, in his own view: 'Teachers at our school have become completely overloaded by all the changes in the educational system and with the hysterical demands of the national curriculum. We hardly ever get to talk to them any more – not even the infant teachers. The *System Rules OK??*'

He was not alone in holding this view. Many of them felt that even the most sympathetic of their teachers now had little time to spare (this point is further taken up in Bird and Ibidun's chapter). Some of those young people had themselves been victims of abuse from their early years and we have enough sad evidence to support their view about 'adults not listening' for whatever reason. By taking seriously what young people like these have said we should be able to learn from some of our earlier mistakes.

There is tape recorded evidence available in Britain which shows how many questions teachers and other people in positions of authority ask children; even in normal conversations. In the chapter by Rhys Griffith in Volume Two (John 1996) he takes up the imbalance of teachers' questions in relation to pupil initiated interactions. There is also evidence which shows that believing the questions we ask to be sensible ones (because we are adults?) children try to answer those even which, to them, make no sense at all. It can be seen as part of the game called 'talking'. In that game there are often two or more sides and many of the rules for playing are carried on so often that they have become more like habits. When children play opposite adults the sides are not very well balanced. In other words, the adult is in a position of power and often has control over what is being talked about and how it is being managed. In addition to this, the adult is able to use a large variety of voice tones and many of these at school are concerned with social control.

The reasons for some children's confusion or misunderstandings seems to stem from people seeing things from their own point of view and making assumptions that everybody else saw things in the same way. The adults' realities and the children's realities were usually quite different but often the adults assumed that the children shared their meanings and knew exactly what they meant and vice versa. This is a normal and very complicated part of communication. Even some of the most confident children who asked a lot of questions at home became speechless in certain school situations when things did not match their own reality or when they were unsure about what they should say or do. It was also noticeable how few children asked questions at school or let their teachers know that they didn't understand; even when their teachers were the most sensitive and sympathetic people.

This was never the case with Sonnyboy because he was not only very self-confident but he was also used to questioning and challenging other's sense of things. It can be speculated that this part of language is stronger in some cultures than in others. In the case of Sonnyboy it could be tied in with the sad history of his people which includes the persecution of Gypsies and Travellers.

Needing to make sense of things is probably a crucial part of their attempt to survive. Even in their day-to-day lives as nomadic people they need to be able to talk well to those in positions of power so that they won't be 'moved on' unjustly. They learn to use their language strongly to argue and to negotiate.

Sonnyboy was one of the first members of his group to go to school and he was trying hard to survive and to make sense of school and of becoming a pupil. (Some of the difficulties he might have encountered are outlined in Chapter 4 by Cathy Kiddle.) Nobody in his family knew very much about the day-to-day life there. In his early days, Sonnyboy simply sat and watched. Later this changed, but he certainly hadn't learnt one of the first unspoken rules of talking at school – which seemed to be that children have to be quiet and listen while the teacher or adult takes the lead or asks questions. He also found waiting for his turn to speak difficult and unnatural. All of this meant that Sonnyboy had to adjust to significant shifts in the power relationships between home and school conversations. He was also so puzzled by the continual questioning which went on that he asked: 'Why do you keep asking the kids questions when you knows all the answers? Like...like...what colour is it then? You can see for yourself it's red...so why you keep asking then?'

James and Thomas, at seven, were very interested in my work with Sonnyboy. They clearly identified with him when he challenged some of the 'taken for granted' rules of school. These included rules about such basic things as eating, playing, or talking at certain times only. They also included knowing how to answer teachers' questions. James explained that they aren't real questions because they aren't supposed to be finding out anything new. In his words '...teachers and grown-ups always have the answer to those sorts of questions in their own heads'. Thomas took the idea further 'Yes, that's true! Children just keep trying different answers until they hit on the one that they want to hear. Then they say, very good...that's right...very good'.

This probably has a ring of truth for all of us but if that is how children hear our questions what sort of effect does it have on the way they answer us? (see Donaldson 1986). Do the majority join in the guessing game and give us the answers which they think we want to hear or think will please?

Like Sonnyboy and Thomas, and many other young children, James is also very tuned-in to the unspoken language of the eyes or to the meanings behind the smiles, the frowns and the tone of voice. They can sense deception and puzzle over and question the hidden messages which we give to children in our conversations but which we are probably not aware of ourselves as they have become unconscious. Many of these are concerned with our own attitudes and values or what we like or dislike. Thomas described this to me like this:

> The talking says one thing...like we all have to get on well together and things like that...but they show you something different in what they do...it's hard to describe what I mean...but it's like when those children never get chosen to be the leaders. Everyone knows the teacher or dinner

person doesn't like them and so do they. Then they get very naughty and start pushing. You know what I mean.

James described many similar hidden messages which centred on giving rewards to good children but not to those who were naughty. He thought that quite a lot of people would think that Sonnyboy was very naughty for asking so many questions. He also said: 'Grown-ups often say one thing but mean another or use funny voices to persuade children to say what they want to hear or to do what they want children to do…but…so do children. I whine a lot to get my way'.

I found out that some of the tears and silences of the young children starting school came about because they didn't understand what adults mean by choices or choosing.

CHILDREN CHOOSING: ADULTS ENABLING

Being able to make choices at home and at school often means completely different things. A little boy, of under five, called Ross was able to describe this:

At school what you do is all your writing and all they sums like colouring balls and things. Then you get to choose. Not choose to go down to the Hoe and look at boats and look for dad's fishing boat and say…got any fish for supper? Not that sort of choose. Mrs A sticks hooks on pictures of bricks and sand…and I can't remember all the hooks…and then you stick your name on and that's how you choose…and that's not called work in school that's called choosing.

What Ross was describing was a very common way in which teachers organise their classes and allow free choice. They often have over thirty children to occupy positively and there is no one way in which this has to be done. The limits of choices are set and for obvious reasons Ross would not have been allowed out of school to go to the Hoe to look at the boats. Sonnyboy experienced similar difficulties when his choices were interrupted by either bell or clock. One day when the bell went for playtime I heard him grumbling: 'That don't make no sense…I just got to the interestin' bit…I don't care about the time…that's plain stupid…time's as long as it takes!'

James talked a lot about conflicts in the messages from adults:

Everyone wants their kids to be independent…and to grow up, grow up…don't be a baby…it's like that with cuddlys. Then it's like it when you want to go to the park on your own to play…you're not allowed because it's too dangerous. You get murdered and that…where can we go to play and be independent.

James also talked about his 'tatty blanket' (cuddly) and said that there was a lot of pressure on him to give it up. Even threats to take it away from him for ever and 'put it in the bin' because he was too big. Compared to the troubles of many children these are very small issues. But aren't small issues like this the stuff of childhood? Small personal things from children's points of view often make the most impact and from adults' points of view they raise serious questions. Such as isn't it the small things over which children can have control which help them later on to sort out the big things? What messages do we give to children about autonomy? How often do we trust children with real choice? Where are their safe places to play which allow normal risks? How do we show or explain about danger without taking away children's confidence? How soon can autonomy begin and how do we adults really encourage it in practice?

BEGINNING TO MAKE CHOICES

Just as there has been a great deal of progress made in the research of young children's language so has there been into the early play of babies. Some of this addresses all those questions. We have been particularly lucky in Britain to have had the wealth of experience of early years' educational pioneers as well as families and carers who are specialists in this early stage of development. They have all added to our knowledge about young children and their learning.

We are now even more fortunate to have had such work of quality formalised further and have had videos produced on the subject by Elinor Goldschmeid. These are available from the National Children's Bureau (Goldschmeid 1989, 1990). They have been filmed in inner city centres where Elinor's approach is used with all the children for a part of each day. Before their production Elinor had already made an enormous contribution as a practitioner, lecturer and trainer in the field of child care in the UK, Italy and Spain. Her imaginative work shows us empowerment and autonomy being achieved very simply and inexpensively in practice. Any thoughts about the aggressive interpretation of power fades as the calm and peaceful atmosphere of these babies and infants playing is captured by her on the screen with their carers.

Under the apt title of 'Infants at Work' Elinor produced a first training video of babies from eight months in 1984. This is of particular value for all people who care for babies; whether individually or in a group setting. Her second video 'Heuristic Play', in which she collaborated with Anita Hughes, extends this early work to involve young children of under three who are inevitably more active and more skilled in their use of materials. Elinor took the meaning of the word 'heuristic' to be 'serves to discover or to reach understanding of'.

Both these videos show that babies and young infants are able to make their own choices in their play in babyhood, to sustain interest over materials or objects which puzzle them and to play sociably from much earlier ages than was assumed from previous research. Even very young babies can be seen choosing their favourite items positively and exploring them happily for long periods of time. Most of these objects are everyday things which can be found around the home or natural materials such as cones, shells and pebbles which come from the environment. At these early stages, real interest usually consists of all the positive body language including our smiles; all of which enhances the babies' early self-esteem and helps to build their confidence.

The second video shows how many simple and inexpensive objects appeal to the increased skills of the young children. It shows a number of ways in which the various junk materials are used by the infants; filling and emptying, slotting, selecting and discarding, recognising similarities and differences, piling, poking and balancing. Sometimes the children can be seen succeeding in their intention, sometimes not, but always trying to achieve their own purpose. The notion of sharing is not forced upon them and they are not continually interrupted. If needed, gentle intervention by the carer enables the infants to learn how to negotiate for belongings without needing to resort to aggression. This valuable skill develops further as they learn from their carers' example how to use their language to such ends. Some of the infants do choose to play with others and to work together but on the whole they chose to play alone and nothing is artificially forced upon them by the adults who sit near them. All of this work is important for us when we begin to examine children's rights; what we need to do in practice to enable young children to claim them.

This work is founded on a strong belief about the capabilities of babies and young children; knowledge about how their curiosity shapes their early learning and about the quality support which empowers them and allows their autonomy.

CHILDREN'S 'QUALITY' PEOPLE

Elinor fits the following analysis of children's views of the sort of adults who are needed by them to put the Articles into practice. From the many things which children and young people have said or written, they fit into three distinct groups, or the Children's Alternative 3 Rs:

Adults should be:

- *related* to children positively, loving towards them, able to talk to children truthfully and find time to listen to children seriously

- *respectful* enough to acknowledge that babies and young children are already people, can be trusted to make their own choices and of eventually expressing their own views

- *responsible* in the way that they care and provide for children and in the example they give in their own attitudes, choices and use of power.

RECENT CONFERENCES

Tenth Annual Conference of Association of Beziers Enfance: Partnerships wiht Families. September 22–24 1994, Beziers, France. Organised by L'Association Beziers Enfance.

International Early Years' Conference: Shaping the Future. October 12–14, 1994, Manchester, UK. Organised by Manchester Metropolitan University and Save the Children.

National Conference: Teacher Education Under Threat. July 8th, 1995, University of Nottingham. Organised by TACTYC (Professional Association of Early Childhood Educators).

Fifth European Conference on the Quality of Early Childhood Education. September 7–9, 1995, Paris, France. Organised by ECERA (European Early Childhood Education Research Association) and INRP (Institut National de Recherche Pédagogique).

FURTHER READING

Bruce, T. (1987) *Early Childhood Education.* London: Hodder and Stoughton.

Bruner, J. and Haste, H. (1987) *Making Sense.* London: Methuen.

Cousins, J. (1990) 'Are you little Humpty Dumpties floating or sinking?' *Journal of Tutors of Advanced Courses for Teachers of Young Children 10,* 2.

Cousins, J. and Hughes, M (1990) 'Teachers' perceptions or children's language.' In D. Wray (ed) *Emerging Partnerships: Current Research in Language and Literacy.* Clevedon, PA: Multilingual Matters.

Donaldson, M. (1986) *Children's Minds.* Glasgow: Fontana.

Goldschmeid, E. (1989) 'Heuristic play with objects.' In V. Williams (ed) *Babies in Daycare.* Daycare Trust/National Children's Bureau.

Goldschmeid, E. (1990) 'Play and learning in the first year of life.' In D. Rouse (ed) *Babies and Toddlers: Carers and Educators Quality for the Under Threes.* London: National Children's Bureau.

Grieve, R. and Hughes, M. (1983) 'On asking children bizarre questions.' In M. Donaldson, R. Grieve and C. Pratt *Early Childhood.* Oxford: Blackwell.

Grieve, R. and Hughes, M. (1990) *Understanding Children.* Oxford: Blackwell.

Harris, P. (1989) *Children and Emotion.* Oxford: Blackwell.

John, M. (ed) (1996) *Children in Our Charge: The Child's Right to Resources.* London: Jessica Kingsley Publishers.

National Children's Bureau (1992) *Children Now.* London: NCB.

Pinsent, P. (ed) (1992) *Language, Culture and Young Children.* London: David Fulton in association with Roehampton Institute.

ACKNOWLEDGEMENT

I would like to thank Elinor for her kind permission to use her work in this chapter and for her generous time in listening to me during its preparation.

Watt, J. (1990) *Early Education:The Current Debate.* Edinburgh: Scottish Academic Press Report.

Wells, G. and Nicholls, J. (1985) *Language and Learning: An Interactional Perspective.* London: Falmer.

Willes, M. (1981) 'Children becoming pupils.' In C. Adelman (ed) *Uttering and Muttering.* London: Grant McIntyre.

CHAPTER FIFTEEN

The Construction of Autonomy
Some Paradoxes of Socialisation

Rudi Dallos

We often hear that some people can't make their minds up about things, they have difficulty making decisions or fail to see that they have other options open to them. To allow children rights and freedom is commendable but we need to think also about how they learn to exercise their rights to make decisions about their own needs and welfare. Existentialist philosophers such as Jean Paul Sartre (1943) see freedom as a burden, we are condemned to be free; as opposed to humanistic psychologists such as George Kelly (1955) who see choice as the positive potential to change and grow.

How do children develop a sense of autonomy and how might this be nurtured? Without asking these questions, talk of rights might simply run the risk of assuming what children want and imposing adult wisdom on them. However, in efforts to encourage or *teach autonomy* we encounter a paradox: how can a child act autonomously if we have merely taught them to do so? It is like saying:

PARENT: I wish you wouldn't always agree with me, think for yourself.

CHILD: OK I will... No I won't...

Yet this is the dilemma that parents face. How do we enable children to think for themselves, to disagree with our views if they want to, to stand up for themselves and their rights but without coercing them into simply conforming to our liberal sentiments? Underlying this question are assumptions our society makes about what it is to be human and whether children are in some fundamental ways different to adults. George Kelly argues that all of us, including children, are intrinsically autonomous and that we do not need to learn to be free. The problem instead is that society constantly tries to remind us that we are not, and should not be free. Skinner (1971) pointed out that it is not only coercion and punishment which restricts freedom but the seductive power of rewards for 'appropriate', socially-approved behaviour.

What does psychology have to offer to help us here? Traditionally the debate has been phrased in terms of nature versus nurture: are we born as formless blobs of clay to be moulded by experience or do we have fundamental qualities? Evidence from studies of mothers and young infants suggests that both are true. Almost from birth babies not only respond but initiate interaction with their mothers and others. Parents do however provide a 'scaffolding' or framework that either facilitates or impedes children's development of autonomy. Autonomy can be encouraged by constructing situations in which a child can experiment and gain a sense of influence over his or her physical and social environment.

Mothers as double-agents: When a young child is playing, for example with some bricks, a mother may say 'That's a clever girl, you're building a little house aren't you?' This frames the child's actions as deliberate and purposeful, and also starts to provide a vocabulary whereby the child can reflect on her own actions.

Teasing: Game-playing and humour may serve to underline the deliberateness of action, for example, a father offers a sweet and, as the child grabs for it, pulls it back and says 'Do you want it. You do don't you...'

THE DESTRUCTION OF AUTOMONY

Such examples tell us something about the construction of autonomy but work with families in therapy tells us also about its destruction. Children's development of autonomy can become stunted when they become immersed in the marital conflicts, power struggles and stresses preoccupying their parents. There are a number of core concepts from the field of family therapy, each of which offers some insights about freedom and choice and show a sense of autonomy is constructed within the dynamics of the family.

Enmeshment

Members of a family can become so immersed in each other's thoughts and feelings that a child may subsequently find it difficult to have a sense of privacy. Experiences of pleasure and pain – as in food, sexuality or even illness – can, rather than becoming within the control of the child, remain the property of the parents, for example, when parents 'know' what the child needs to eat or whether they are really ill or when they intrude on the child's early sexual explorations. Similarly, there may be diffuse rules in a family about personal space – does the child have rights about the state and contents of 'their own room?' Without some such boundaries she may find it difficult to function autonomously in the world outside the family. We could say she has been *taught* to be *unable to think for herself.*

Conflict detouring

When parents are in conflict, or are too emotionally drained by a variety of stresses, a child can become pulled in to take sides or become a scapegoat, for example by developing a problem such as truanting from school. The child is, in a sense, compelled to make a choice – usually an unconscious one – to save his parents by becoming disturbed or ill, which distracts them from their own conflicts and worries.

Double-binds

One or both parents may construct no-win situations for a child, for example, when a child is encouraged into a flirtatious or sexual relationship with a parent and then punished for being provocative. If they refuse their parent's advances they are punished for being unloving and if they accept they are also punished. Attempts to reveal these games are denied and it may be suggested that the child is deluded or mischievous. This can lead a child to develop a sense of guilt and 'helplessness', a belief that whatever they choose to do in life will be wrong.

OPTIMISIM?

We can end up with a fairly bleak catalogue of the damage that families can inflict on children's emerging sense of self and autonomy. The increased awareness of abuse in families and moves to protect children can at least halt some of the more grotesque forms of abuse. However, we also need to be more aware of how the day-to-day, ordinary dynamics of family life can result in a stunting of children's development of autonomy. There is no simple formula about how to get it right but some potentially positive factors can be identified.

- Meta-communication: discussing with children what is going on in the family, how people are feeling and, most important, giving children the right to comment on what they think is going on.

- Reflexivity: encouraging self-awareness, for example, by parents both talking and encouraging children to reflect on what they are doing and why.

- Clear boundaries: it is important for children and adults to have privacy, rights to their own emotions and time to think. Talking in families can often mean that children have their parents' stuff dumped on them whether or not they want it, and whether or not they can handle it.

In families, liking each other helps, of course, but this in itself is dependent on understanding, empathy and allowing space for a child to decide what he feels and wants to feel – to be allowed to think about and for himself.

COMMENT FROM THE YOUNG PEOPLE'S EVALUATION PANEL [1]

We thought the talk was very interesting and useful. There are a few points on which we would like to comment. Dr Dallos used the word 'autonomy' which we, and other members of the Young People's Evaluation Panel, did not understand. This meant that our understanding of this talk was slightly limited. Rudi should've explained what 'autonomy' meant.

We would like to commend him on the way he talked about us; being young people ourselves, we agree that parents do seem to mould 'clay-selves' into their own image. This is inevitably going to be the case as children tend to copy their parents' actions. As this case is so inevitable, we feel that parents should set a good example to their children, but what indeed is a 'good example'? We think Rudi made a valuable point when he said 'children are what we make them'. Children are bound to copy their parents because they want to please them and be like them because they look up to them. Looking at it from the parents' view, it could be hard because it's impossible to set a good example when important factors of life, like other people the child is going to meet, are going to contribute to the child's attitude. Parents should find the time to sit down with their child, and discuss things, and find out that what the child's views are on matters. They shouldn't force their views on the child as the child, later on in life, won't succeed in making decisions and forming opinions.

The things he talked about we found especially interesting as we could relate to such situations as the 'double-bind' and 'enmeshment'. I was surprised when he talked about 'enmeshment'. My mother is an 'enmesher' if you like, and up until now I didn't realise that there was a name for this kind of behaviour. Where my mother is concerned, I sometimes have to take the back seat in situations and I always thought I was supposed to, but now I know I don't, I'm going to say what I want to say, and I think children should know about 'freedom of speech' – basically, the points that Dr Dallos made – for example, letting children have their own emotions, letting them reflect on their own experiences and letting them make their own decisions, rather than the complete enmeshment situation that occurs so often in our lives today.

---

1   Names withheld to protect the 'enmeshing' mother!

FURTHER READING

Burham, J. (1986) *Family Therapy*. London: Tavistock Publishers.

Brazelton, T.B., Kislwoski, B. and Main, M. (1974) 'The origins of reciprocity: the early mother–infant interaction.' In M. Lewin and A. Rosenblum (eds) *The Effect of the Infant on its Carer*. New York: Wiley.

Dallos, R. (1991) *Family Belief System, Therapy and Change*. Milton Keynes: Open University Press.

Pollner, M. and Wikler, L. (1985) 'The social construction of unreality.' *Family Process* 24, 241–259.

REFERENCES

Kelly, G. (1955) *The Psychology of Personal Constructs*. Chicago: University of Chicago Press.

Sartre, J.P. (1943) *L'Être et le Néant (Being and Nothingness)*. Paris: Methuen 1969 (English edition).

Skinner, B.F. (1971) *Beyond Freedom and Dignity*. London: Penguin Books.

CHAPTER SIXTEEN

Children Teaching Adults to Listen to Them

Jeff Lewis

Articles 12 and 13 of the UN Convention of the Rights of the Child make it clear that children have a right to express their views. This involves not just the expression of those views but also having them listened to and taken into account in any matter which affects the child. Much of the work included in this volume has concentrated on the expressive elements of those Articles. This chapter turns attention to the responsibilities for effective listening that those rights imply. It recounts, as an exploratory case study, the preparations and theoretical background to a workshop that was run at the World Conference on the UN Convention held at the University of Exeter in 1992. This modest project is used here to focus issues that arise from a number of concerns which are intrinsic to research and practice in children's rights and also central to the way in which the whole educational process is connected with securing the rights of children. In planning such a workshop we had a desire to include children of all ages in the conference, not just as observers, but as active contributors and, in some instances, as chairs, evaluators or leaders of some of the sessions. This workshop was discussed, negotiated with, planned and presented by a group of school students and run as an interactive session with conference delegates thoroughly involved in it. Such a presentation involving active participation is often daunting – even to a seasoned professional conference performer, let alone an inexperienced group of nine- and ten-year-olds. Nevertheless, it was in the spirit of the conference but it tested our faith in the belief that facilitating the voice of children in this way was a pedagogic reality and that the final result would demonstrate not a polished pro-adult performance, but the very real fruits of giving young people the responsibility for raising consciousness about their own needs and views. The subject of the workshop was to be practical ways to help children to find a voice and be heard. The Children Act in the UK stipulates that a young person must have their views heard on any matter relating to their treatment. In order for this aspiration to be translated into practice the following pre-conditions must be met:

1. The young must be aware of their rights relevant to the situation they find themselves in.

2. They must have the necessary skill and confidence to state their case.

3. They must have an audience that is willing and able to listen to them.

What, then, is the role of education in meeting these pre-requisites? It could be argued that programmes of instruction could fulfil the first and second conditions listed above, but that without a receptive audience their words could fall on deaf ears, and thus the provisions of the Children Act would become a mere piece of rhetoric encapsulating a pious wish but unable to alter the status quo. The theoretical background to the workshop was based on the idea that a successful programme of communication skills for young people would also help them to help others listen. This idea is based in counselling psychology (particularly Egan 1975), Group work theory (see Thacker *et al.* 1992; Feest 1992), and the pioneering work on creative listening by Rachel Pinney (1981).

Pinney suggests that our society is marked by a failure to listen, and that this failure runs through all sections of society. Young children are probably the group who are least listened to in any meaningful way, often being deliberately kept in ignorance of the matters that concern them, being encouraged not to speak up for themselves (seen but not heard, cheeky, precocious, 'a right little madam' and many other common phrases give a telling picture of the model of appropriate communicative behaviour we expect of children) and having most of the decisions that affect their lives made for them on the grounds that they are not yet able to make wise decisions on their own behalf. The child's 'best interests' and adult doubts about the child's competence have often been excuses for not involving them in the decision-making process. An elegant challenge to such paternalistic notions is raised by Rosenak (1982). One of the first, and most well known of Pinney's techniques, the Childrens' Hour, in which the child is given a regular period of uninterrupted, non-directive attention by an adult, was claimed to give the child a quality of inner peace largely unknown in the West. This may seem to be an immodest claim, but if the frustrations that arise when one is not listened to are surveyed, and the large numbers of adults seeking counselling and therapy may be some small indication of a desperate need to be listened to, a picture emerges of a society which indeed fails to listen and in so doing fails to satisfy a basic human need in its members.

It is not difficult to identify the source of our society's failure to listen, especially where it effects the youngest members of our society. The first source of this failure probably resides in the socially necessary practice of conversation. To converse with others fulfils many social and personal needs, yet the skills of pleasant conversation are not the skills of good listening; in fact we become systematically practised in unhelpful listening behaviours. As our minds work considerably faster than the tongues of others, we have a great deal of mental capacity to use whilst someone else is talking. Amongst the things we use our mind for are thinking about what we will say next, noticing what else is happening, starting to wander off into thoughts about experiences of our own that the speaker has reminded us of, seeking for witty, wise or helpful responses, looking for an opportunity to interject or to change the subject so that we can talk rather than listen, thinking of something else entirely, or wishing we were involved in that altogether more interesting conversation on the next table. All of this can be taking place whilst attempting to give an appearance of interest and involvement. As conversation thus typified is about passing time and making convivial, if sometimes ritualised, contact with others and not listening in any meaningful way, no harm is necessarily done. It is quite possible to spend an entire evening in non-stop conversation in a group of friends and remember very little of what was said, only that a good time was had by all. On the next occasion when this company assembles much of the same conversation, jokes and anecdotes would be repeated without detracting from the bonhomie thus engendered. When it comes to the situation where someone actually needs to be listened to, however, these habits arising from social conversing can be very unhelpful. It is my view that young people, in attempting to be heard, will be treated to more than their fair share of interruption, questioning, well intended advice and oft-repeated anecdote, causing them to give up hope of actually being listened to and quickly being transformed into a less than attentive spectator whilst their older and wiser 'listener' waxes lyrical on some cautionary wisdom for the benefit of the frustrated victim.

The realities of life in schools make it inevitable that teachers will often deploy the very worst of listening habits. It is simply impossible to attend simultaneously to the listening needs of thirty or more individual children, especially as the teacher needs to attend to her own agenda of actually teaching the curriculum and directing classroom traffic. The teacher therefore becomes skilled in preventing interruption, often in a non-oppressive way, so as to secure conformity in the class and give herself sufficient 'space' to get on with the things she has to get through. In order to do this she will learn how to delay interjections until a more appropriate time, move children gently back onto task, cut children off in mid-sentence with an appropriate answer, stop all conversation in order to direct a general instruction to the class, or engage a repertoire of verbal and non-verbal techniques to indicate that speaking is not appropriate or welcome at this time.

This may be necessary, one could argue, in many aspects of the social world, and has benefits in allowing the purposes of schooling to be expedited. It is known, however, (see Jackson 1968) that constant, unremitting exposure to such experiences lead school students to become resigned to the fact that some important human communications are unavailable in the normal school situation, and that in order to achieve the task of being schooled without too many admonishments they must learn the hidden curriculum of rules, routines and regulations which leads to them leaving their personal anxieties, interests and concerns largely at the school gate such that when a parent asks them what they did at school the inevitable answer is 'nothing'. Problems really arise when teachers and other adults are called upon to genuinely listen to a child, and old conversational and teacherly habits combine to ensure a less than ideal listening transaction.

Whilst the difficulties we encounter in learning run through all levels of society, they are heightened in the case of young people due to structural inequalities in transactions with adults. The theoretical work of Habermas (1989) on ideal speech situations helps us understand why this might be so. An ideal speech situation rests on certain assumptions, among which are equality of the participants and freedom from conventional restraints, so that each participant's assumptions are rendered problematic, and that the validity claims of each utterance are open to scrutiny. It is clear that most adult/ child speech situations are not of this type, neither, as Blake (1994) reminds us, is it desirable that they should always be. If, however, true discourse, as Habermas characterises it, should be necessary – as it would be if an adult were to attempt to genuinely understand the viewpoint of a child – it is likely that our normal unproblematic assumptions and conventions that govern child/adult interaction would make such a discourse exceedingly difficult. Again, our habits may override our good intentions when a young person needs to be listened to.

The optimistic feature of the work of Pinney and others is that we learn that if the programme of communication skills offered to those who rely upon certain qualities in their listeners is of a certain type, then the very practice of these skills helps the listener to be more effective almost by proxy, that is, the child, by learning about listening and communication skills, can help to shape and improve the listening skills of the adult. If the activity of listening can be defined as helping others to speak, then the act of effective communication may be said to include helping another to help oneself speak, that is create a context in which real expression of ideas, opinions, hopes and fears can genuinely take place. It follows then that in order for the three pre-requisites listed above to be met, young people need to be helped with the first two in such a way that their practice makes the third more likely.

In order to make these ideas available to the conference delegates in a concrete form, the group of school students were to present a session based on helping adults to listen to them. The children were from a middle school in Exeter where groupwork and listening skills had been developed for some years based on the Developmental Group Work system devised by Leslie Button (see Thacker *et al.* 1992 and Feest 1992). The children had considerable familiarity with listening skills activities as they had experienced these as part of their groupwork programme. Moreover, older children from the school had been invited to come to the Faculty of Education at the University of Plymouth to lead sessions in groupwork for student teachers. For this particular group of younger children, and for their teacher, their going out to offer instruction to adults was a totally new venture. Daunting though this prospect may have been for all concerned, it was decided at an early stage that the class would have as much control as possible over the programme for the conference presentation. This meant that the teacher and I would have to overcome our desire that the class put on a credible presentation and place trust in them to devise and present an authentic offering and confine ourselves to supportive and facilitative roles. However much we might have been ideologically committed to such a position, in practice it was not easy.

The class, having been briefed about the conference and its background, quickly agreed to take part and set about deciding what it was that they would like to draw to the attention of the conference delegates. We had a class groupwork session on Rights as they saw them, and from this they identified their central need as being for the actual views of young people to be taken into account when their rights were being discussed by adults. In order to begin selecting appropriate tasks for the conference presentation they then brain-stormed the qualities of good and poor listeners, and reflected upon feelings when we are not listened to, and by contrast, the way we felt when someone took the time and trouble to really listen to us.

Slowly a possible pattern for the presentation began to emerge. The class would introduce themselves, demonstrate some negative listening behaviours from a child's point of view, engage the audience in some listening and communicating activities and then evaluate the session with the audience. The class divided into small groups and devised short sketches which encapsulated their experience of not being listened to. To my surprise, none of the scenarios depicted professional interactions. They all involved domestic events; a child with something important to say being ignored by a mother and her neighbour, a young boy vainly attempting to communicate with his Dad while a football match is on television, and a girl being taken shopping for clothes and having all her wishes ignored or overridden by her mother and a shop assistant. All the scenarios neatly captured the frustrations experienced by these young people, and it is highly probable that some of the watching adults winced as they recognised some of their own behaviour behind the sketches.

As work continued on preparing the presentation I often had to 'sit on my hands' in order to suppress the teacherly urge to suggest ways in which they could improve aspects of their delivery, reminding myself that the aim was to present the issues from a young person's viewpoint, not to put my own ideas into their heads. Eventually they honed the event down, fitting it to a time schedule so that enough time was left for feedback and evaluation. The group were then left to write the introductions and links. The final rehearsal allowed the very natural nervous tension to be vented through embarrassed giggles and tongue-tied introductions. Nevertheless, there was a strong feeling that it would be all right on the day and that what was really needed was the context of reality provided by an expectant and interested audience.

And so to the Conference itself. As we had hoped, the group rose to the occasion being heartened by the willingness of the audience of sympathetic professionals to be directed by this group of young children. The scenarios described above were followed by a series of communication exercises. In threes, the audience took turns in listening to each other and noting effective listening behaviours, both verbal and non-verbal, and evaluating each other's perform- ance. Clarity of instruction was explored as pairs of participants sitting back to back, possessing sets of different shaped blocks, assembled them into a pattern and tried to convey the exact configuration to their partner who had to assemble an exact replica; this exercise certainly reminded some professionals how easily we can fail to give clear instructions, and then blame our classes for not listening! We then all sat in a circle and evaluated the occasion. The participants were warm in their appreciation of the group's efforts, which was an extremely heartening experience for the group members. They in turn expressed their pleasure at being given an important opportunity, and at the evidence of respect which they felt came from the participants. The class teacher was clearly proud of her class and felt gratified that the trust and faith she had in their ability to carry out the presentation had been so adequately repaid. The Young People's Evaluation Panel who were present at all conference sessions saw it as a unique session, though I feel that they had questions as to how much control the group really had over the content and conduct of the session. My own recollection of the event was the tangible growth in mutual respect engendered by the simple expedient of adults and young people fully attending to each other from a position of equality.

Taken simply as an event, the session justified our decision to involve young people at all levels at the conference. It may be that one of the greatest obstacles to children securing their rights is simply the adult belief that they are not as able as they manifestly are. When they are given the opportunity, they rise to the occasion and their confidence in themselves seems to grow. Beyond this, the planning and presentation underlined for me the importance of structured programmes of group work, communication skills and assertiveness, together with authentic opportunities to practice these skills in a context of meaningful transactions, as a means to helping children find the voice that the Children Act and the UN Convention indicates they have the right to use.

As I suggested at the beginning of this chapter, whilst it is necessary for young people to be fully informed concerning their rights, and to have the necessary skills to give voice to their own wishes, the greatest imperative is to engender a listening culture amongst the adults to whom they must direct their voice. It was perhaps the lesson of all the work connected with this session, and the session itself, that by involving young people fully in their education, and allowing them to learn and teach alongside adults in conditions approaching an ideal speech situation, that all of these aspects of children's rights within the educational process could be usefully incorporated within a single approach.

BIBLIOGRAPHY

Blake, N. (1994) *Ideal Speech Conditions, Modernism Discourse and Education.* Papers of the Annual Conference. Philosophy of Education Society of Great Britain. Oxford.

Egan, G. (1975) *The Skilled Helper.* Fifth Edition. Monterey, California: Brooks/Cole.

Feest, G. (1992) *Listening Skills.* Crediton: Southgate Publishers.

Habermas, J. (1989) *Moral Consciousness and Communicative Action.* Cambridge, Mass: MIT Press.

Jackson, P. (1968) *Life in Classrooms.* New York: Holt, Reinhart and Winston.

Pinney, R. (1981) *Creative Listening. A to Z.* London: R. Pinney.

Rosenak, J.N.L. (1982) 'Should children be subject to paternalistic restrictions on their liberties?' *Journal of Philosophy of Education 16,* 1, 89–96.

Thacker, J., Stoate, P. and Feest, G. (1992) *Groupwork Skills.* Crediton: Southgate Publishers.

PART EIGHT

A Fair Hearing?

CHAPTER SEVENTEEN

Listening to the Street Children of Mwanza[1]

Rakesh Rajani and Mustafa Kudrati

ABDALLAH'S STORY

In the early morning of 16 November 1992 there was a loud banging on our door. It was Abdallah, breathless, with a terrified expression on his face. He blurted out what had happened. Just before sunrise the police had begun to round-up all the *walala nje* and *waombaomba*, the 'outside sleepers' and 'beggar' street people. They were woken up with sticks and told to get into a big lorry. Those who were slow or resisted were hit harder and brutally dragged into the lorry, their few belongings scattered about. In the days that followed the police and the traditional *sungusungu* defence patrols made the nights hell for the children. They were harassed, beaten, chased, made to hop like rabbits, dunked in open (and very filthy) gutters and locked up in cramped, mosquito infested rooms for the night. The children we met late at night (in the back kitchen of a local restaurant) looked exhausted, like weary old men. They were terrified of the night, having run out of places to hide. It appeared to us as if the intention was to make the lives of the street children as difficult as possible, so that they would go away somewhere, disappear, cease to be a problem.

Through it all we were astounded by the children's resiliency. They nursed each other's wounds, using cigarette packets and sellotape. They helped each other find safer places. They made deals with the police and night-watchmen, using bribes and sweet-talk, to let them sleep undisturbed. They used their plight to extract special gifts from sympathetic friends, like getting bigger

---

1 This is an abbreviated version of a report 'Street Children of Mwanza; a situation analysis' which was published in 1994 by *kuleana* center for Children's Rights, PO Box 27, Mwanza, Tanzania, Tel/Fax 255 68 50486 (from whom a copy of the full report can be obtained) in association with UNICEF – Tanzania.

helpings of food for less money and cajoling us to follow-through on treatments for scabies and worms. The few among them who went to school amazed us by being punctual and cheerful in the morning when they had hardly got any sleep at night. They revelled each other through the night with stories of how they had managed to avoid arrest – finding pleasure and strength in thinking of themselves as fugitives from injustice living on the edge.

But we also found out, in quiet conversations, that these tough little survivors were also hurting. They told us of how they missed their mothers, of how a friend was wetting his pants in his sleep, of not being able to handle a single more night. They grieved for the loss of their family through AIDS, although they do not let themselves name it as such, and for the loss of their childhood, a cherished bicycle, a secret tree-tunnel, lost brothers and sisters. Girls especially worried about physical and sexual violence at the hands of adults, often recalling their own horrible experiences of the past. They worried about their friends who had been taken to Butimba Prison. When we gave them crayons, they drew pictures of big people beating little people, and of themselves swirling around in stormy circles.

INTRODUCTION

The idea for carrying out a situation analysis of street children in Mwanza emerged from our personal experiences and commitments. Both of us had worked with homeless and troubled youth in the USA for a number of years. Our later academic work focused on the situations of children in especially difficult circumstances in the third world urban contexts. Our thinking about children was challenged in powerful ways during the process of preparing the UN Convention on the Rights of the Child.

Upon return to Tanzania, these experiences influenced our perceptions and shaped our concerns about the life of children on the streets. In 1991 the number of street children was increasing rapidly; their situation appeared to be especially difficult; the need for action felt urgent. Several groups had established themselves in Dar es Salaam, but nothing was being done in Mwanza. It made sense to respond to the situation by working with the children to improve their present lives and prospects for the future.

We realised the need to carry out a situation analysis with the children first. It was clear that we needed to understand their lives – their histories, present situations and future aspirations – to inform the planning and implementation of our response. The study began in September 1992 with funding from UNICEF.

In the course of the seven months of the study, events revealing a complete disregard for children's rights occurred with an astonishing frequency. These troubling experiences have become a major focus of this study. Abdallah's story and the events of 16 November 1992 are a case in point. It represents many of the themes that characterise the situation of street children in Mwanza: violence, sexual abuse, stigma, prejudice, emotional trauma, a lack of voice, the denial of their right to speak and to determine their own lives; as well as remarkable resiliency, ingenuity, and a fierce determination to live.

Within a year, the situation was very different. The violence had ceased. The children were less withdrawn and depressed, more lively and cheerful. At *kuleana* the children felt they had places and people to turn to, a community that would stand with them. Allies had been made in the police, *sungusungu* forces and the courts. The public was more aware, more thoughtful, and less prone to harass indiscriminately.

Yet Abdallah's story continues to provide a warning to what can go terribly wrong when a community fails to respect and to take care of its children. The reasons for which children end up on the streets are outlined in our full report, likewise a description of the situation of children on the streets. We have made every effort to verify the accuracy of information through direct observation and cross-checking sources. The final section focuses on issues that are a cause for major concern and that form the dominant experience of street children in Mwanza.

Our study's most important conclusion is this: the well-being of children is inextricably linked with a respect for the rights of children. Welfare and piecemeal approaches outside the rubric of children's rights only go so far and ultimately fail. Project planning cannot afford to ignore the larger issues. We need to learn to listen to children and to build genuine partnerships based on trust and respect. The task is enormous. It will take no less than challenging and unlearning the debilitating relationship of hierarchy between adults and children.

Our study was carried out to help to understand the situation and to prepare us for our work with the street children of Mwanza. We hope that it will also be useful to others concerned about street children in Tanzania. Nothing would delight us more than to find out that it has inspired people to action to promote the rights of children.

RATIONALE FOR THE STUDY

The following text was written in August 1992. It outlines the background and rationale for carrying out the situation analysis.

As in other urban centers in Tanzania, the number of unaccompanied children on the streets of Mwanza is growing very fast. Children as young as four years old are seen roaming about engaged in various kinds of activities and survival strategies. Explanations such as increasing poverty, urbanisation, and more recently AIDS and its effect of weakening extended family systems, are given to account for the 'problem'. Street children are viewed as poor and deprived, lacking the care of parents, desperately in need of somebody to help them. They are seen as needing to be rescued from their plight, usually to be housed in orphanages, and in this way spared from the bad socialisation of the streets that may lead them into 'vagrancy' and 'criminal activities'.

While these explanations bear truth, and while the concern and action that they sometimes inspire are important, the extent to which they are accurate and in the interests of the children remains questionable. All too often historical stereotypes distort the images of who street children are, their reasons for being on the street, the relationships in which they are engaged, and their desires for the present and future. As a consequence, the kinds of responses adults organise may not be appropriate and welcomed by the children.

At the heart of this difficulty is that most of us have very limited relationships with children on the streets. These interactions may be no more than passing observations, brief transactions or annoying confrontations with pathetic faces begging for food or picking pockets. In turn, children know, and will, deliberately feign the kinds of behaviours that will get them what they want. In these circumstances a convenient and 'safe' distance is maintained. Unrepresentative images are reinforced. Mutual relationships between street children and adults are hardly initiated or encouraged.

The experiences of working with children on the streets in Latin America and Asia have shown that many patronising efforts to take care of street children have ended in virtual disaster. Orphanages in particular have turned out to be disastrous places that children hate, that are much too expensive to run, difficult to control and not conducive to appropriate child socialisation.

The increasing awareness of children's rights has raised important questions of whether organisations purporting to work on behalf of children are actually working in the interests of children. The need to learn about the children's lives from the children themselves has become apparent. As such, children are less to be 'contained' and more to become the protagonists of their own struggle, supported by adult partners.

The experiences of working with street children in various parts of the world can be useful in thinking through the situation in Mwanza. Substantive relationships with street children will need to be established, on as mutual a basis as possible, before any programme planning is undertaken. These relationships take time, but are necessary, to learn about the histories and situations of street children and to ensure their participation in informing and implementing the kinds of responses that make sense.

This is especially important because the situations of street children are not monolithic. For instance, if most street children maintain some sort of links with their families, interventions that encourage a stronger re-integration and support to the family should be encouraged. However, if a child avoids her home because she is abused there, the intervention will need to be considered more carefully. The situation of children of adults who are homeless also requires special attention. In all likelihood the responses in this case will need to be worked out in terms of their larger family units.

Not all interventions ought to aim to remove children from the streets. In certain circumstances, *given what is possible*, the streets may provide the most viable form of livelihood for some children. In these sorts of cases children may seek assistance to enhance their street survival strategies. For instance, those running small businesses may want more reasonable working hours, better profit margins and less police harassment. They may prefer better service facilities such as access to showers, lockers, and informal literacy classes arranged along a flexible schedule. Others may desire a place to play and crayons with which to draw. In some cases no interventions whatsoever are required. For instance, weekend door-to-door vegetable sellers have carefully negotiated an independent and healthy life between home, school, and street.

The situations of children are complicated and made more urgent by the AIDS epidemic. We have heard numerous troubling accounts of the difficulties of children whose parents are ill and unable to provide adequate care. Reports from counsellors emphasise the need to respond to children orphaned because of AIDS. Our limited work on the streets listening to children's stories confirms the serious impact of the epidemic. It affects basic livelihood needs such as food, shelter, clothing, and the capacity to attend school, forcing some children to engage in inappropriate survival strategies on the streets. Moreover, it is also clear that AIDS causes immense emotional trauma that needs special attention for healing to take place. While we can draw on some community resources to respond to the crisis, we also need to think harder and deeper to learn to provide adequate care.

Appropriate responses need to be worked out carefully in different communities, social circumstances, and between different groups of children. The particular ways in which numerous socio-economic and personal factors relate to, and are complicated by, the AIDS epidemic need to be better understood. Programme responses can only be intelligibly constructed by first doing a situation analysis of the sort we propose to do. It is critical that this be done with the active participation of street children, so that their concerns and hopes can help guide action.

METHODOLOGY AND APPROACH

There are many kinds of children on the streets of Mwanza. Our study focused on children who live and sleep on the street, of which there were approximately 240 in July 1993. (There are considerably more children who spend their day time on the streets and go home at night.)

Our extensive research background in working with street children served as a useful framework to conceptualising and implementing the study. Several documents were consulted in preparation, including academic papers, socio-economic data, newspapers, project experiences and government publications. Two texts were particularly useful in designing the study: the UNICEF Methodological Series 'Children in Especially Difficult Circumstances', especially the Methodological Guide on Situation Analysis (Series no 6) and the Guidelines for the Application of No 6 (Series no 8), and Fabio Dallape's (1987) 'An Experience with Street Children', based on work of the Undugu Society in Nairobi.

Before we began, we were acutely aware of the special issues involved in approaching street children. Many of them were likely to have had extremely negative experiences of adults, both at home and on the street. In this context it would have been natural for children to mistrust our work and intentions. Therefore, our most important aim was to build relationships of mutual trust with the children. We tried to be mindful of this throughout the study.

The following approach was used.

Street Work

We began the study in September 1992. Initially we observed street children's movements and talked with them informally. Our primary aim during this stage was to get to know some of the children and establish relationships of trust and interest. While we had the objectives and themes outlined above in mind, our approach was relaxed and avoided probing. We also encouraged and elicited the children's input in determining the shape of the study. Information gathered was unstructured and not recorded in the presence of children. We listened to their stories, and shared our own. When they needed medical attention, we tried to facilitate care at local health centres. We intervened when we saw them being harassed.

Team Approach and Building up Case Histories

In Phase Two a group of four male street children and ourselves began to work together on definitions, areas to be covered, basic questionnaire outline, how to go about interviewing, and so on. Our primary aim in this phase was to build up accurate case histories and learn about the basic characteristics of street life. We consulted each other often, but did not work as a formal team. The children in the group introduced us to their peers and served as our primary informants during the first four months of the study. They also participated in carrying out action-research alongside us. A baseline matrix, containing over 200 specific and open-ended questions, was developed and information collected over time. During this time relevant authorities – such as community leaders, welfare officers and police – and adults close to street children – such as taxi drivers, street vendors, restaurant owners and night guards – were consulted.

In January 1993, in the fifth month of the study, some of the children began to come to our apartment for informal conversation over tea or for medical attention (first aid needs and basic illnesses were common among street children). These occasions allowed for longer, more personal discussions to be carried out in a relaxed and safe atmosphere outside the public glare. A special relationship was developed with five children who were enrolled in, and supported through, a nearby primary school.

By this time we had founded a non-governmental organisation – *kuleana*. In April 1993 the *kuleana* center for children's rights was established on Post Street next to the New Mwanza Hotel, at the heart of the city centre. The Centre offered essential services, non-formal educational activities, health care and legal advocacy. This strengthened relations with the street children and facilitated contact in a wide range of issues. We were able to learn a lot about children/community relations, especially related to legal matters.

Study Write-Up and Creative Presentation by Street Children

We wrote a first draft of the situation analysis in February 1992. However, it was clear that we were learning more all the time, especially after the centre was opened in April. A decision was made to extend the duration of the study by four months (from March to July 1993). The additional time was used to clarify information, consolidate baseline data, and learn more about difficult areas such as intricate laws and sexuality. We also spent this time consulting with a core group of six children and two colleagues at *kuleana* about the implications of the study for planning interventions.

A final statistical analysis of the data was made in August 1993, using information updated through to the end of July 1993. A draft of the study was first presented publicly at a workshop in Mwanza in October 1993.

A group of street children, including most of the core group involved in carrying out the situation analysis, formally closed the study through a presentation made at the workshop. The content and style of their presentation was determined by themselves. The theme of their play highlighted street children's resiliency and support for each other in the face of tremendous discrimination.

WHY DO CHILDREN END UP ON THE STREETS?

The reasons are complex. Typically children do not end up on the streets due to a single cause but are pushed onto the streets by a combination of several factors that make life impossible within a home. These factors are societal – related to international economic relations, the inferior position of women, the AIDS epidemic – and individual – having to do with the specific circumstances of a child's family. Our research into these issues is continuing. At present six inter-related factors appear to be the most significant.

Poverty

Most street children come from poor families (only five out of 122 described their backgrounds as relatively affluent). While the amount of food available within the home varied, it was usually neither regular nor sufficiently nutritious. Fifty-three per cent of the children cited 'hunger' as one of their reasons for leaving home. Several of the older children (aged 12–18) were pulled out of school by parents or guardians who could not afford fees, or because they needed the children's labour to supplement family income. Most children describe their homes as crowded, lacking direct water and electricity, and being in generally poor repair.

Recent International Monetary Fund (IMF) sponsored economic policy changes have resulted in the removal of subsidies on essential food staples and in health and education budget cuts, shifting a greater burden on to the poor. In this context, any delay or shortfall in income can push a family living on subsistence over the edge. Many families are already over-burdened and unable to take care of their own or their relative's children.

The daily grind of abject poverty is, perhaps, the oldest cause for pushing children on to the street. It is also something that makes the children want to stay away from home. With all their difficulties, the city streets are still a place where one can be quite sure of finding some food and money every day.

Urban newcomers

Poverty in rural and peripheral areas is associated with migration to the cities. The population of Mwanza municipality has increased dramatically in the last decade; its current annual growth rate of 8.3 per cent is one of the highest in the world. Because it is usually the poorest who migrate, newcomers can call on few resources to make the transition to urban life. Often many can only secure makeshift housing without adequate water, sewage or electricity facilities. Living conditions tend to be crowded, and afford little privacy. These circumstances make it difficult to prevent infections within the household and frequently lead to family tensions.

Most significantly, street children's families may not have the supportive links of rural communities to draw on. The majority of street children in Mwanza are not *Wasukuma* (the major ethnic group in Mwanza), which suggests that their families may not have been able to call upon kinship networks for support.

Traditionally the extended family provides insurance, social security and emotional support. But for urban newcomers these links are often weak or absent. In such circumstances individuals and nuclear families have little resort in times of economic or social hardship. There may be nobody around who feels the obligation to supplement family needs, or to help with caring for children.

Traditional practices that specifically prevent child abuse and neglect are considerably weakened in the urban context as well. Living far from the clan and not actively subscribing to many of its values, many young men in the city may be particularly unlikely to subject themselves to sanctions placed by parents and elders. Cultural mechanisms to mediate conflicts, or to regulate child abuse and neglect may be ineffective in this context.

Changing sexual patterns

A striking feature of the children on the streets of Mwanza is that they come from families that are relatively 'unstable' or 'fluid'. In almost half (58 out of 122) of the children, the mother had had children with another man. In almost as many cases (54 out of 122), the mother had been living with a man who was not their biological father. In 17 out of 122 cases the children had been living with a stepmother or 'aunt-mother' just prior to moving on to the streets.

These changes in sexual cohabitation patterns have tremendous significance for children. In fluid relationships, parental and financial obligations remain ambiguous and this can cause various difficulties. A typical scenario, described by several children, is one in which their parent (usually the mother) lived with a new partner who refused to assume responsibility for those that were not her or his biological children. In other cases, male partners were reported to have identified their relationships as 'temporary' affairs with no long-term responsibility for fatherhood.

Situation of women

Many street children described their mothers as working at several jobs, for many hours a day, and still have more to do. The children reported that their fathers (or mother's husbands) did not contribute to the household budget, chores or caring for children; and often used up the family income for activities outside the home. In some cases, children made comparisons with neighbours and overtly identified their mother's lack of wealth as their reason for being on the street.

The economic and social position of women has a significant bearing on the situation of children in the home. Since the household and child rearing are traditionally female responsibilities, the situation of children is inextricably linked with the situation of women. Women who are poor are caught in a double bind: they need to work extra to earn the family income and take care of children at the same time.

Women who are economically or socially dependent upon men are also in a poor position to insist on a larger share of resources being allocated towards the care of their children. Patriarchal social structures make it difficult for women to insist on their own and their children's health. Leaving an abusive husband, or choosing to be single, is often not an option for many women in Tanzania.

Violence

A striking 89 per cent of the children in our study cited violence or neglect at home as one of their reasons for choosing to live on the streets. Virtually all the children reported that they had been physically and/or sexually abused. Some children have told us that staying at home would have meant 'dying'.

We know of a child who was rescued in the last moment from being split in two with an axe, of one whose parent kept throwing him to the wall when he was an infant, of one whose drunken father would beat him every night, and of one whose older male cousin would rape her at home. Girls who have been sent to work as 'housegirls' are at special risk of being over-worked and abused. In many of these instances there is a strong association with alcohol. Offenders are drunk or pouring out their anger from being abused by a partner who is drunk.

There are few mechanisms to help mitigate the effects of violence against children. Traditional means of regulating such conflicts have weakened considerably, particularly in the city. Seen as the property of their parents, children are perceived to have few independent rights.

AIDS

The family backgrounds of many of the street children suggest that one or both of their parents have become ill or have died from AIDS-related complications. This is particularly true of new arrivals. Many of them (26 out of 122) come from Kagera, an area with a high incidence of HIV infection. Twenty-nine per cent of the children cited being 'orphaned' or 'abandoned' as one of their reasons for being on the streets.

Orphaned children are forced to move on to the streets when extended family systems do not accept them or fail to provide adequate care after the death of a parent. The situation is made especially worse in cases where unscrupulous relatives disown children of the family house, land and other resources. Three children known to us have attempted to claim such rights without success. These situations are also obviously very traumatic to children.

The number of children affected by AIDS will continue to increase dramatically. At present approximately 50,000 people in Mwanza region, over 10 per cent of the sexually active population, and over 20 per cent of young people in Mwanza city are estimated to be infected with the HIV virus. The May 1992 report of the National AIDS Control Programme (Ministry of Health) estimates that approximately one million children in Tanzania will be orphaned as a result of AIDS by the year 2000.

THE SITUATION OF THE STREET CHILDREN OF MWANZA

There are many ways in which to research and characterise the situation of any particular population of street children. Through the duration of the study we have come to learn of intricately complex realities, individual quirks, communal survival strategies – a wealth of remarkable information. It was difficult for us to decide how to sort through this information and to decide what to edit. In the end we felt it was important to stick to our original mandate, and describe the *basic* situation affecting street children in Mwanza. Inevitably, there will be an emphasis on those aspects of their situation that are a cause for major concern.

What follows is what the situation was like in July 1993. Since the report of our study, on which this summary is based, was written there have been a number of changes. The Centre for Children's Rights has moved from its original location to larger premises with grounds for children to play. The new centre houses up to 100 children, 85 boys and 15 girls. Over 100 children have been successfully reintegrated back into their communities. Fifteen older children have found steady jobs and are established in the job market. Free and accessible health care is available for over 400 street children and youth through *kuleana*'s health clinic. About 65 children regularly attend non-formal education classes during the daytime. Fewer than four children a week appear in Primary Court in Mwanza due to *kuleana*'s interventions. *kuleana* continues to raise community awareness through 50-foot murals on children's rights in the busiest streets of Mwanza, through regular workshops, publications and public forums. All of these events are organised with full participation of street children. Children at the centre and on the streets regularly get counselling from our team of educators and street workers.

Shelter

During the first six months of the study, harassment and beatings by members of the *sungusungu* or police were regular and merciless. Hardly a night used to go by without reports of violence against street children. However, there has been a dramatic improvement in the safety of the street at night between September 1992, when we began our study, and the situation in July 1993. The violence is down significantly. Arrests of sleeping children still happen, but they are now isolated cases rather than a daily pattern.

Between 75 and 90 children sleep at the *kuleana* temporary shelter on Post Street next to the New Mwanza Hotel. The street girls used to prefer the stalls at the main bus stand because of the protection offered by passengers sleeping nearby, until they were continually harassed by a small group of police recently. *kuleana* has now made arrangements for them to sleep on a covered shop-front under the protection of a night guard.

The remaining 150 or so children make do in various locations. The street children of Mwanza have found or created an impressive array of places (offering varying levels of protection) to sleep at night: on shop pavements, underneath food stalls and public benches, in buildings undergoing construction, inside a box or underneath a tree.

These places are far from ideal. They are usually dirty and cold, may not keep out the rain, and offer little privacy. They offer little protection from sexual assault by adults or street youth. Those who own houses and shops in the vicinity can always decide that they do not want the children and order their 'clearance'.

Some of the children have reciprocal arrangements with their adult 'friends': night guards who let them sleep in sheltered places in exchange for money or cigarettes, women caterers who let them sleep in food stalls in exchange for 'guarding' and fetching water in the morning, Indian families who allow them to sleep in their alleys in exchange for sweeping the area and running errands. In a few cases (four out of 122) the children sleep in the homes of the people for whom they do odd jobs, and three of the children who work for a local restaurant sleep on its kitchen floor.

Health

Street life is hazardous. Moving around on streets (usually barefoot), digging in dumps for food or scrap, fighting with each other and being beaten by adults results in frequent cuts and bruises. Eating food at street-side stalls (often cold leftovers), that may be left uncovered and exposed to flies, in dirty plates with dirty hands, leads to diarrhoea, dysentery and worms.

Children who lack places to shower and wash clothes get dirty very quickly. This encourages infections of the skin and slows down healing of wounds. Children who wash and bathe in Lake Victoria are exposed to various infections, including the bilharzia parasite. Many of these illnesses can be easily treated in 'normal' contexts, but street children have limited access to health services. Small wounds easily become large pus-filled sores, simple cuts can lead to tetanus, common infections take long to heal because of the lack of restful environment.

At present, most of the street children use the health room at *kuleana*, because it offers free, prompt treatment in an accessible and caring environment. On average, 23 children receive treatment and/or preventive health education at the facility per day.

This situation is quite different from the one at the beginning of the study in September 1992, one year ago. At that time medical care was officially free and universal in Tanzania. However, street children's experiences of health care facilities and health workers were almost always negative. In our survey children complained of being treated badly in clinics and hospitals, made to wait or told to come back the next day, asked awkward questions, spoken to rudely and denied medicines.

Sexual life

Like street children throughout the world, many of the children in Mwanza are sexually active. Sexual relations are complexly related to pleasure, initiation rites, a need to belong and be accepted, and power relationships among children. Sexual partners among the younger boys are usually younger boys among their peers; some of the older boys have sex with street girls and commercial sex workers who are their 'friends'.

Life on the street puts the children at increased risk of acquiring sexually transmitted diseases (STDs). Our survey showed that nine out of 122 street children (of whom four were girls) had acquired one or more STDs in the past 12 months. Since only about half the children were specifically examined for STDs, this figure may be actually higher, particularly among some of the girls who are sexually active.

Sleeping outside, children are vulnerable to sexual attacks from adults and older children. In at least two cases (one boy, one girl), children were infected with syphilis by being raped at night. Several of the children who had been remanded or imprisoned at the Butimba prison reported cases of children being sexually abused by adult prisoner's gang leaders.

kuleana has carried out several counselling/workshop sessions with street children on reproductive health in the past six months, focusing on mutual relationship and protection from the HIV virus. Awareness of safer sex practices, including the use of condoms, is relatively high. However, the use of these practices is not consistent. Clearly more needs to be understood about both street boys' and girls' sexuality to plan effective interventions.

Education

Most of the street children (93 out of 122) cannot read or write. Only 32 out of 122 have been to primary school, and in most of these cases schooling was terminated early. At present six out of 122 children attend formal primary school with sponsorship from *kuleana*. This represents 50 per cent of the total 12 children who were originally enrolled.

The six children who dropped out, and 70 plus other children in our study, expressed no desire to attend formal school for similar sorts of reasons: the school routine was too rigid and too stifling; the school day was boring and failed to stimulate; in contrast many more 'interesting things were happening' on the streets; teachers were sometimes unfair, arbitrary and vindictive in their punishments; the responsibilities of school life – showering every morning, washing uniforms, taking care of books, doing homework – were difficult to maintain when the rest of their lives were so often in turmoil; attending school took many 'prime' hours of the day and conflicted with the need to earn money. Some children felt that they were too old to begin school.

Street children who have never attended school or have dropped out are mistakenly viewed as stupid, dumb and intellectually deficient; or as lazy, spoilt and psychologically immature. They are seen to need 'rescuing' from their 'vices'. Our survey revealed an opposite reality: much of what children did – in their work strategies, in dealing with discrimination, in their play – showed high intelligence and creativity.

While most children have a low written literacy and numeracy, they are remarkably articulate orally and visually. For instance, few children could write down the answer to '15 x 3 = – in an exercise book, but virtually all were immediately able to calculate the total cost of three bananas at 15 shillings each. The toy cars children construct from scrap display tremendous ingenuity and skill. Their spontaneous role-plays, story-telling and discussions about surviving violence show an acute understanding of their situation and a shrewd sense of practical justice. The camaraderie among street girls involving a strong element of self-support counselling about how to safeguard their health. Their drawings 'speak' volumes about their realities, concerns and desires. It was clear to us that the street children actively used their minds every day to survive the harsh circumstances of their lives.

Virtually all the children in our study (98%) expressed a strong desire to learn. The children have been enthusiastic and participated actively in non-formal educational activities at *kuleana*. Highly motivated peer-tutors have emerged among the children.

These experiences point to a basic conclusion: formal education is inappropriate and will not work for most street children. However, street children are intelligent and eager to learn; and their education can best take place in flexible, participatory, non-formal environments.

Street children have to work to survive, and they do so through a whole range of activities. Many children do not stick to one particular occupation for a long time but shift between activities or do several things within a short period. These activities required varying levels of time and effort. In our survey the work-load ranged from one hour a day for car washers to about 12 hours a day for some street vendors, restaurant workers and housegirls. Earnings per day ranged between fifty and one thousand Tanzania shillings.

Many children talked about the risks of making a living on the streets and low rates of return as their main difficulties. Street vendors complained that their assets and money were often stolen by older children and adults. Children who worked for others talked about having to work long hours with irregular and little pay in return. Those who worked in restaurants reported having to wait until late to eat cold leftovers scraped from the bottom of the pot. In most cases, the 'steady' occupations were considered low paying.

As a result children sought odd jobs from adult friends and patrons who often paid up to eight hundred shillings and provided a meal for a few hours of work.

While street boys' occupations varied widely, none of them appeared to be particularly hazardous to their health. The girls situation contrasted sharply. While we observed overt prostitution in only one case, virtually all the girls were pulled into relationships in which they were exploited sexually. A complex combination of protection, affection, gifts and threats was offered in exchange for sex.

The situation of girls who live on the margins, but not on the street, is especially worrying. Some girls who worked for relatives were pressured into having sex with 'friends'. There is also anecdotal evidence that housegirls as young as 10-years-old are made to work extremely long hours and are physically and sexually abused. Besides emotional and physical damage, these practices put girl children at tremendous risk of acquiring sexually transmitted diseases, including HIV/AIDS.

Discrimination

Discrimination against children has been reduced during the course of the study and the kinds of round-ups described in Abdallah's story in the introduction are now more isolated events, rather than daily occurrences. Allies who help children have emerged from many different backgrounds, including the police. However, discrimination still pervades the lives of street children. Much of the public perceives them as lazy, dirty, dangerous and good-for-nothing. Street children are treated badly in many of their interactions with society. Shopkeepers push them away, restaurants refuse them entry and travellers want them out of sight. At schools, health centres, parks and other public institutions the children are rudely dismissed or forced to become the subjects of paternalistic curiosity.

Harassment and physical abuse from the police and traditional defence groups (*sungusungu*) continues to be a major problem. Our study revealed that 77 per cent of the children had been arrested and 72 per cent beaten by the police in the past 12 months; 43 per cent were arrested by and 91 per cent experienced beating from the *sungusungu*. These authorities are quick to assume that children are responsible for various street crimes. Vagrancy laws instituted during the colonial era (especially the Removal of Non-desired Persons from Towns Ordinance) give wide and arbitrary powers to round up street children, when their only crime is not having a home.

Discrimination fosters violence against children and allows it to pass without outcry. Virtually all street children identify violence as their greatest fear and concern. Many of them come from backgrounds filled with violence. They face violence from security forces and older street children and, to a lesser extent, from members of the public. Beatings from the police (though far from life-threatening) cause enormous cumulative damage. According to the children police custody, the Butimba prison and the Bukumbi 'disabled' people's camp are notorious for both physical and sexual abuse.

These practices contrast sharply with existing legislation that is generally pro-children. Laws that provide special privileges in juvenile justice procedures relating to arrest, remand, the court process and imprisonment are frequently and flagrantly violated. For instance, 34 per cent of the children have spent time at the Butimba prison, usually in mixed facilities with adult offenders, when this is a clear violation of the law.

The role of the Department of Social Welfare in relation to the legal protection of children is unclear. Most members of the police, courts and prisons appear to be unaware or unwilling to involve probation officers during their proceedings. Existing legislation requires a probation officer to represent the interests of children in custody. However, our study revealed that this is often not followed. Only 10 per cent of the street children reported having had any personal contact with welfare officers in the past 12 months. In cases where the probation officers were present in court, they often did not actively defend the rights of children.

Tanzania has ratified the UN Convention on the Rights of the Child, but there is very little awareness of its content, and its principles have not been embodied in new legislation or codes of conduct. Discrimination against children takes place in the context of a hierarchical cultural tradition in which adults are permitted to do what they wish to their children. There is very little sensitivity to children's rights. Children are not permitted to protest adult decisions and actions or determine their own destinies. Adult priorities and concerns almost always take precedence over actions that would promote the best interests of children.

Emotional needs

The physical and social needs of street children – shelter, food, clothing, medicines, education, reasonable working conditions, protective laws – are visible. In these areas it is relatively easy to identify violations and plan interventions. Children's emotional needs are harder to observe.

We are only just beginning to understand the trauma of a violent childhood and the immense emotional strain of living on the street. That children are deeply affected is clear: many urinate while sleeping, wake up screaming in the middle of the night, have psychological 'breakdowns' and draw pictures that depict tremendous pain and confusion.

Where children need love and belonging, violence and loss have marked their lives – at home, in schools and other public institutions, in the hands of authorities and on the streets. Children of people with AIDS have had to nurse ill parents and watch them die. Family tensions and alcoholism have contributed to regular physical abuse of children. Children's trust has been shattered when they have been sexually abused by parents and relatives. Turmoil at home has led to losing contact with siblings and friends.

Instead of care and concern, children have experienced adult institutions as places of violence and disregard. 'Security' forces have often carried out activities that undermine children's sense of safety. Instead of protection and assurance, life on the street is a long ordeal of uncertainty: of where to sleep for the night, of where to get food, of how to avoid rape and being beaten. Despite the children's remarkable resiliency, these circumstances can only crush their spirits and leave them with diminished hope for the future.

The cumulative effect of these experiences is tremendously painful and heavy, and has systematically eroded children's esteem and sense of self worth. Street children have created remarkable support networks among themselves, and used various strategies to deal with their trauma. But these cannot replace the need for supportive relationships with adults and acceptance by the communities in which children live.

REGARDING PREVENTION

Children are forced on to the streets when community capacity to take care of them is eroded and weakened. Various measures may improve their situation:

- Research the specific situation of children in communities, especially the relationships between adults and children, paying particular attention to issues of violence, abuse and specific needs of children orphaned by AIDS.

- Increase and expand basic services to poor communities, especially in health, education, water and sanitation.

- Identify and strengthen community approaches of caring for children.

- Conduct an assessment of the situation of children for all interventions, projects, programmes – prior to planning, in evaluating the effects/benefits to children, and during the evaluation of the intervention. Special efforts should be made to elicit and incorporate the views of children in this process.

REGARDING PROTECTION AND PROMOTION OF THE RIGHTS OF STREET CHILDREN

- Improve street children's access to health facilities. Sensitise and train health workers to better respond to the needs of street children. Consider organising special time(s) during the week when street children would have access to health care and education tailored to their needs. Pay special attention to issues of sexuality; and the prevention and treatment of sexually transmitted diseases in particular.

- Sensitise and train primary school teachers better to respond to the needs of street children. Encourage NGOs and communities to establish small, low-cost, innovative, flexible and highly participatory non-formal education programmes for children.

- Research the situation of working children in Tanzania. Provide advocacy on behalf of street children seeking reasonable employment. Organise small-scale income-generating activities on a business basis with street children.

- Make concerted efforts to raise awareness and mobilise communities to promote children's rights. Involve the media and cultural forums to further these aims.

- Sensitise and train people in key sectors, including the police, *sungusungu*, courts, prisons and social welfare, to protect and promote children's rights within their institutions and the community. Encourage and facilitate the writing of 'practical working guidelines to promote the rights of children' within each key institution. Facilitate the building of pro-children coalitions and networks among these sectors.

- Review all legislation relating to children's rights and protections. Identify existing pro-children legislation and seek ways and means to ensure its enforcement. Amend or repeal laws that discriminate against children. Identify areas in which new legislation needs to be drafted to protect and promote children's rights.

- Research the ways in which girl and boy children are physically, sexually and emotionally abused within the home, in schools, in custody, in other institutions and on the street. Pay particular attention to the nature of relationships between children and adults.

GENERAL

- Actively promote awareness and new legislation to implement the UN Convention on the Rights of the Child.

- Promote the UNICEF-initiated principles of 'first call for children' and the 'best interests of the child'. Write a practical framework/guide to evaluate all development programmes and activities from a 'child-centred' perspective (similar to doing a 'gender analysis' for women).

- Actively pay attention to the specific needs and rights of girl children at all levels, including programme-situation analysis, planning, implementation and evaluation.

- Establish a special national commission to monitor the situation of children's rights in Tanzania, to set national policies, and to ensure that issues of children's rights are given the highest priority at the highest levels. Consider the benefits of appointing a children's ombudsperson, as has been done in several other countries.

- Encourage adults to listen to children, and to pay attention to children's views, ideas, concerns, priorities and feelings. Design and implement effective programmes to promote children's voices, including publications, recordings and special forums. Encourage and elicit children's participation in planning and evaluating programmes related to children and community development.

REFERENCES

UNICEF Children in Especially Difficult Circumstances, Series 'Menores en circunstançias Espeialmente Defiles, La Paz Bolivia' Analisis de Situacion No 8 Bogata, Columbia UNICEF.

UNICEF (1988) *Methodological Guide on Situation Analysis.* UNICEF Methodological Series No.6. Bogota, Columbia: UNICEF Regional Office for Latin America and the Caribbean.

Dallape, F. (1987) *An Experience with Street Children.* Nairobi: Undugu Society of Kenya. Paper prepared for the Urban Child Project, UNICEF International Development Centre, Florence.)

CHAPTER EIGHTEEN

The Time of Your Life?
Children's Knowledge of Crime

Richard Kinsey

This chapter has two primary concerns. First, I would like to outline some of the empirical findings from a large-scale research programme on young people, crime and policing. In this context, particular attention will be given to the crimes routinely committed both *by* and *against* young people frequently by adults. Second, I shall consider the extraordinarily virulent responses the research itself has generated: the frequent disbelief and intense (methodological?) criticism which has been levelled against it and – closely related? – the assumptions which have led criminologists to focus upon juvenile *delinquency* rather than victimisation.

A recurrent theme of the paper, therefore, will be to explore the everyday practices and common-sense perceptions of childhood, as revealed both by the findings of the research itself and the reactions to it. To begin with, however, I will need to alert a non-Scottish readership to some of the legal and political institutions and cultural practices which have shaped the agenda of the particular research programme. Of course, this can only be very brief. But, for my immediate purposes, two matters are of particular importance:

1. the juvenile justice system in Scotland, which, unlike the system in England and Wales, for example, is premised upon the *welfare* rather than *criminal* responsibility of the child

2. the pattern of crime in Scotland – particularly juvenile crime – which again is very different from that found in England and Wales.

Before doing so, however, I want to make a further, general point. There are many other specific differences in the policy, practice and organisation of juvenile justice in Scotland – the political accountability and organisation of policing and social services, for example, to which one might wish to attribute the comparative 'success' of juvenile justice policy and practice. I believe there is much of positive value to be learnt from the experience and practices established in Scotland over the past twenty years. Furthermore, these institutions and practices are now central to an understanding of current political and cultural responses to juvenile offending in Scotland. (For example, findings from the last British Crime Survey to include Scotland 1988 showed an extraordinarily widespread depth of support for non-punitive, welfare responses to young offenders.)

However, it is, in my view, essential to recognise that the cultural practices upon which such institutions are premised are both prior to, and yet consequent upon, the practices of those institutions themselves. In short, the process of cultural *reproduction* cannot be divorced from its particular history and, in this case, from the political and legal institutions which both *form* and *are formed by* that culture. In considering the findings of our research, therefore, one cannot focus simply upon the Children's Hearing System in Scotland in the pious hope that one could transplant one set of discrete policies or institutions from one culture to another. To do so would be to abstract them (literally) from their time, place and history.

In making this (fairly obvious) point, I am aware that there are those who argue that we are living at 'the end of history' and 'the close of modernity'. In fact, I have a lot of sympathy with those who perceive 'intimations of post-modernity' in contemporary social order (e.g. Bauman 1992) but the important word, it seems to me, is 'intimations' not 'post-modernity' itself. Certainly, we live in a world which is riven by discontinuities, ambiguities and, crucially, the reconstruction and re-reordering of time and place. But as important, surely, are the *continuities* which inform the reordering of time and the reconstruction of past, present and future. As I shall try to elaborate in this paper, current debates on childhood and youth seem to lie at the heart of this process.

INTRODUCTION: SCOTLAND IS NOT ENGLAND

The differences in Scottish law, the structure of Scottish local government and the organisation of policing and social services – although clearly important for any detailed comparative analysis of the research to be discussed – cannot be covered here (a useful introduction is to be found in Flyn and Spencer 1990). Rather, for the immediate purposes of this chapter, I think it is more important to emphasise two particular points: the distinctive patterns of crime in Scotland, and the system of juvenile justice which, again, is radically different from the system in England.

As a European readership will probably be aware, the 'crisis in law and order' played a central part in the British election campaign of 1979 and was to remain a continuing issue in domestic politics throughout the 1980s (Hall *et al.* 1978). It is now of particular interest to note, therefore, that in 1981, i.e. in the year of the first Brixton and Liverpool riots, the first British Crime Survey found no significant differences between victimisation[1] rates in Scotland and those in England and Wales (Chambers and Tombs 1984). This is, perhaps, of particular interest since, every year since the summer of 1981, serious urban disorders and riots have occurred in English towns and cities while such problems have been noticeably absent from Scotland – though, rarely, a matter for comment or curiosity in England itself (e.g. Benyon and Solomos 1991).

It is also notable that, although throughout the 1980s increases in *recorded* crime were to be observed in police statistics both north and south of the border, the British Crime Surveys have revealed that in England and Wales this reflected a real increase in the underlying level of victimisation. In Scotland, on the other hand, where victimisation levels decreased, the increase in police-recorded crime over the period appears to have reflected a greater readiness and increasing propensity to report crime to the police (Chambers and Tombs 1984; Anderson and Kinsey 1992).

In relation to patterns of crime, the differences between England and Scotland are relatively easy to illustrate but, inevitably, more difficult to explain. As Table 18.1 shows, the last British Crime Survey which included Scotland (BCS 1988) found statistically significant differences between Scotland and the remainder of mainland Britain in the incidence of both household and personal offence.[2] These findings were all the more remarkable as cultural stereotypes represent Scottish urban culture as particularly violent in comparison to England. Indeed, the higher levels of both household and personal crime found in England are even more 'surprising' if conventional indicators such as unemployment rates are taken into account. (See Figure 18.1).

Unfortunately, the British Crime Survey has to date included Scotland on only three occasions – 1982, 1988 and 1993 – and *at the time the study we report on here* was undertaken the results of the 1993 survey were unavailable. What is very interesting, however, is the present fall in police-recorded crime reported by individual forces throughout Scotland. Again this would seem to indicate a

---

1   There is a difference, not often appreciated, between official police statistics (that is numbers of crimes that have been reported to the police and investigated by them) and the information that was provided by a scheme introduced by the Home Office and the Scottish Office, namely the British Crime Surveys and the victim surveys. What happens is that a large random sample of households is taken and individuals are asked whether or not they have been a victim of crime. On the basis of the information gathered in this way it seems that only 50 per cent of crime experienced by such victims is actually reported to the police. It is therefore thought that 'victimisation' surveys give a more reliable picture of what is actually happening. Clearly, if only 50 per cent of experienced crime is reported to the police, much of it does not appear in police statistics which therefore underestimate the actual crime rates

2   It is important to recognise that the various reports so far published by the Home Office under the title of the 'British Crime Survey' do not include data for Scotland or Northern Ireland. In contrast, the data for Wales are not analysed separately from the English data.

Table 18.1: Comparison of crime rates: British crime survey Scotland and England and Wales 1988

| | Crime rates | | % Change 1981–1987 | |
	Scotland	England and Wales	Scotland	England and Wales
Household offences				
1. Vandalism	1073	1521**	-25	+3
2. Theft from a motor vehicle	907	1083**	+8	+54
3. Housebreaking	652	612	+60	+50
4. Theft of a motor vehicle	145	200	-7	+28
5. Bicycle theft	151	201	+57	+70
6. Theft in a dwelling	44	58	+42	-28
7. Other household theft	796	946*	0	+12
All household offences	3768	4610**	0	+22
Personal Offences **(Rates per 10,000 adults aged 16+)**				
8. Assault	463	513	+19	+4
9. Theft from the person	85	79	-37	-29
10. Robbery	30	44	-21	+5
11. Sexual assault	20	29	-41	+93
12. Other personal theft	324	447*	-29	+9
All personal offences	912	1099*	-12	+3

Note: Starred figures indicate statistically significant differences between Scotland and England and Wales. Two-starred figures indicate a statistically significant difference at the 5 per cent level and one-starred at the 10 per cent level.

Source: Anderson and Kinsey 1992

significant difference from England, where police figures have shown continued increases and the 'law and order' debate, particularly in relation to youth, has once again assumed a key role in domestic politics. Now that the 1993 data is available (although in 1993 a separate Scottish Crime Survey was produced), what is revealed from the Scottish material is that the actual level of victimisation has fallen in complete contrast with what has happened in England and Wales.

Of course, until the results of the BCS 1993 became available, we could only speculate about the significance of the fall in police-recorded crime in Scotland. It could have been that the greater propensity to report crime found

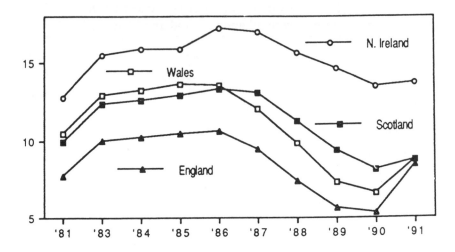

Source: Compiled by Richard Kinsey with data provided by Labour Market Statistics
          Group, Central Statistics Office

Figure 18.1 Unemployment Rates in UK, 1981–1991 (%).

in the previous surveys in Scotland had suddenly diminished and that such falls
in police-recorded crime were disguising an actual increase in victimisation.

Evidence from other surveys, for example the British Social Attitudes Survey,
continued to show marked cultural differences between Scotland and England
(especially the south of England) whilst our own research with both young
people and adults provided little indication of any recent changes in attitudes
towards the police and the criminal justice system (see Kinsey 1993). But as
the results of the 1993 BCS (Scotland) did in fact show, levels of criminal
victimisation were in fact lower in Scotland and rates of reporting crime to the
police had remained constant.

For present purposes, however, explanation of the differences between
England and Scotland is not my immediate concern. Rather, I have emphasised
the point because there is, I think, a very real risk that those reading the findings
of our research from outside Scotland may be tempted to interpret the high
rates of offending found in our research as symptomatic of the same or similar
problems and difficulties experienced in England and Wales. This, I believe,
would be mistaken and I would again draw your attention to the findings shown
in Table 18.1 and, in particular, to the findings on vandalism and car crime.

Again I am forced to speculate as we do not have adequate comparative
research, but it is instructive to note that significantly lower levels of both
vandalism and theft from cars were found in Scotland – both of which, we
might be assume, are offences frequently committed by young people. I stress
this point here as one of the most important aspects of Scottish criminal justice
and welfare policy relates to the Children's Hearing System. Thus, in sharp

contrast to the juvenile justice system in England and Wales – which is premised upon conventional categories of the individual culpability and criminal responsibility of young people over 14 years of age – the Children's Hearing System was introduced under The Social Work (Scotland) Act 1968.[3] Under this system which openly and self-consciously adopted a strategy of *decriminalisation* for young people under the age of 16, a policy of the welfare of the child was prioritised so that offending is only one of the grounds for referral for decision by 'lay panels'. Thus, whether a child has been involved in law-breaking or is vulnerable to abuse or otherwise regarded 'at risk', the Hearing System is concerned with the needs and the welfare of the child for which purpose it has a range of disposals available to it which might include, where deemed appropriate, attendance at a residential school or supervision orders.

A second, equally radical break with convention, saw the attempt to avoid the intimidating complexity of the traditional juvenile justice system (Carlen 1976) with a strong emphasis placed on the informal setting and procedures. Thus the Hearing System provides for lay membership of the new 'panels', permitting representation from all sections of the community. Where innocence or guilt is disputed, the case may be taken to the ordinary (adult) criminal court but in practice this is now exceptional. From the outset, the 1968 Act required that only those prosecutions involving the most serious offences should be taken to the criminal courts and that any such prosecution must first be formally submitted to, and sanctioned by, the Lord Advocate.

Many of these provisions have provoked criticism. There are those who have argued that the informal procedures adopted by the Hearings System deny children full rights under the rule of law and have demanded – under the slogan of 'justice for children' – the introduction of formal rules of procedure and evidence. On the other hand, there are those who regard the welfare philosophy of the Hearing System and the underlying policy of decriminalisation as too lenient and as an out-dated 'liberalism' born of the 1960s.

In truth, it is the rhetoric of the latter lobby – with its confused demands for punishment, deterrence, incapacitation and suchlike solutions to the problems of juvenile offending – which might cause the greatest anxiety when considering the political use which might be made of the research findings I shall outline below. For example, the research found that well over half of the young people who completed questionnaires (3,500) had committed an offence of some description within the previous nine months. Obviously, without full and careful interpretation, such findings can very easily be taken as evidence of the failure of the Children's Hearing System. In my view, this would be an improper interpretation.

---

3   The Children's Hearings System was introduced following the report of the Kilbrandon Committee in 1964.

LISTENING TO CHILDREN: RHETORIC, THEORY AND PRACTICE

The purpose of the research was to allow young people the opportunity to express their own views about crime and, so far as possible, to avoid imposing preconceived adult definitions upon them. From the outset, therefore, the conventional criminological focus upon 'the juvenile delinquent' or the 'persistent offender' was deliberately abandoned. Of course, there are young people who persistently offend and who, in different ways and for different reasons, are marked out from the norm. Self-evidently, understanding such processes is a legitimate and necessary criminological concern. But in other ways, even within criminology, the concentration on juvenile delinquency can be seen more as a reflection of adult concerns about crime and the problems caused *for* adults *by* young people. Rarely, it seems, have criminologists and policy makers considered the reverse of this question: the problems crime causes *for* young people.

The research itself, therefore, has involved young people from the city of Edinburgh, smaller towns and villages and rural areas in south Scotland. In total, more than 3500 young people – aged between 11 and 15 – have completed questionnaires in schools throughout the region. In addition we have recorded and transcribed small group interviews with approximately 1000 girls and boys. In this chapter, however, I draw mainly on the research in Edinburgh, where, following an earlier pilot study, questionnaires and group interviews were carried out with approximately 1000 pupils attending schools in four very different areas of the city. Without going into the history of Edinburgh – which has been described as one of the most socially segregated cities in Britain – it might be noted that the structure of the city is such that, for purposes of comparison, we were able to select schools which provided samples from four spatially and demographically distinct areas, to each of which are attached different histories, reputations and understandings. Thus one area selected is a deprived, 1960s council estate on the periphery of the city; second, in sharp contrast, we took an affluent area of central, south-west Edinburgh, very much at the upper end of the private housing market. The third area is a more middle-class, 'commuter' area on the outskirts of the city with a considerable amount of smaller detached and semi-detached post-war private housing. The fourth area, close to the centre of the city, is the most socially mixed – although not deprived – including owner-occupiers as well as private and public authority tenants.[4]

Through the combination of quantitative and qualitative methods, we have explored young people's experiences of crime: as victims of crime as well as

---

4   In graphs, etc., the four areas will be described as (i) 'peripheral council', (ii) 'affluent S.W. Edinburgh', (iii) 'middle-class commuter' and (iv) 'central Edinburgh'.

offenders; their contact with the police and their perceptions of social justice; their use of time outside the home and outside school; their worries and anxieties about the present (including their concerns about crime) and, more generally, their hopes and aspirations for the future.

These latter questions – young people's perceptions of their present and future aspirations and possibilities – provide a key to one of the underlying theoretical questions informing some of the more practical issues I shall address in this chapter: namely the way in which adults including the decision takers and policy makers responsible for social work, policing and criminal justice practice in relation to young people conceptualise youth and how, as part of that process, adults in general conceptualise or perceive their own past and the extent to which this shapes the perceptions of the present problems of young people.

Young people's understandings of their past is, of course, is at the very least problematic. As Walter Benjamin (1985) pointed out many years ago in his biographical 'Chronicle of Berlin' children have no past, therefore no present and no future which is in any sense equivalent to the taken-for-granted 'reality' of adults. At the same time Benjamin was writing – coincidentally? – Henri Lefebvre (1991) made a related and, for me at least, an extraordinarily powerful point in his 'Critique of Everyday Life'. In a few words on the films of Charlie Chaplin, Lefebvres catches something difficult to put into words:

> The point of departure for this 'vis comica' peculiar to Chaplin is therefore the simplicity of a child, a primitive and wonderfully gifted barbarian, suddenly plunged (as we all are at every moment) into an everyday life that is inflexible and bristling with ever new difficulties, some foreseeable, others not. In his first films Chaplin takes up battle in a duel which is always different and yet always with the same objects, everyday objects: an umbrella, a deckchair, a motorbike, a banana skin... Always surprised, always delighted by the strangeness and richness of things, always awkward when faced with ritualised practices (essential behaviour, necessary conditioning), Chaplin captures our own (surely adult? R.K.) attitude towards these trivial things and before our very eyes. He makes it appear suddenly amazing, dramatic and joyful. He comes as a stranger into the familiar world, he wends his way through it, not without wreaking joyful damage. Suddenly he disorients us, but only to show us what we are when faced with objects; and these objects become suddenly alien, the familiar is no longer familiar (as for example, when we arrive in a hotel room, or a furnished house, and trip over the furniture and struggle to get the coffee grinder to work). But via this disorientation and strangeness, Chaplin reconciles us on a higher level, with ourselves, with things and with the humanised world of things. (p.11)

The contrast between 'wreaking joyful damage' and the self-righteous *adult* indignation provoked by current television images of 'mindless vandalism' and 'hooliganism' could not be more clear adult conceptions of childhood are double-sided. At one moment, the mystery, wonder and unrecognisablity of the (now) mundane and the (now) trivial is a source of adult amusement and nostalgic reminiscence, at another – in Anglo-American culture at least – it becomes a harsh cause for complaint: the failure of socialisation, the collapse of family values, the inadequacy of school discipline, etc.

The extraordinarily intense suspicion with which our research methodology has been greeted seems based on the assumption that young people will deliberately lie, cheat or deceive 'naïve' researchers such as ourselves who, ironically enough, of course, as 'academics' are typified as 'childishly naïve' and unused to 'the real world'. Indeed, on many occasions, one feels such methodological doubts – which have been much more vigorously expressed in relation to this particular research than in any other empirical research I have undertaken – say more about the culture and attitudes of those who express such doubts than they do about the problems of research itself. The research seemed to have touched an exposed nerve – the *aporia* of conventional theory, policy and practice?

This is not the place to go into the full detail of the collection of data and the statistical analysis (see Anderson *et al.* 1994). An extensive pilot study was undertaken and revision of both method and content of questionnaires and interview technique continued throughout the early stages of the research. Researchers were present at all stages of fieldwork –including questionnaire completion[5] – and considerable care was taken to establish the trust, confidence and consent of all those who took part. I might simply ask readers to note the (surprising?) consistency of findings across very different areas and between demographically very different groups of young people. (See, for example, the patterns of victimisation shown below).

Most convincing of all, however, was the way in which young people talked to us: the intonation and expressiveness of their language, the matter of fact descriptions of their victimisation (the full resonance of which, sadly, is lost in transcription) and, most important, the level of detail and prosaic realism of the accounts they gave us. Thus, impressionistically, we were convinced that the young people who took part in the research did so willingly and with considerable commitment. Indeed, our subsequent surprise at the findings was matched only, perhaps, by the surprise of the young people themselves on being asked to take part.

---

5   We were frequently surprised by the relief teachers expressed when they were informed that we would administer the quenstionnaire. Often, it seems, researchers are content to leave such 'mechanical' tasks to the teachers.

YOUNG PEOPLE'S EXPERIENCE OF CRIME

Young people's understandings of crime are arrived at in many different ways; by getting into trouble, by seeing others committing crime and witnessing the consequences of it and, not the least, by being the victims of crime themselves. The process is complex and long term, often, one suspects, continuing well into adulthood. It is a process which, as we shall see, young people often find confusing, ambiguous and unjust yet the practices upon which their *common-sense understandings* of crime are based are frequently very sophisticated and, even at the simplest level, demand an extraordinarily sensitive appreciation of social relations and cultural practices. This is all the more extraordinary as, very often, the acquisition of such practical knowledge seems more intuitive than rational, more subconscious than conscious and rarely, if ever, is it – can it be? – the subject of formal instruction or education.

For example, during the course of our research we would ask young people to explain the difference between shoplifting and breaking into a house. Typically, by the age of eleven or twelve, children would have no difficulty in recognising or 'sensing' that stealing personal possessions from someone's house was wrong; the experience of such a crime was something concrete with which they could readily empathise. Shoplifting, in contrast, was far more difficult to understand – if goods have yet to be bought, who do they belong to? Not surprisingly, perhaps, the abstract relations of the market economy – the concepts of private property, money, exchange value and profit – were too complex to grasp.[6] The following comment from a twelve-year-old girl was typical of many: 'Breaking into a poor person's house? I mean that's a sin. You mustn't do that. But stealing from a shop...that's different. I mean, it all belongs to the Council. doesn't it?' Few people would expect children of this age to make moral judgements of a high level of abstraction. But how much more confusing is it for the young person, when such decisions are overlaid by even more complex and unspoken practices of race, gender or social class?[7]

It is not difficult to see how, from the child's point of view, adult values and practices appear inconsistent – if not incomprehensible. For example, many of the young people from poorer areas of the city felt it unfair that they were moved on by the police, refused entry to shops or cinemas or, worse still, rejected for work experience simply because of the way they dress, speak or where they live.

---

6   In this respect, the method employed was taken from Piaget's work on moral development and the child. Our theoretical conclusions, however, are very different.

7   It was only during analysis of the transcriptions of such discussions that it became very noticeable how often a discussion between young people themselves would end with a question directed at the researchers.

Practical, common-sense knowledge of such subtleties is gained through routine practices but, unlike the nostalgic reconstructions of Charlie Chaplin, such encounters are neither harmless nor classless. In the following case, a cadet uniform becomes a passport out of one of Edinburgh's most deprived estates:

> I go to cadets with my mates on Fridays. The police don't like people from my area up there but they never bother us because we're in uniform. The other night we didn't have our uniforms on – we'd been cleaning the hall. They pulled us straight away. I just don't go there now except for cadets.

In this instance, although he clearly resented it, the boy concerned had come to accept the way in which a uniform altered his status in the eyes of the police and his own ways of living had been modified to take account of his class position (Anderson et al. 1994). As we shall see later – especially among younger children – such experiences can fuel feelings of uncertainty and confusion as often as, if not more often than, resentment.

It is as important for present purposes, however, to appreciate the wider context of such experiences. Young people do not learn about crime and policing simply through thinking about it or reflecting upon the principles of deterrence in the classroom – no matter how ideologically attractive 'rational choice' and 'neo-classicist' theories of crime may appear to the conservative theorist. Rather, it is through their day to day experience of crime – whether as victim, witness or offender – that young people, from all class backgrounds, acquire the essential practical knowledge of dangerous places, things and people, of the social norms and practices – and the injustices and inequalities – which typify their relations with an adult world.

However, the cultural, institutional and structural conditions within which police officers work bear little comparison to the open-ended and unpredictable life of young people. Indeed, as Bourdieu observes, even among adults, routine practices are frequently better understood in terms of uncertainty and 'fuzziness' rather than informal rules.[8]

Such fuzziness – so much loved by Chaplin – seems nowhere more evident than when the child is outside the institutions of family and school, that is in

---

8   '...if practices had as their principle the generative principle which has to be constructed in order to account for them, that is a set of independent and coherent axioms, then the practices produced accordingly to perfectly conscious generative rules would be stripped of everything that defines them distinctively as practices, that is the uncertainty and 'fuzziness' resulting from the fact that they have as their principle not a set of conscious, constant rules, but practical schemes opaque to their possesors, varying according to the logic of the situation, the almost invariably partial viewpoint which it imposes, etc. Thus, the procedures of practical logic are rarely entirely incoherent.' (Bourdieu 1990, p.23).

the ready-made adventure playground of the street. Indeed, the complexities and uncertainties which children encounter when outside the family and school – the ambiguity, the confusion, the fun they confront, experience and make in the street – are no different from our experience as adults when visiting – or, indeed, writing for – another culture. But to the insider the complexities of such practices – their subtle shifts and adaptations over time – are often invisible and certainly not understood in terms of rules or theories until, suddenly, they become self-evidently obviously 'old-fashioned' and 'out of date'.

As a schoolboy growing up, I soon learnt when and where to wear a cap but it was only much later – perhaps only recently – that I recognised the way in which a cap told so much more than which school, which part of town, which social class. Thirty years later I heard the same story being told by a boy cadet who was out of uniform, out of his area and out of place.

ADULT KNOWLEDGE OF YOUNG PEOPLE AND CRIME

Surveys of the adult population have shown, beyond doubt, how official knowledge of crime – especially as recorded in police statistics – is, at best, partial and, at worst downright misleading. The British Crime Surveys, for example, have shown that as much as two-thirds of crimes and offences committed against adults are never made known to the police. The situation in relation to juvenile offending is even more difficult to assess. For example, recent figures for Scotland show that in 1989 police action taken against juveniles – including police warnings, reports to the Reporter to the Children's Hearings System and reports to the Procurator Fiscal – was at the lowest level since present records began in 1977 (The Scottish Office 1991). In relation to drugs offences, throughout Scotland reports were made on just 98 children – that is less than one (0.5) per thousand. In relation to handling offensive weapons, reports were made on 500 children (1:1000) while for car theft the figure was 1,035 (2:1000)in comparison with 3,080 for vandalism (6:1000).

Of course, as the Scottish Office made clear at the time of publication, these figures refer only to those cases in which the police took action and, therefore, cannot be taken as an accurate indication of juvenile offending (the accompanying press release read as follows: 'Only those children who are subject of police reports are included in the statistics. Those whose crimes are undetected or who are informally dealt with are excluded'). But, even with such caveats in mind, the difference between police action taken and the actual incidence of juvenile offending is stark. For example, according to our study, 18 per cent of 11- to 15-year-olds in Edinburgh had taken drugs – usually 'hash' (marijuana) – one or more times during a period of nine months (i.e. from the beginning of the summer holidays in 1990); 10 per cent had bought or sold drugs; 30 per cent had carried a knife or weapon; 35 per cent had shoplifted; 30 per cent

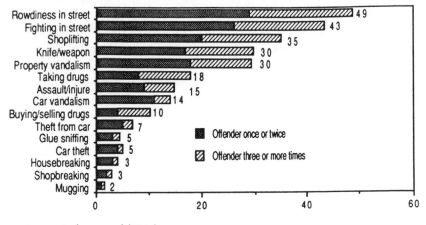

Source: Anderson et al. (1994)

Figure 18.2 Offending: Percentage committing offences

admitted vandalising buildings and 14 per cent had vandalised cars while 5 per cent admitted car theft.

Indeed, where the Scottish Office figures show police reports made in relation to 52 children per thousand (12% of whom were aged under 11), as Table 18.2 shows, our study revealed that as many as two-thirds of young people resident in Edinburgh aged 11 to 15 had committed at least one of the offences shown during the previous nine months.

Table 18.2 Young People's Survey: Variations in self-reported rates of offending (%)

Two-parent family		Single-mother		Adult home after school	
No adult in FT or PT work	Two or more in FT work	No adult in FT or PT work	One or more in FT work	Usually at home	Not usually at home
46	59	57	74*	45	70*

Source: Survey of Young People, University of Edinburgh, 1992

Notes:
1   * statistically significant at 0.5;
    ** statistically significant at 0.01.
2. Figures for those in full-time employment may include adult siblings and other relatives

Two essential points should be made in relation to these findings on offending. First, the results of the survey show very clearly that offending is not restricted to any particular social group or 'hard core' of young people. Although some kinds of offences are slightly more prevalent among children from poorer backgrounds, what is much more striking is the similarity in patterns of offending across social classes and different neighbourhoods. Put simply, 'rule-breaking' and petty crime would seem to be very much a 'normal' feature of young people's lives wherever they come from and whatever the economic-social status of the family. Furthermore, as Table 18.2 shows, there is no simple relationship between parental unemployment, family structure and the incidence of offending and levels of offending by young people. Rather, what appears central is the presence or absence of the parent or parents from the home, which in the case of both single-parent and two-parent households appears to be a function of their employment status. But again, the taken, for, granted assumptions of conventional criminology are reversed: the lowest levels of offending were found among children from two-parent families where neither parent was in employment, and, while the higher levels were found among lone-parent families, where the single parent was unemployed offending rates were lower than among children from the relatively affluent households where both parents were working.

The second point to be stressed is that while juvenile offending is relatively evenly distributed across social class, for the vast majority of young people it is, nonetheless, a relatively infrequent form of casual behaviour. Thus, while most young people in Edinburgh commit occasional offences, very few can be described as persistent offenders. Furthermore, those who can properly be described as persistent offenders are responsible for only a very small proportion of the total number of offences committed by young people. Yet, given the limited resources and policy priorities of agencies such as social work, the police and the juvenile justice system generally reinforced by the consequent gaps in official knowledge, it is those children, labelled as 'problem cases' (i.e. typically, those from poor and from single-parent households) who are seen as constituting the problem of delinquency.

This gap in official knowledge and the consequent bias in policy and practice is evidenced by the survey findings on contact with the police. For example, when asked whether they had been moved on, questioned or searched by the police over the nine-month period, levels were again surprisingly high – very much higher than is suggested in official statistics. But in this instance the figures were more clearly skewed in terms of social class and neighbourhood. Thus, as can be seen from Figure 18.3, adversary contact between the police and young people in Edinburgh decreased as the affluence of the

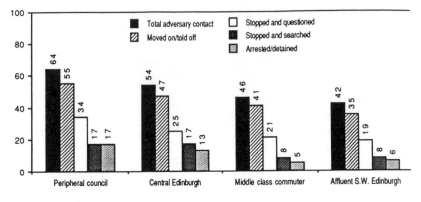

Source: Anderson *et al.* (1994)

Figure 18.3 Young People's Survey: Adversary contact with the police in area (9 months)

residential neighbourhood increased. Total adversary contact is thus highest in the council scheme (64%); it falls in the socially mixed, central area of the city (54%); in the more middle class 'commuter' area it falls again (46%). However, the lowest level is found in the affluent areas of south west Edinburgh (42%).

Despite the differences between areas, however, it is more important for present purposes to note that over half of the total sample of 1000 children surveyed in Edinburgh reported adversary contact with the police – a finding which stands in marked contrast to the official rate of 52 per thousand children against whom the police took formal action and which lends particular force to the Scottish Office caveat that the official data exclude 'those who are informally dealt with'.

I shall argue presently that, alongside their own experience of offending, this level of 'informal' contact with the police is critical to the way in which young people learn about crime and respond to the problems it poses for them. Before doing so, however, I want to bring a further factor into the equation – again one which, like offending, is almost entirely hidden from official knowledge – namely young people's experience of victimisation.

Over the nine months covered by the research, no less than half of those interviewed had been victims of non-sexual offences against the person – i.e. assault, threatening behaviour and theft from the person. (Note: this does not include incidents occurring at home or in school). In this instance, the extraordinary consistency of the findings across different areas of the city is worth reflection.

This consistency is reinforced when the results are analysed by type of accommodation. Thus, with victims of assault and theft from the person we find only minimal differences between those who live in council houses (40% and 20.5% respectively) and those in owner-occupied accommodation (36.5%

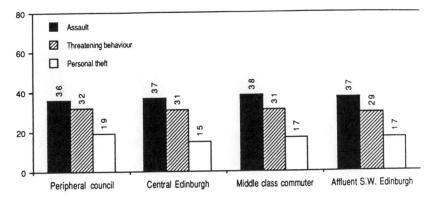

Source: Anderson *et al.* (1994)

Figure 18.4 Young People's Survey: Percentage victims of offences against the person (9 months)

and 17%). In relation to threatening behaviour, there is a larger difference (34% to 29%) but again it is not substantial.

Perhaps not surprisingly, the majority of offences against the person involved other young people under 18, however, we should be very careful not to dismiss such experiences as merely 'part of growing up', 'the rough and tumble of the street', as 'not *really* crime' – especially as the impact and subsequent anxiety is often considerable. However, the real meaning of the problem for young people rests in the fact that between a quarter and one-third of these offences were committed *by adults*. Other findings from the survey make the point even more forcefully.

Take, for example, the incidence of sexual propositioning of girls by adult men. No less than 30 per cent of 13-, 14- and 15-year-old girls had been victims of at least one incident of: 'indecent exposure', 'men touching or trying to touch them', 'trying to get them to go away with them' or 'trying to get them to touch them' (each one of which is a criminal offence). Again this was in a period of only nine months and again the findings were repeated across the city; nor, as the following graph shows, were such offences limited to girls. (It is perhaps worth noting that the graph suggests quite clearly that as boys get older and bigger such offences become less frequent, while the opposite is the case for girls. This perhaps suggests more about the nature of adult sexuality and the conventions which define the behaviour of adult males than it does about the behaviour of young people).

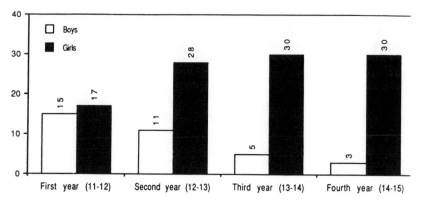

Source: Anderson et al. (1994)

Figure 18.5 Young People's Survey: Percentage sexually propositioned by adult men (9 months)

CONFLICTS BETWEEN PRACTICAL KNOWLEDGE AND OFFICIAL KNOWLEDGE

Offences committed against young people are rarely made known to the official agencies or, indeed, to parents. For example, girls reported fewer than one in five of the incidents described above to the police, while even fewer young people reported non-sexual offences against the person. There are many reasons for this. Very commonly, young people will not tell their parents because if they do they won't be allowed out with their friends or, very frequently, because they don't want to worry them. Others are simply inured to the problems they confront – it's something they have to put up with. As one girl from central Edinburgh put it: 'I've been followed (by men) loads of times. Loads. It's horrible. You don't worry so much like thinking if it's going to happen, but when it does, honestly...'

But there is a further and wider issue: many young people simply do not trust adults to take them seriously. The following account of reporting a serious sexual assault was given by a 12-year-girl:

INTERVIEWER: Did you tell anybody?

GIRL: I went down the police station.

INTERVIEWER: And did he ever get caught?

GIRL: No. They never found him. I ran down to the police
                station because it was just down the road and they got
                my dad over. They didn't believe me at first, then when
                they got there they found my hairband lying on the floor.

INTERVIEWER: Was it bad when folk didn't believe you?

GIRL: Uh huh (yes). Because when I was at the police station the lady didn't believe me and she phoned my dad and she said we'll go up and have a look anyway. And she took her torch and she was looking about the floor for clues and she looked over at a coloured bit and my hairband was lying there from when I was running away from him.

INTERVIEWER: Do you think the police are unfair?

GIRL: Aye, they don't give you a chance to talk.

Such incidents and adult responses to them rapidly enter the common stock of the stories about crime and policing that young people tell each other. Indeed, the 'cautionary tales' they tell – sometimes based in personal experience, sometimes in anecdote and fantasy – are one of the ways in which young people learn that to minimise the risk of crime, avoid dangerous places, persons and situations. Talking about such incidents is also a way of dealing with the impact of crime and many times during interviews we became aware of the sophisticated level of support young people provided for each other. Frequently, however, tales such as the following take the exaggerated form of the horror story or urban myth:

I can't go up blocks of flats. I can't, I'm scared of them. Wester Hailes or Clovey, I can't remember which, and I went into a lift and there was blood all over the lift, you know, at the top. My pal told me this story – there was a man in the lift and the wifey walked in and he just sort of grabbed her when the lift was shutting and her head got caught in it that's why there's blood all over it... There's a lot of murders in those high flats, eh?

While such 'horror stories' have the positive effect of conveying warnings between young people about people and places to avoid, there is a corresponding – and very real – risk that adults will dismiss *all* young people's talk about crime as exaggeration or fabrication; as 'childish nonsense'. Ironically, this is especially so given the very offences of this nature which are subsequently made known to the police. Thus, they *are* reported to the police or to the social services. Far from being seen as commonplace, to adult (especially male) eyes, they appear to be exceptional and hard to believe – a response which is reinforced by the paternalism 'grown-ups know best' which underpins so many official dealings with the young.

Taken together with the level of victimisation suffered at the hands of adults, it seems hardly surprising that young people are reluctant to place very much confidence in the protections offered to them by the adult world. For example, adversary contact with the police results largely from adult complaints about misdemeanours and incivilities committed by young people. (The double standards of the adult world seem only too evident.) This can lead to a level of cynicism and a relatively widespread belief that the police have little understanding of their problems. Over half of those we interviewed described police understanding of the problems of young people in their area as 'quite poor' (32%) or as 'very poor' (20%). As one 13-year-old boy put it:

> They're wasting their time chasing you for a minor thing when they could be chasing someone else for a big thing. They should be more understanding about what goes on instead of picking on people all the time. They never give the young ones a chance to explain or anything.

Indeed, very often young people are confronted by adult responses which not only appear unfair but seem out of all proportion to the seriousness of the offences they do commit. In the following extract it is easy to see how the anger and irritation experienced by adults leads to confrontation, incomprehension and resentment among young people. Here we see that what starts as 'just colouring in' ends up with the police being called and a belief that 'the woman's mad':

INTERVIEWER: What about vandalism, why do people do that?

A: 'Cos they've got nothin' else to do.

B: Its not only that is it? 'Cos if you're standin' in a stairway and you've got a marker in your hand you just write.

C: You just colour in or something, you don't really think of it being bad or something.

B: Remember that stair we used to stand in, it was covered.

A: That was the same stair next to this woman's stair. She comes out chasing us with frying pans and everything. She come out swearin' at us and everything and she had a fight with a wee lassie. She had a fight with the wee lassie, she was batterin' the wee lassie. She was pullin' her hair and everything. That was the woman, but she's mad... We were goin' to get charged before it got painted over. The police and all that were coming.

The apparent over-reaction of the adult world to 'harmless' incidents such as 'a bit of colouring in' is only compounded by the apparent failure of adults to take seriously the offences young people themselves experience as anything but trivial or harmless. This leads young people to seek their own solutions to their problems, which, however, often serve only to intensify their difficulties. For example, among the young people we spoke to in Edinburgh the most common response to crime, among girls as well as boys, was to seek safety in numbers. And not only does going around in 'a gang' in this way provide protection, it's also a lot of fun – but then, precisely for that reason, it can cause trouble of a different sort. The following comment from a 14-year-old girl living in central Edinburgh was echoed by others throughout the city:

> There's no youth clubs in this area, right? Up there…up there at the church there's one but it's crap 'cos all the big laddies are being cheeky, you know. So you muck about in the park and you're moved by the police. You muck about at the square and you're moved on by the police. You go back to the park and you get moved on by the police. What do they want us a do? Muck about up the town and get mugged? So, you've got to stick together…(Directly to interviewer) But, you'd be frightened, wouldn't you? If you were walking through the park and you saw maybe thirty or forty of us together? But what are we supposed to do? We wouldn't do anything bad. It's good. We've got a really healthy crew (gang) since we joined up with Trinity. I mean, we maybe go fightin' an' all. But we're not thieves. I mean, they wouldn't dare go up to an innocent person just walking along the street and say 'you', know what I mean? Like they all say we're goin' to steal old grannies' bags an' that. Who do they think we are? They do! We're not like that, we're not thieves. I mean it's good. A whole bunch of us. It's just exciting being together.

This element of fun should never be under-estimated but then hanging around in groups or 'gangs' is also one of the most common causes of adult complaints to the police; this in turn helps to explain the high rate of adversary contact between young people and the police. The following is comment from a police officer who works in the same area of Edinburgh as the girl whose words I have just quoted:

PC: We need to get about them. To have more police on the streets and hassle them a wee bit… It possibly won't solve the problem, but they need to be aware that the police are there. They give everybody a hard time. So we select the areas where they congregate. We make them aware of our presence. We need to take a hard line view.

INTERVIEWER: Under what circumstances do you move young people on?

PC: If they are causing a disturbance or shouting abuse, or if I recognise them as troublemakers, or if I thought they are going to cause trouble. If they are 'casuals' I move them on right away. They cause us and the public a lot of bother.[9]

---

9 It is very difficult to find police officers who can actually define what they mean by the term 'casual'. Most often it refers to the style of dress – baggy jeans, trainers, etc.

Even so, young people are by no means uniformly anti-police. For example, in total 55 per cent of those surveyed said they would feel safer with more police foot patrols, and 49 per cent with more car patrols. Indeed, as Figure 18.6 shows, this was so even in those areas where the level of adversary contact with the police was highest.

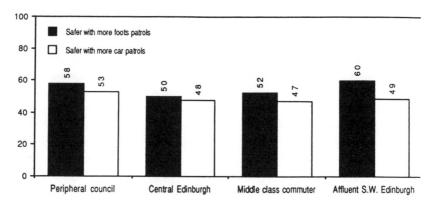

Source: Anderson *et al.* (1994)

Figure 18.6 Young People's Survey: Percentage 'would feel safer' with more police patrols in area

When these findings are broken down more finely, there is no simple correlation to be found between those who think the police are unfair to young people in their area (46%) or that the police have a poor understanding of their problems (52%) and those who say they would not want a greater police presence in their area. Indeed, from the interviews we carried out, we were left in no doubt of the ambivalence young people feel towards the police borne out of the contradiction between their needs as victims of crime, their worries about getting into trouble and the desire simply to have fun and enjoy the sense of freedom that the streets can offer. This was so, even among the youngest of those we interviewed:

INTERVIEWER: Why would you like there to be more police about?

A: All the men, the weirdos.

B: You're always bein' followed and that…flashers.

A: I was in the lift at my auntie's house with my wee sister. And this man got in and took down his trousers. We screamed and screamed but we couldn't get out till we got down. Then we ran off…but he didn't chase us or anything.

B: You're always frightened of getting jumped on.

INTERVIEWER: What do you mean 'getting jumped on'?

B: Gettin' raped and that.

C: The alkies and the junkies. They come up to you saying things. They try to get into your clothes.

INTERVIEWER: So is that why you want more police?

ALL: Yeah.

A: Mind, you wouldn't want too many, eh? I mean, they'd be watching you all the time, catching you an' that. It wouldn't be any fun if there was too many.

THEORETICAL KNOWLEDGE ABOUT YOUNG PEOPLE AND CRIME

Throughout this chapter, I have pointed to the dangers of adopting a narrow focus on rule-breaking when trying to understand young people's attitudes towards crime and the police. As soon as the topic is mentioned, it seems, the problem is posed in terms of delinquency, lawlessness and pathology. I have also suggested that, more often than not, this approach is informed by another agenda – namely, the problems young people cause adults – and that, by denying the legitimate claims and needs of young people themselves, the problems are further compounded.

Even within the narrow terms of reference of 'delinquency', however, further assumptions are made. For example, most empirical research on young people and crime not only focuses solely on offending. Almost always it is undertaken among the poor thus reinforcing (often unintentionally) the belief that it is the children of the poor who are the problem. Such research, of course, generates its own theoretical knowledge about crime in which the Edinburgh findings appear not only anomalous but, for many people, quite threatening. Thus, time and time again when we have given seminars on this research, we have been met with outright disbelief and unusually *personal* comments: 'you're not suggesting that children like mine go shoplifting' or 'things like that just don't happen in areas like ours'.

From such a perspective, it is hard not to conclude that conventional thought about young people and crime is simply more comfortable – a kind of 'not in my backyard' criminology. Indeed, in part at least, I think this helps explain the extraordinarily sympathetic reception and pervasive influence in this country – especially among Home Office Ministers – of the work of the two American authors James Q. Wilson (1985) and Charles Murray (1984) . Both authors take as their focus the poor – the so-called underclass – and both present crime as a problem of the ghettos.

Of course, both authors are ideologically driven by the image of the 'market society' (Currie 1992). Much of Wilson's work, for example, has directly undermined the idea that the causes of crime can be addressed through social policy and political intervention. The ultimate causes of crime, he maintains, rest in human nature which, for Wilson, is universally selfish and bleakly Hobbesian and as such lies beyond the possibility of change. The best we can do, therefore, is to contain the problem of crime (typically, for Wilson, predatory street crime committed by young males) through policing and the use of both formal and informal sanctions. Again, policies of containment are comforting.

Murray's work proves equally attractive and reassuring. Celebrated architect of the supposedly new idea of 'the underclass', Murray argues that the 'incentives for failure' offered by the welfare state have undermined respect for private property and the person leading to a 'dependency culture' of the poor. For Murray the process is indexed on the one hand by rising lawlessness and violent crime in the ghettos and, on the other, by the collapse of the family and the disintegration of the values of self-reliance, independence and self-control especially among 'the children of welfare'.

It is not my intention here to challenge either of these authors' comments on American culture and the problems of crime in American cities.[10] Nor do I intend to address directly Murray's more recent anecdotal inroads into Scottish culture and his highly contentious notion of the 'emerging British underclass' (Murray 1990). Rather, I would simply suggest that, in the context of British criminal justice policy, their work has supplied not only a spurious intellectual legitimacy but an enormous ideological plausibility to a series of arguments and political initiatives which have little connection to the reality of crime in Britain, especially as it affects young people. For example, the findings of the Edinburgh research would appear to undermine such claims in three ways:

1. Juvenile offending is by no means restricted to the children of the poor. Indeed, as we have seen, there is no evidence at all to support the proposition that those living 'in dependency' – whether as children of the unemployed, single parents or as children of council tenants – commit more crime than the children of the affluent.

2. There is no evidence to suggest that the children of the poor are any more or less likely to be victims or perpetrators of crime. Indeed, one of the most surprising findings of the survey is the inadequacy of social class as an indicator of either rule-breaking or victimisation. These findings in themselves not only challenge common sense theories of rule-breaking – i.e. what Bourdieu refers to as

---

10 I would simply refer readers to Elliot Currie's extraordinarily powerful book *Confronting Crime* (Currie 1985) and to an equally impressive work by William Julius Wilson *The Truly Disadvantaged: The Inner City, the underclass and public policy.* (W.J.Wilson 1987).

'spontaneous sociology' – but also question some of the most ideologically charged imagery of childhood itself and the paternalist culture within which and upon which such imagery thrives.

3. While the survey provides evidence of the differential policing of the poor, there is little to support James Q. Wilson's proposition that intensive policing and the enforcement of 'decent values' will contain crime. Indeed, the evidence of the research suggests almost the opposite: for as long as the emphasis is placed on containing juvenile crime as opposed to providing support for young people and their protection from crime, there is every reason to believe that problems will intensify.

CONCLUSION

The Edinburgh research raises more questions than it answers. For example, as researchers we found the absence of a class dimension counter-intuitive. Certainly the evidence suggests a class bias in policing, but, in relation to the other elements of the (equation for example, young people as victims or offenders) what stands out are more the similarities than the expected class differences. Indeed, as the research progressed such similarities became much more significant than any statistical differences. Thus, the broad patterns we found in the city have been reproduced among young people living in the small towns, villages and rural areas.

Not surprisingly, there were differences. For example, boys in rural Scotland are more likely to steal wild salmon from the rivers than those living in the city and young people in the city were more likely to 'vandalise' the schoolyard or the local park than those living in the country, where throwing stones into a stream offends nobody.

Of course, such differences are quite compatible with that version of individualist, rational choice theory which seeks to explain such differences in terms of 'opportunity' and to introduce pragmatic solutions through design-ing-out crime (for example, by surrounding school playgrounds with barbed wire and floodlights). Common sense, perhaps. But an explanation, no. Strate-gies of 'environmental crime prevention' simply reconstruct a material world within which the practices of exclusion, class and 'otherness' are reproduced – keep out...stay away.

The similarities in the findings across social class and area may be difficult to accept, but politically and culturally rather than methodologically. For example, in the later stages of the research we found that the sexual proposi-tioning of 14–15-year-old girls by adult men was no greater and no less in city, town and country. But, if we had found statistically significant differences, should such differences drive our explanations? Perhaps the similarities are more important? Certainly, we need to challenge the common-sense assumptions of the 'criminal area' – 'the bad part of town'. But, as important, we need to challenge the simple assumptions of class structure.

It is possible to construct a plausible explanation of the extent of adult crimes against young people (and vice versa) simply in terms of *status* (of childhood) rather than *class*. The systematic exclusion and victimisation of young people is in many ways analogous to other forms of discrimination against women, blacks or catholics, for example. It could be argued that the problems of a middle-class child of 11 or 12 years of age, coming to terms with the complexities and inconsistencies of the cultural practices of a world outside school or the home, will not be so different from a child from the poorest area of the city or the country (though the context and the content of the practices elaborated might be very different.)

Even so, one is left with the feeling that 'class' is conveniently lost in any such analysis. As we continued with the research we knew – as criminologists – that, as they grew older, only some of the young people we interviewed would confront systematic exclusion and economic disadvantage; only some predomi-nantly male, working class and poor would end up in prison; only some would join the homeless sleeping on the streets of Edinburgh. On the other hand, for many, the exclusion they experienced as young people would be short-lived. They would be granted full access to the privileges of adulthood – to jobs, homes and security. And yet, at the same time, we also knew that many of the girls – of all classes – who expressed such resignation when talking about adult male behaviour in public would confront more of the same – but alone – in the domestic violence of the private house.[11]

Of course, many of these 'unanswered questions' remain conceptually and empirically disputed but, as I have emphasised, one of the difficulties with the Edinburgh research has been that while we were attempting to describe and analyse the everyday lives of young people in different areas of the city, small towns and rural areas, the most intransigent problem we encountered was the response of policy-makers and decision-takers and the meaning and under-standing of childhood they carry *as adults*. Perhaps, therefore, as complex as the everyday lives and practices of the young people – and just as central to the theory, method and practice of criminology – are the shifts in the political and ideological construction of *adult* practices in relation to the everyday percep-tions of childhood and youth.

---

11 Analysis of the Scottish findings in the British Crime Survey 1988 revealed, for example, that domestic violence against women in the home was as common as violence between men in pubs, clubs or other places of entertainment (Anderson and Kinsey 1992) *Crime and the Quality of Life*, Scottish Office). On the extent of domestic violence in England, see Painter, K. and Mooeny, J. (1991) *Wife Rape, Marriage and the Law*, University of Manchester.

In this context, therefore, I find myself drawn to the commentaries and critical debates on the construction of 'the other' occurring within critical anthropology (e.g. Fabian 1983). The parallel, however, is not the way in which both criminology and anthropology constructed their objects – a debate which, within critical theory at least, is (by definition?) unfinished and must therefore continue. Nor is it simply that contemporary concerns with 'youth', 'juvenile delinquency' and the repetitive focus upon the wrong-doing, rule-breaking, etc., of the young working class poor is symptomatic of a cultural reconstruction of an imperial/colonial past (Clifford 1988) – although, certainly, 'the other' is now much closer to home: in the same city, region or country (but not in our own backyard).[12] Rather, it seems, we are witnessing the elaboration of continuing (albeit contradictory and diverse) metaphors and rhetoric of childhood – a rhetoric which, in its familiarity and continuity with a past, is all the more powerful in a re-structured present. For example, in writing of his own infant son, Charles Darwin himself shares more with the contemporary television images (and Alison Lurie) a century later than much post-modern cultural criticism seems ready to acknowledge: 'May we not suspect that the vague but very real fears of children, which are quite independent of experience, are inherited effects of real dangers and abject superstitions during ancient savage times?' (Darwin 1877, p.469).

Is it far from here to Piaget's stages of cognitive development or to the everyday comment on adolescence that 'it's just a stage that he or she is going through'? Surely not. And perhaps – just perhaps? – such 'very real fears' are (still) justified. And perhaps, therefore, the object of our research should not have been young people but the continuing representations of childhood and the 'techniques of neutralisation' employed by those adults who commit offences and incivilities against young people, who (routinely) push past them at bus queues or at the supermarket counter and who similarly ignore them in the definition of policy priorities.

But then, perhaps we would have to start with our own childhood memories. When Lefebvre watched Chaplin or when we recall how long the school holidays once seemed – was it really so very different? With hindsight, they were the happiest days of our life. Or were they? When judging children, devising youth policy or simply complaining about young people today, to whom and about what are we talking?

---

12 Nor, very definitely, am I suggesting that current 'moral panics' about youth can be read as a radical break or rupture in common-sense and everyday discourse about youth. (The history of hooliganism, as Geoffrey Pearson put it so well, is 'the history of respectable fears').

REFERENCES

Anderson, S. and Kinsey, R. (1992) *Crime and the Quality of Life: Public Perceptions and Experiences of Crime.* Edinburgh: Scottish Office.

Anderson, S., Kinsey, R., Loder, I. and Smith, C. (1994) *Cautionary Tales; Young People, Crime and Policing in Edinburgh.* Aldershot: Avebury.

Bauman, Z. (1992) *Intimations of Post-Modernity.* London: Routledge.

Benjamin, W. (1985) 'Berliner Chronik.' In *One Way Street and Other Writings.* Verso.

Benyon, J. and Solomos, J. (1991) 'Race injustice and disorder.' In S. McGregor and B. Pimlot *Tackling the Inner Cities: the 1980s Reviewed: Prospects for the 1990s.* Oxford: Clarendon.

Bourdieu, P. (1990) *In Other Words.* London: Polity.

Carlen, P. (1976) *Magistrates Justice.* London: Martin Robertson.

Chambers, G. and Tombs, J. (1984) *The British Crime Survey Scotland.* Edinburgh: Scottish Office.

Clifford, J. (1988) *The Predicament of Culture: Twentieth Century Ethnography, Literature and Art.* Cambridge, MA: Harvard.

Currie, E. (1992) 'International developments in crime and social policy: market and society and social disorder.' In *International Seminars on Crime and Social Policy.* London: NACRO.

Currie, E. (1985) *Confronting Crime.* New York: Pantheon Books.

Darwin, C. (1877) 'A biographical sketch of an infant.' In *Darwin's Early and Unpublished Notebooks.* Transcribed and annotated by Paul H. Barrett. London: Wildwood House.

Fabian, J. (1983) *Time and the Other: How Anthropology Makes its Object.* New York: Columbia University Press.

Flyn, R. and Spencer, J.R. (1990) *The Evidence of Children: The Law and the Psychology.* London: Blackstone Press.

Hall, S. (1978) *Policing the Crisis: Mugging the State and Law and Order.* London: MacMillan.

Kinsey, R. (1993) 'Crime, deprivation and the Scottish urban environment.' In H. Jones (ed) *Crime and the Urban Environment.* Aldershot: Avebury.

Lefebvre, H. (1991) *Critique of Everyday Life,* Volume 1. London: Verso.

Murray, C. (1984) *Losing Ground: American Social Policy 1950–1980.* New York: Basic Books.

Murray, C. (1990) *The Emerging British Underclass.* London: IEA Health and Welfare Unit.

The Scottish Office (1991) 'Children and crime, Scotland 1989.' *Statistical Bulletin CRJ/91/3.*

Wilson, J.Q. (1985 Revised edition) *Thinking about Crime.* New York: Vintage Books.

Wilson, W.J. (1987) *The Truly Disadvantaged: The Inner City, The Underclass and Public Policy.* Chicago: University of Chicago Press.

The Contributors

Jo Bird is 24 and lives in Manchester and was a founding member of Underground Power in 1990. She is actively involved in pioneering work and building a young people's voice movement in the UK.

Jaqui Cousins is an Early Childhood consultant, lecturer and researcher in education and a family support worker. Her life includes communicating with babies and young children to find ways in which their needs can be fulfilled and their rights understood. Jaqui is a member of an international inter-agency network which supports Gypsies and other threatened people. She works with Governments and young people alike.

Olivia Croce is now aged 16. Between the ages of 7 and 12 she attended an independent democratic junior school. The next four years were spent at a state secondary school. At this school she was in the top stream and had to take a minimum of 8 GCSEs. She found the competition, high expectations from teachers and the size of classes stressful. She described her first day at Sands as the nicest day she had ever had at school. She is able to negotiate the subjects she is to study and enjoys being able to interact freely with people older and younger than herself during the school day, rather than having to spend most of the time with her peer group. In addition to formal subjects she plays the piano and sings and composes songs.

Elsa Dawson was for eight years the Save the Children Fund's Research Co-ordinator for the work of Non-Government Organisations and at the time this work was undertaken Elsa was Field Director for Save the Children Fund in Peru. She is now on Oxfam's Strategic Planning and Evaluation Team responsible for providing advice and support in programme methods to Oxfam Overseas Division.

Rudi Dallos is a Senior Lecturer and Clinical Psychologist at the Open University specialising in work with families and other relationships. His research interests include studies of family beliefs, adult mental health and processes of change.

Kristen Eskeland was working for the Norwegian Campaign for the Environment and Development and the campaign that she writes about was the result of the first Children's Hearing in Norway in 1990. Since the Global Children's Hearing in Rio de Janeiro she has been the main co-ordinator. She used to be a teacher teaching young people between 13 and 16 years of age. The concept of the hearings grew out of her experiences as a teacher. She saw the need for children to speak up about their concerns and their need to act. She saw the whole project as a way of increasing the children's self-confidence and thereby strengthening democracy.

Sarnia Harrison wrote the piece included in this collection when she was 17 and at Sixth Form College. Although initially the subject was suggested to her by her mother when she was searching for a project to undertake for her project for her A Level studies in Communication, she found it increasingly therapeutic to have written it and felt it had given her a new perspective on the problems she had experienced. She is now 18 and working as a waitress and saving up to go to America to work au pair.

Stuart Hart is Director of the Office for the Study of the Psychological Rights of the Child, Purdue University, Indianapolis, USA. He was formerly a president of the International Schools Psychology Association. He believes that it is essential that the perspectives of children about their rights and treatment be acquired directly from them. Acquisition of the perspectives and knowledge of children, he believes, is consistent with the general theme of the Convention – that children are persons of dignity and worthy of respect – and this information will also assist in determining whether the Convention and efforts in relation to it are truly serving the interests of children. He writes about a research study on the perspectives of children and their teachers which has been underway at his University since 1989.

Bonnie Hill is now aged 16. She went to a state primary school until she was 9 and then transferred to Britain's first 'flexi-school' in Ticknall, a small village in Derbyshire. From the age of 12 to 14 she was home-educated, with about one hour per week spent with a tutor helping her with anything she particularly wanted to study (Latin mostly). She chose to go to a Further Education College part-time for one year at the age of 14 and achieved good grades. Now, after one year at Sands school – where she did some A levels but chose not to take any exams – she is planning to study AS level Maths and English Literature, A Level Psychology and French and take courses in massage and aromatherapy. She was a delegate at the Third International Democratic Schools Conference in Vienna this year and hopes to go to the fourth conference in Hedera, Israel next year.

Kunle Ibidun is a 23-year-old student in Manchester. His encouragement of young people to think, take action and take themselves seriously has been invaluable in the development of Underground Power into a national organisation.

Mary John is a psychologist whose research work has largely been with minority rights groups on issues relating to the transformation of power relationships. Early work was with John and Elizabeth Newson as part of their longitudinal study on child-rearing and it was from them she first learnt never to trust any information that does not come from the horse's mouth! Since then she has acted as a psychological consultant to Head Start in the United States and then as an expert adviser to the Centre for Educational Research and Innovation, OECD, Paris and later on disability matters to the EEC. She is a Professor of Education at the University of Exeter and Dean of the Faculty of Education.

Cathy Kiddle started working with Gypsy families in 1976 and after several years teaching in a variety of situations with pre-school children and right through the school years to adults. For the last 20 years she has continued to work with travellers, first in London and latterly in Devon. She is currently co-ordinator of the Devon Traveller Education Service.

Richard Kinsey was Reader in Criminology at the University of Edinburgh and is now Principal Lecturer in Criminology at the University of Teesside. His research has included children as victims rather than offenders. His recent research interests are in oral history particularly the oral history of childhoods.

Jeff Lewis is a Principal Lecturer at Rolle Faculty of Education, University of Plymouth. He has, for a number of years, been particularly concerned with research and teaching in Special Educational Needs.

Alex Mellanby is a Research Fellow in the Postgraduate Medical School at the University of Exeter with a background in General Practice. The Project he reports on was funded by the South Western Regional Health Authority and was directed by Dr John Tripp.

Sara McCrum is a freelance radio journalist and producer. She used to be a teacher and has taught in both primary and secondary schools. She has worked extensively for the BBC on programmes concerned with children putting forward their own views. Most of her work has involved getting children to talk. She has contributed to 'Education Matters' on Radio 5 and recently to the 'One World' Programmes. She has worked with the Child to Child Trust and has been involved in the Children's Hearings in the UK and the Global Voice of the Children presentation at the Earth Summit in Rio de Janeiro. Her extensive work empowering them to use the media as a resource in making their feelings and views known is distinctive in that it provides a very practical illustration of new ways of working with children that resources the child's own voice.

Fran Phelps at the time of the research reported here was a Research Fellow with a background in education. She now works in Shropshire as a Health Education Adviser.

Zoran Pavlovic has a Ph.D in Psychology and is a senior researcher at the Institute of Criminology at the Faculty of Law in Ljubljana, Slovenia. He is president of the Commission for Children's Rights at the Association of Friends of Youth of Slovenia and a member of the international co-ordination team for the Cross-Cultural Study on the Rights of the Child initiated by the International School Psychology Association.

Rakesh Rajani and Mustafa Kudrati are directors of the *kuleana center for children's rights* in Mwanza, Tanzania. *kuleana* is involved in child rights advocacy and runs programs in research, publications, training and awareness and policy development. *kuleana* also runs the largest street children's program in Tanzania. Both authors also have extensive experience in adolescent sexual health.

Penny Townsend is the 19-year-old co-ordinator of Devon Youth Council. She has now come to the end of her term of office and will be going on to assist the County Council in some of the work they are currently undertaking with young people such as the 'next generation' project – the project on young people and drugs, etc.

John Tripp is a Consultant Paediatrician and Senior Lecturer in Child Health in the Postgraduate Medical School, University of Exeter. He has worked in Exeter since 1980 after training at Guy's Hopital and the Hospital for Sick Children, Great Ormond Street. Clinical interests are in general paediatrics with special interest in adolescent medicine, gastro-enterology, cystic fibrosis and physical handicap. Dr Tripp's main research activities are now concentrated in two related areas of social paediatrics: the effects of family breakdown on children and the sex education programme reported on in this paper.

Geraldine Van Bueren is a Barrister and Director of the Programme on the International Rights of the Child in the Faculty of Laws, Queen Mary and Westfield College. She represented Amnesty International at the United Nations during the drafting of the Convention of the Rights of the Child and other subsequent UN instruments. She is an adviser to UNICEF and the United Nations High Commission for Refugees. She is also law consultant to Save the Children Fund and also advised the Ugandan Government in its review of child legislation. She is the author of a book for Save the Children Fund on the International Law on the Rights of the Child and has edited books for the Swedish Refugee Council on Unaccompanied Children. She has recently edited the book *International Documents on Children* (1993, Martinus Nijhoff) and *The International Law on the Rights of the Child* (1995, Kluwer).

Matthew Williams is now 14 and has lived in Devon from the age of six weeks. He went to a state primary school then to a democratically run private primary school until he was 10 when he started at Sands. He had been home-educated for short periods when he, and/or his parents, did not like the education provided locally by state schools. At Sands he has just successfully taken a number of GCSE's and is planning to do Drama, German and AS level Maths. His other interests are role playing, music, drama and computers. He was a delegate at the Third International Democratic Schools Conference in Vienna and plans to attend the next conference in Hedera.

Ella Young lived in the tropics for 15 years in Uganda, Nigeria, Indonesia and Nepal. She taught in the UK and overseas from playgroup to University level with a special interest in middle school science and biology. She has two sons. She recently edited the book 'Health into Science' as part of the Health Across the Curriculum series. She is currently involved in voluntary work including therapeutic horticulture and publicity training for the Child to Child Trust. Her late husband, Bev Young of the British Council, was one of the co-founders of the Trust.

Moshe Zeidner is a Professor of Educational Psychology in the School of Education, University of Haifa, Israel, and Director of the Laboratory for Cross-Cultural Research in Personality and Individual Differences. He is Associate Editor of the mainstream journal *Anxiety, Stress and Coping*. Among his recent books are the *Handbook of Coping: Theory, Research, Applications* (with Norm Edler, Viking) and *International Handbook of Personality and Intelligence* (with Don Saklofske, Plenum). He is currently doing basic and applied research in the area of coping with stress in evaluative settings and individual differences in stress and anxiety.

Subject Index

Numbers in *italics* refer to figures and tables

Author Index